Good
Luck

Dad
4/18/00

SQUANDERING AIMLESSLY

- -

MY ADVENTURES IN THE AMERICAN MARKETPLACE

- -

DAVID BRANCACCIO

Simon & Schuster

New York · London · Sydney · Singapore

SIMON & SCHUSTER
Rockefeller Center
1230 Avenue of the Americas
New York, NY 10020

Designed by Kyoko Watanabe

Manufactured in the United States of America

10 9 8 7 6 5 4 3 2 1

Library of Congress Cataloging-in-Publication Data

Brancaccio, David.
Squandering aimlessly : my adventures in the American marketplace /
David Brancaccio
p.   cm.
1. Consumption (Economics)—United States.
2. Consumer behavior—United States.   3. Finance, Personal—United States.
I. Title.
HC110.C6 B665   2000
332.024—dc21   99-055141
ISBN 0-684-86498-3

For Mary,
who still laughs at all my jokes

Acknowledgments

I am profoundly indebted to all the people who favored me with their time and wisdom during my adventures. They were my teachers.

I am deeply grateful to Dominick Anfuso and Annik LaFarge at Simon & Schuster, who, along with my intrepid agent, Jonathon Lazear, saw potential and made it reality.

I want to recognize my very cool bosses, the creator of public radio's *Marketplace,* Jim Russell, and the program's executive producer, J. J. Yore, who provided the support I needed to work what became a second job.

I also wish to thank:

All my colleagues who warmly took up the slack, including Michelle Brier, Walter Cabral, Deborah Clark, Eve Epstein, Sarah Gardner, Cheryl Glaser, Mitchell Hartman, George Lewinski, Carla Mozee, Quinn O'Toole, Stuart Seidel, and Rob Wood at *Marketplace,* as well as Mary Hawkins and Julia Mears at Public Radio International.

My sister, Lisa, my brother, Peter, Josh Fischman, Chris Houston, Barry and Rosalie Howarth, David Johnson, and Harriet Rubin for commenting on drafts of the manuscript.

Economist Jack Albertine, John Maxwell Hamilton at Louisiana State University, Michael Iannazzi at the Yale School of Management, economist Sam Kahane, economist Lisa McGowan, Paul Merenbloom at Prudential Securities, economist Howard Rosen and University of Southern California professors Warren Bennis, Morton Owen Shapiro, Jonathan Aronson, Ian Mitroff, and Michael Renov for their wise counsel.

John Barth, Elizabeth Bakos, Harriet Baskas, Janet de Acevedo, Maureen Glazier, Joe Gwathmey, Richard Laermer, Ellen James Martin, Herb Mayer, Phil Shuman, Joel Toso, and Jason Zweig for their help.

Michael Fortkort and Alan Zelon for their legal assistance.

Deanna and Tom Fortkort, my in-laws, for their encouragement and support.

My mother, Ruth, for teaching me the joy of performance; and my father, Patrick, for showing me how Dante Alighieri, Henry James, and Ralph Waldo Emerson could guide me on this quest.

And this book would not exist without Mary Brancaccio, my charismatic collaborator, who never stopped imagining the possibilities of this project, even in the middle of the night.

Contents

"Please, Lord, give us another boom. We promise not to screw this one up."

—West Texas oil country bumpersticker

"One must come out of one's house to begin learning."

—West African Proverb

SQUANDERING
AIMLESSLY

1

The Naked Truth About Money

I once saw a naked Belgian accountant carrying nothing but her purse. She made it look easy. Her money was exactly where she wanted it. I, however, used to have a much tougher time knowing where to put it. I had a surplus once and didn't know what to make of it. I wanted to acquire that walk, that confidence, because I was determined not to make the same mistake with money again.

As host of a public radio program about money, I am asked all the time about what to do with it. During a time of great surplus for some, this is an acute occupational hazard, like that of the chiropractor at a convention of contortionists. I needed to answer the question for myself before I could have anything meaningful to say about other people's money.

What I really wanted were street smarts, so I went out on the road. Ten trips sprinkled over sixteen months of a busy work schedule. It was to be a pilgrimage to places that evoked ten plausible ways to use a lump sum. I didn't start out with a surplus, but I came back richer and no longer prone to breaking out in hives if I found myself in the clutches of a bonus payment, a severance check, a capital gain of one sort or another, an inheritance, a lottery win, a tax refund, or simply the realization that the passbook savings account finally contains some serious money.

I had figured a personal finance pilgrimage would be an amusing and productive way to "Do the Knowledge," as London cabbies refer to their apprenticeship in that city's confounding, gridless geography. It would be less painful than going to business school, given my math scores. It would be a pilgrimage to see what other folks were doing with their money as the century closed with a boom and to explore those possibilities in three dimensions, not just as data on one of my flat market screens. A pilgrimage, because you hear stories and because strange things happen, perhaps an encounter with another naked accountant.

Let me say more about the first accountant because it was she who got me going down this path. I didn't know her well, but I am convinced of one thing. There is no chance she would ever have broken out in hives when presented with a surplus. And she despised me for even needing to ask. Just where is the best place to put your money? That question became especially urgent for me as I, too, stood naked in the middle of a French town.

I had been passing through France when an editor for my program, *Marketplace*, telephoned with an oddly incomplete assignment. The mayor of a French seaside village would be expecting me at ten the following morning. The normal set of follow-up questions were met with suspicious pauses and dissembling.

"The story? You'll figure out the story when you get there."

I felt like Robert Mitchum's character in the noir classic *Out of the Past*, who tells a cabby, "I think I'm in the frame, but I still can't see the picture."

Cap d'Agde was just a couple of centimeters away on the Michelin map. I parked the car, grabbed a bag with a tape recorder and microphone, and then saw the sign: *"Nudité Obligatoire."* Obligatory nudity, no ifs, ands, or buts. I was in a town, population 20,000 in the summer, where no one wears clothes. It was not a nudist colony in the traditional sense but rather an entire nudist city. I swallowed hard, for when in Rome . . . .

The interview with the naturist quarter's ranking official was memorable. There was no air conditioning in the mayor's office, and the Naugahyde chairs seemed to belch rudely when brushed by my bare thighs. In the nude *supermarché*, shoppers skated clear of the waste-high frozen-food section. In the one-star restaurant, diners with cloth napkins stretched primly across their loins enjoyed a three-course seafood lunch. Here was the real horror of the situation: French health and safety regulations allowed me to be naked, but not the waiters, bank clerks, or shop assistants. You haven't seen a French waiter really condescend until you are sitting there in the altogether trying to order the *crudité*. I am not ashamed of the human form, but it was all so incongruous.

But the most perverse moment for me was changing money in the naked financial institution, Banque Dupuy, Perseval. It was like my recurring nightmare: I stand up to do my solo and find the rest of the orchestra is in black tie while I am wearing only a black tie.

My challenge was figuring out how to "cover" this story. As the saying goes, there are a thousand untold stories in the naked city, but I was desperate for just one with a business angle.

A roly-poly pair of naked elderly folks nodded politely and offered the pleasantry used by German hikers when they squeeze past you on a narrow mountain trail. A jovial Brit in a tank top and no bottoms ominously asked if I wanted to try my hand at *boules*.

In the midst of this, I became increasingly aware of a cramping in my right hand. I had been tightly clutching a wad of French bank notes and franc coins since entering the place sans trousers. It was the call of the elusive business angle: how does one run an economy in a place without pockets?

I began my inquiries. A T-shirt vendor suggested the old credit card in the shoe trick, only I had left my Reeboks back in the car. Merchandising and innovation proposed another solution. I could purchase a rather jaunty round-the-neck, hermetically sealed money holder, now available in three designer colors. The vendor pointed with his chin at the striking sight of a woman striding confidently down a path to the shops.

"Now *that* is where you put your money," he said.

It was the Belgian accountant with her purse. When I say naked, that is not entirely true. She was wearing a wide-brimmed raffia sun hat, golden earrings, and golden sandals. She proved to be less eager than I for an interview about where to put money. I managed to get from her the Belgian part and the accountant part and not much more. She knew exactly what to do with money, unquestioningly. It was not just her profession; she was probably born that way. Nor was she about to discuss it with the likes of me. My lack of savoir-faire in these matters must have been plain to see. She vanished into some shops, leaving me standing there with my microphone dangling.

Chastened, I strolled down toward the beach to sort out my notes. At the edge of the boardwalk, the white heat was taking its toll on a group of naked volleyball players. The rest of the beach was packed cheek-by-jowl. For a passing moment I felt queasy forging into the crowd, unprotected as I was. Then reason prevailed. Who would notice one more pair of buttocks in a crowd this size?

Reason failed. No less than ten thousand people stopped what they were doing and watched intently as I walked from the sidewalk down to the cool sand at the water's edge. I had no idea why I was worthy of such scrutiny. Was it my tan line? Or my "skeptical reporter" tattoo?

One tends to look inward after a near-death experience like this. It wasn't so much the embarrassing stares on the beach. It had something to do with the Belgian accountant. She had judged me as unworthy; I could feel it. What kind of question is that, what do you do with money? It was an opening line that was doomed to fail with someone like her, someone who appeared to have the knack. I didn't intuitively have the knack, and somehow I would have to devise a way to acquire it. The idea of a pilgrimage would not gel for several more years. At that moment I was too busy blowing the most cash I had ever seen in one place.

The cash had materialized during the George Bush administration, those dark ages before the dot-com era, a time when money had to be earned the old-fashioned way. My wife and I saved it by being cheapskates. A rented apartment. Embarrassing, collegiate-style furniture. We ate in unless an out-of-town relative with a credit card was in town. When a second job teaching a college course forced the purchase of a second car, I found an eleven-year-old thing for $800 that I could keep running by threatening it in Italian.

That is how we managed to put $17,000 into our savings account. For the first time in my life, I had a positive net worth. I was liquid. I was home free, or so I believed. But just as I thought I was crossing into the end zone to score seventeen thousand points, the game changed. Now that I had some money, what exactly was I supposed to do with it? That was when the hives started.

I imagined a financial adviser's eyes lighting up at the sight of this little nest egg. Seventeen thousand dollars has "home mortgage down payment" written all over it. Cobble together another $2,000 and we would have had 10 percent down on perhaps a tool shed, given the real estate prices in northern California at that time. A house would bring a tax deduction. It would mean respectability. It would be the mark of a grown-up.

If I had seen fit to consult a financial adviser, I would have been asked about debt. We had very little debt. Every month our credit cards were paid down to zero and the student loans were nearly done, so debt relief wasn't a pressing need.

The adviser might have urged me to save some taxes by opening up an Individual Retirement Account. That is, saving it for old age. But at that time the nonprofit radio station where I worked had no pension plan. I had no broker. I knew one guy who was an arbitrageur who boasted he was a personal acquaintance of Ivan Boesky. But at the time I wasn't completely clear on what an arbitrageur did.

I did know one thing. I wanted to be a foreign correspondent when I grew up.

So my wife and I quit our jobs, sold the cars, moved with our infant son to London and blew the money in nine months.

But as our last few pence were circling the drain, a process hastened by one of the lousiest exchange rates for the dollar since the demise of the gold standard, something happened. Just about the time of the naked Belgian accountant assignment in France, other people's money started coming in to my little overseas bureau. The enterprise blossomed, and after three years it was possible to argue that the overseas lark was a good investment. We were enriched by the travel, the chance to break old patterns and try a new way of life. It was instrumental in getting the job I have now.

This is my rationalization, anyway. It is very easy to rationalize spending money. But the fact is, I can't prove that moving my family to London was the right thing to do with it. In other words, buyer's remorse has set in.

I think a lot about the wisdom of blowing our nest egg the way we did, because in my job now I am surrounded by such responsible people. I spend much of my day exchanging knowledge with eminent men and women of business and finance. Talking with two or three economists and analysts a day has an effect. One day who should walk into my office but someone as confident about what do with money as the naked accountant. It happened to be a U.S. Secretary of the Treasury, Robert Rubin, in the flesh. Well, not *flesh*. He was wearing a suit that probably cost more than another trip to London for my whole family, and he wanted to talk about investment capital working to help inner cities. How was I to look a guy like Secretary Rubin in the eye and admit that I once flushed away on some European fling seventeen thousand of the very dollar bills that bear his signature? I was living out a version of the Mel Brooks film *Young Frankenstein*. It was as though I spent much of my life menacing the villagers, then in some kind of twisted lab experiment, I exchanged my brain with an eminent financier. In the final scene I was the monster, propped up in bed next to Madeleine Kahn, reading the *Wall Street Journal* through banker's spectacles.

My transformation into *Homo capitalis* was nearly complete. Plugged in as I now was, I should have had all the answers. I consumed it all: live data pumped into my hands still warm from the market; electronic retrieval of nearly every English-language periodical on earth; correspondents in world hot spots just a button away; phone numbers for Wall Street sources that even their mistresses didn't have. One would think the wisdom about what to do with money must have been hidden in this ocean of information somewhere, if only I could find it. And there is no doubt that this tidal wave of information gave me a good handle on the state of the economy, the direction of interest rates, and the ability to make the occasionally decent call when it came to picking stocks. But months of pointing and clicking yielded more data, more questions, and not much in the way of synthesis and no useful answer to the question of what should I do with the proceeds, should I ever really score on a stock. It had become obvious to me that a piece of my education was still missing. But I couldn't just go. I needed a sign.

One day something terrifying happened at work that would be the catalyst that would push me out the door on my pilgrimage. With about a minute and a half to go before airtime, I was walking toward the studio, giving a script about the day's financial news a final, preflight check.

"While the Dow was in the dumps," the script read, "the gnostic was doing better, with the gnostic composite index rising 1.2 percent. . . . A gnostic trader is quoted as saying, 'Everywhere investors look, they see reasons to buy.' "

I paused in midstep, about to recuse myself from further broadcasting duties that day on the grounds that I was losing my mind.

Did it really say "gnostic"?

I blinked twice and fearfully shuffled back to that page again, praying I would find instead the word "Nasdaq," the electronic stock market run by the National Association of Securities Dealers, the NASD. But it did not say Nasdaq. Settled before the microphone, in the remaining moments left before the show's opening gong, I was forced to go on a furious hunting expedition, crossing out as many gnostics as I could find.

"Thirty seconds," the director said into my headphones.

"What does 'gnostic' mean?" I asked, pressing the intercom button. The producer's eyes widened in panic.

"Number one, I don't know. Number two, you've got ten seconds. Number three, forget gnostic, they'll think you mean Nasdaq."

Greek isn't listed on my résumé as one of my languages , but I managed to recall that gnostic has something to do with knowledge, maybe self-knowledge. Somebody must be trying to tell me something with this gnostic thing, but what? It occurred to me that I could study all I wanted about money and how it works, but until I knew myself, I would never understand what to do with it.

The on-air light glowed red.

A forensic reconstruction of the events leading up to what has come to be known as the Gnostic Incident concluded it was "pilot error." An intern had thought he was doing me a favor by running an electronic spell checker on the script displayed on my computer screen prior to its posting on our Internet site. WordPerfect's spell checker did not recognize the word "Nasdaq." The spell checker had taken it upon itself to make the substitution. Gnosis does mean knowledge, but the kind of intuitive knowledge that is more at home around the word "insight" than it is around the words "curriculum" and "training." It is about coming to an understanding of yourself and then using that kind of knowledge to help interpret what is going on. It was the sign.

I concluded that it was time to get out and Do the Knowledge, just as we like to say we "Do the Numbers" on the radio program. Still, there were some practical preparations in order.

First, I had to secure an advance from a publisher to pay for the trips. Enough said.

Second, I had to arrange for some vacation time from a boss who would sooner put out his own eyes than give a fellow a day off. Actually, that was my paranoia talking. In reality, the boss turned out to be magnanimously flexible in return for me saying so here.

Third, I had to persuade my brilliant wife, Mary, to do all the research for the pilgrimage at no pay while allowing me to get all the credit. As a special bonus, she could shoulder all the extra child care duties for our three offspring during the ten times I would be away from home. That was my plan. The final bargain was if I got to do this, she got to go to an expensive graduate school.

All that remained was determining the route. A Ouija board seemed a tad random, so I combed through newspaper accounts about lottery winners for inspiration about ways to spend a surplus. Lottery winners have eclectic opinions on how to answer the legendary class of hypotheticals that includes: What if my ship comes in? What if I hit pay dirt? What if I get the Big Score? Newspapers cover this subject with loving dedication, perhaps because of the rags-to-riches human drama, perhaps because state lotteries are big newspaper advertisers. The lottery clippings that spoke the most to me fell into these categories:

- Spend it on a shopping spree.
- Do good.
- Start a business.
- Gamble with it.
- Give it away.
- Invest it in the markets.
- Buy a house.
- Go back to school.
- Retire early.
- Save it for a rainy day.

Once I knew the categories, the destinations for my travels would fall into place. I was summoned to a school reunion that would take me near the mother of all shopping malls, just the place to confront my own passionate impulse toward spending. Getting smart about money has to start with getting smart about consumption. I wanted to know if I could take a surplus to the mall and still get out alive.

2

Going Back to Shop Class

Spending at the Mall of America, Bloomington, Minnesota

From the clipping file: A twenty-six-year-old political science student and mother-to-be in Boise, Idaho, won more than $87 million in the eighteen-state Powerball lottery. *People* magazine reported she uttered the "consumerist manifesto, 'If I want it, I'll buy it,' took off on a couple of shopping sprees and then settled into her new life." October 16, 1995

*Y*ou *know and I know that we would both spend a surplus if no one were looking. It might be at a car dealership, a Napa vineyard, an art auction. It might even happen at the Mall of America, which is to consumption what the Statue of Liberty is to another cherished national ideal, freedom. It is also a piece of kitsch the size of a domed stadium, and I had the chance to see it for myself at little cost, since I had a rendezvous already planned with old friends nearby anyway. I wanted to force myself to understand why I spend, what I get out of it, whether money used for immediate gratification has an acceptable rate of return.*

To focus the mind, I had decided this trip needed to be a bit of an ordeal.

The goal was to get in there and not spend a penny, to get the powerful forces at work in this kind of space to reveal themselves by applying some resistance. Without the control of consumption, a surplus would simply vanish and this money trip would go no further. I went to the mall to confront my demon.

Let me first tell you about the demon, then the mall. You can surmise that I got out alive because I am here to tell the tale. What you don't know is how close it was.

It's happening again.

I don't drink nearly enough. I do not smoke. I have no ribald Web sites bookmarked. But I am possessed by another urge so powerful it is a wonder everyone around me isn't inquiring why I'm so happy to see them.

A mysterious envelope has arrived and it is starting all over again. The envelope contains a check, the payment for a long-forgotten gig. Chuck Norris's people began one of his movies with the sound of a radio to set up a plot in which Chuck and a scruffy-but-winsome dog chase terrorists. I was the voice on that radio. No pictures, no name, I didn't even get to meet Chuck. It was all over in one take, thirteen seconds' worth of work. Until the money arrived.

As I hold the check in my hands it starts to morph, turning from two dimensions into three and taking on weight. I seem to be holding some kind of camera, but it is much more substantial than the 35mm body I already own. I can almost smell the leather from its heaving bellows. The camera's logo resolves out of the mist of my imagination: this isn't a check for $500; it is a vintage Speed Graphic press camera of the sort made famous by Weegee, the celebrated forties crime photographer. If only I could run my fingers along the dimple of its four-by-five-inch back.

Now the inevitable downward spiral begins. I already know how it will play out. I will spend evenings prowling magazines and the Internet for signs of the object of my desire, ignoring the kids' pleas for bedtime stories. I will pass restless nights planning my conquest, and if sleep comes, the press camera will even enter my dreams. I can feel myself tumbling into another one of my infatuations of Shakespearean proportions, an out-of-control, tongue-lolling, bug-eyed crush on a thing.

Talk about an all-consuming passion.

Now on the theory that everyone needs a hobby, what is the problem here? The guy works hard, so he should be able to treat himself now and then. It is not like he wants to use the money to buy crack cocaine or something.

The thing is, it is not just the camera.

I have just crossed from St. Paul to the Minneapolis side of the Mississippi River, hunting. In the cockpit of the car, I am indulging my habit of leaning on the radio's "seek" button until something interesting happens. The readout comes to rest at 98.5 FM. A fellow is talking with great passion too close to a microphone. The ambiance suggests he is not in a studio but in some public space. The vocal range and vowels are Garrison Keillor's, and he seems to be deep into a monologue.

"God loves YOU," growls the voice. "But God HATES, and I mean HATES, your SIN!"

I know, I know. I try to do the right thing, Garrison, but I am weak. If I ever have money, demons seem to possess me.

It is odd that my man is on such a dogmatic riff on a weekday, but this is Minnesota. Maybe they have developed an All-Wobegon radio format for their native son. The program breaks for an announcement and it becomes clear that I'm tuned to a station run by religious folk. These are Baptists, so the voice can't possibly belong to Keillor.

I am just sneaking off to the mall, for heaven's sake, so why does it feel like the radio preacher has caught me doing something I oughtn't? My immediate goal here is to find the turn for 24th Avenue South, upon which the Mall of America, the eighth wonder of the world, has been built. The Mall of America is presumably good, wholesome fun. So why all the sneaking? Why am I prepared to lie about the day if nice people inquire later about what I did on my day off in the Twin Cities? I checked, and the correct, grown-up answer would have something to do with watching a matinee at the Guthrie Theater or browsing in the Walker Art Museum. These are acceptable answers because they are defensible. I spent the money and the time at the Guthrie or the Walker to feed my soul. But what is not nearly as clear is the answer to the question that sent me on this pilgrimage: what is the return on my investment here? Once I know what I am really getting out of this, I can begin to compare shopping with other ways of using money and see how they measure up.

I am starting my pilgrimage in familiar territory. It doesn't take a forensic accountant to figure out what I tend to do with my money. The checkbook register and the credit card statements tell the story. In so much else I proudly tell myself that I differ from the national average. I read more and watch less TV. But when the average for guys is nearly five hours of shopping a week, I'm as American as I can be. I am not even counting shopping's virtual equivalents, provided by direct mail or online.

When you do something often enough, it becomes second nature, automatic. "Unthinking" is another way to put it. A stand-up comedian once told me what happened after he won the "$100,000 Star Search" competition. "The money just *went away*," he confided. It wasn't stolen. It didn't work its way down his trouser leg through that hole he had been meaning to mend. He just found a few thousand things to buy that seemed like a good idea at the time but left little or no lasting impression. The comedian never got the chance to think about investing. After several months he was pretty much back where he'd started, with no need to embark on a money trip because there was no longer any money to consider.

It's enough to make a financial adviser weep. If only the guy had paid himself first by putting his windfall into something better, imagine the return. If I can use this mall trip to get some insight into my own penchant for allowing money to just *go away*, it will be worth the price of my plane ticket to Minnesota, and I can then begin to imagine other kinds of returns, whatever they may be.

As I follow the arrows that promise parking, I spot a woman sitting on a bench adjacent to the the giant metal spreadsheet filled with stars that marks the mall's main entrance. She is holding her hand to her face as if to conceal tears. The woman is dwarfed by a pole supporting not a flag but a decorative piece of fabric printed with the image of a cartoon clock permanently frozen at the perfect time for shopping, 10:35 A.M. If time heals all, what a nasty trick it is to stop time dead at a bad moment for the woman. It's a foreboding sign, but I shrug it off. To my peril.

I am leaning over the railing, looking down on the Mall of America's centerpiece, an enclosed Knott's Camp Snoopy theme park. A carousel meshes with The Tumbler, which overlaps the mechanical balloon race. The din of the Pepsi Ripsaw rollercoaster and the windowed roof line seem very familiar. The West Market atrium was designed to look like a big European train station. You don't even need a passport for this trip. It is a shrink-wrapped grime-free version of Paddington Station or Gare du Nord, only most of the tracks are ripped out, and those that remain are elevated and twist in a spray of directions.

I am choosing to prove my valor at the Mall of America because the mall is asking for it, begging for it. A shopping center that sets itself up as a *tourist* destination must represent the state-of-art of what America knows about parting me from my cash. I am here to be tested, like a recovering alcoholic signing up for the single-malt tour of Scotland. If any shopping-centric experience in this country is going to pay high enough dividends to justify the cost, it has to be this one. This is, after all, the place its boosters like to compare to the Grand Canyon.

"The Mall of America has more visitors than the Grand Canyon and Disney World combined," reads just about every bit of PR ever created for the place.

It is a riveting statement: forty million people visit the mall every year.

Go to the Canyon and you hear a common line whispered by a succession of visitors as they approach the edge and the bottom opens out into the dizzying vista: "Gosh, it makes you feel so small." Upstairs at the mall, looking out across the grand shopping scape with credit cards in my pocket, I have the impulse to say the opposite. "Gosh, it makes me feel so powerful."

The Mall of America, I quickly learn, offers much more than either Disney or the Grand Canyon. The Canyon, first of all, is seriously deficient in shopping opportunities. The canyon vistas are also a problem: they are impossible to properly capture and package. I imagine a sight-seer sitting at her kitchen table in Winnetka trying to convince skeptical relatives that it really is grand, even if her point-and-shoot camera didn't do justice to it. The canyon is also too cold during the winter and too hot in the summer. At the mall it's always seventy degrees.

The Disney parks aren't as temperate, especially in the summer. And Disney makes you pay for parking. Most of Disney's shopping opportunities are relatively narrow in scope, tending to run along the hat-with-mouse-ears, sweatshirt-with-logo, and soft toys lines. At the Mall of America you can do the rides, and at the end of your day you can take home STUFF. Stuff for your bedroom. Stuff for the den. Stuff to show off.

I locate the mall's information kiosk and scan the long list of stores in the mall. There are twenty-five devoted exclusively to footwear. Feet scare me and I intensely dislike shopping for shoes. Fortunately, I don't need new ones. Scanning the list, I realize that I probably don't *need* anything the mall has to offer. N-240 on the mall map lists a working wedding venue, the Chapel of Love, but I'm already married and Minnesota happens to be one of the states where bigamy is frowned upon. There is a Lake Wobegon, USA store in the mall's West Market area. I'm not sure how much of the proceeds trickle down to Keillor, but as much as he may want my money, he probably doesn't need it as much as I do. If I better understood the distinction between need and want, I'd be able to save more. But standing in this spot, saving money for something I can't yet envision seems remote.

Spending, on the other hand, is tangible. I feel powerful marketing forces encouraging me to buy, not save. But a thought intervenes, the recollection of the stock phrase of Italian museum guards who would admonish me as a boy: *"Non toccare, solo guardare."* Don't touch, just look. Today I'll listen. After all, parking and admission at this theme park are free, so it won't cost me anything to take a good look around. A treacly scent tugs at my nose; it must be the nearest Cinnabon franchise. I would kill to "invest" in one of those. But then I remember my vow of abstinence.

"Shut Up and Shop," reads a Mall of America magnet. Walking past Eddie Bauer, the first stirrings hit me. They come in the form of a phrase: five little words that resolve into focus whenever I am forced into browsing mode.

"I could use a watch."

This is my crutch when I find myself in an airport duty-free shop, at an open market antique sale, or trapped on the first floor of a grand department store waiting for someone with more urgent business there. It is like holding a glass of ginger ale at a cocktail party even when you're not thirsty and the glass and accompanying napkin are a nuisance. You need something to do to make wandering aimlessly in a crowd seem less absurd.

My search for a watch has been wide but not at all deep. I searched for a watch in one of the original nineteenth-century arcades linking Old Bond Street and Savile Row in London. I looked in an underground store in Munich and at a shop on the wharf where Hovercraft embark for Copenhagen in Malmö, Sweden. My wife bore three children, we've moved house four times through three presidential administrations, and still just the right timepiece has proved elusive.

I don't think my requirements are outlandish. I want a recognizable brand name in the $125 range. I need something elegant enough to wear with a suit and without any stylistic cues that would fraudulently suggest scuba diving. My fantasy watch must have a large, clearly marked analog face and—here is the rub—it must include a digital stopwatch so I can time interviews at the office. There is also a political angle: I remember reporting on the controversy that arose when the company behind one popular brand of watches fired more than three hundred union employees at its factory in Scotland.

Alas, while there are pilot's watches, jogger's watches, golfing watches, watches for people with high blood pressure, and watches for those who change altitude frequently, no one has seen fit to mass-produce a wristwatch designed for the radio broadcast professional. TV news inherited Edward R. Murrow's dashing aesthetic. But the public face of radio now looks very much like Limbaugh, Stern, or Imus, three guys who have done much for the commercial side of the medium but absolutely nothing for fashion, and I haven't forgotten about Limbaugh's line of neckties.

So it can be said that whenever I'm stuck shopping, I stare with "watch"-ful eyes. Today, even though I am on assignment and have taken a one-day vow of shopping chastity, I can't stop myself from lingering for a moment over the Eddie Bauer watch collection.

They do sell a plausible contender. It's a model with all the formal attributes I'm looking for. There are two negatives. It's only $85; that is to say, it's too cheap. Second, it has a tasteful Eddie Bauer logo inscribed at the center. A logo, per se, is not a problem for me. But a logo that reads Eddie Bauer is not a logo that reads L. L. Bean, the most famous thing from my home state since lobster and former senator George Mitchell. One shouldn't betray one's roots.

Alas, the great Watch-on-the-Hill is still out there somewhere, so I skulk past the shiny Eddie Bauer concierge at the entrance with my hands open and exposed to show that I am not shoplifting anything. My mother's voice rings in my ears.

"You are impossible about shopping." My poor mother. She thinks shopping is about acquiring in as efficient a way as possible that which one acutely needs. That is why she thinks I am impossible. She sees me investing time and emotional energy into these shopping situations and often coming up empty-handed, without the new watch. She likes me too much to consider the horrible possibility that she raised a son so callow that he sets out on deliberately futile afternoons of thwarted consumption just to fill time.

Reflecting on my watch question takes me a long way toward understanding my relationship with shopping. This isn't, first of all, about real need: I have three watches already, a heavy diver's model, one made from granite, and a very tacky-looking plastic digital thing with timers that ascend and descend. I can spin a pretty good tale about why I need something more integrated, something more stylish, but the impetus remains "I could use another watch," rather than "I have no idea what time it is moment to moment; I can't function without a new one."

What we have here is a pathetic creature who is using browsing in the same way he often uses television, to escape the tensions of the day and to block out sometimes painful thoughts about the big picture. A Mall of America souvenir refrigerator magnet proclaims, " 'Shopping is cheaper than psychotherapy'—writer unknown." I might have gone with "origin unknown." The word "writer" implies that a Faulkner or Hemingway might be behind this lofty thought. The phrase is true, but just barely. The average price tag for a trip to the mall is a little over a hundred dollars; an hour of psychotherapy in Minnesota isn't much more than that. Browsing, real browsing, the kind that tortures sales clerks working on commission, the kind that is never consummated, still has a cost. It is an opportunity cost. I could be doing something else, something more productive, something more real.

Shopping is also about the ability to express the power of your money. If you've got the right wristwatch and some money to spend, you can appear to wield the sort of power that directs entire battalions of service sector personnel to meet your personal whims. That's what you think anyway. The great salespeople are those who let you think that you have gained the advantage over them. But in the final analysis, just who plays the puppet and puppetmaster is far from clear. Perhaps the only consumers to escape the sales transaction unscathed are those who know what they want.

When I was twelve, I remember stopping at a modest camera store in Brooklyn with my uncle Sam, who at the time managed a very serious camera store on Sixth Avenue in Manhattan. My uncle was shopping for just the right roll of film. When he walked into that cramped store, it was like Lord Olivier entering the stage at the Old Vic. He drew all of the energy of the room to him. He walked to the counter and picked up and examined a Kodak mat near the cash register as if he were toying with the salt shaker at his own kitchen table.

"Sixty-four thirty-six" was all my uncle said. The Brooklyn clerk knew he was dealing with a very serious consumer of photographic products and showed respect to his powerful customer by not fooling around with trifles.

"With or without?" the clerk said.

"Without," my uncle replied with a dismissive snort. Just a dozen syllables were exchanged, but the two parties to this transaction knew that it was about the purchase of a roll of Kodachrome 64, with thirty-six exposures to the roll, processing not included. The guy behind the counter knew the price had better bloody well be the best one available on the entire eastern seaboard. My uncle knew it would be.

*   *   *

On the lower level of the mall, at the periphery of a store-cum-play-area known as the Lego Imaginarium, I lean against a pillar, watching the Cubist versions of a seven-foot red Tyrannosaurus Rex and a blue raptor with red spots along his back. Looking up, I spy half-sized Lego men on a yellow Lego arch. Inside the arch is a one-story nutcracker with operational clockwork made from what was probably three railroad boxcars of plastic bricks. Then, as I look into the distance, past a huge yellow globe, a dancing neon display draws my eye to the General Cinemas entrance on the distant top floor of the mall. The images begin to swirl, producing vertigo, even though I am standing firmly on the ground. For a moment they seem to turn into a cornucopia, beckoning me to taste. A little girl's voice brings me back from the brink.

"Wake up, wake up!" she shouts.

She is trying to restart the motorized Lego head of an eight-foot long-necked dinosaur. A pubescent boy with mousse in his hair and way-cool sunglasses reveals his age as the full impact of the Lego vista breaks through the ennui he was trying to cultivate.

"Wow, check this out. It's actual Lego."

Actual Lego. That makes the plastic Tyrannosaurus here an actual dinosaur. And we're not in a Lego museum. It's an actual store.

I need to catch my breath for a moment as I feel a pang of low blood sugar caused by my cinnamon bun–free state. I find a bench. I am hearing what sounds like the noise of a train station somewhere in the distance mixed with the laughter of children. T-shirts parade by: "Give Blood—Play Hockey" on a boy of maybe nine. A woman in her fifties wears "Easily Amused."

There are also the embittered spouses set throughout the mall's four levels like Rodin statues, only they are not just thinking, they are brooding. Each has gone through the same, inevitable metamorphosis. He reluctantly came to the mall for a day of shopping with his partner. But he would rather be anywhere else: at the auto parts store, at home woodworking or just watching the game. Soon his indulgence gives way to anxiety, wondering just what time parameters he has inadvertently committed himself to. What if we have to visit ALL the shoe stores? Impatience sets in as the spouse secretly prays for divine intervention to end the shopping trip. In the next stage he realizes he is all on his own.

He decides to take charge. Leaving no room for debate, he announces to his partner that traffic will be bad if they don't leave NOW. Fast-forward another hour and ten minutes and you have my partner on the bench: shoulders slumped, eyes focused on infinity, motionless. But he'll have his revenge. Next week he'll be the one to initiate the trip to the mall because he's suddenly possessed with the acute need for the Kitchenaid sausage-making attachment or a state-of-the-art post-hole digger.

No one dreams of speaking to me, and it doesn't seem appropriate for me to try to kibitz with them. If malls are supposed to be our new town squares, there is a problem. For all sorts of reasons, folks reserve their public space mode for the game or for the beach. This is private space, and it's clear I am not going to make any friends.

I feel this loss acutely because of where I have just come from. One of the virtues of a pilgrimage is that experiences unfold and rub up against each other in unpredictable ways. This trip to Minnesota was not inspired by the mall but by a reunion of people from this area whom I once went to school with in a very faraway place. It would have been just like me to come to a place like the mall and have a pleasant enough time and not really appreciate the difference between this virtual experience and an experience centered around not shopping but human interaction.

The reunion took place at a campground and retreat center about an hour west of Minneapolis. As a high school student I attended a school run by Lutheran missionaries from these parts. That school was located at the southeastern tip of Madagascar.

I was fifteen when I went there, dragged by a father's fellowship. It was a year that saw a coup d'état, martial law, a devastating cyclone, and intense friendships at a crucial adolescent moment. And hardly any consumption. Five hundred miles away in the temperate high-altitude capital of Madagascar, Antananarivo, was a grand Friday street market— the Zoma. I do remember purchasing a menacing six-foot souvenir spear there. But by and large, for an entire school year, I did virtually no shopping, saw no billboards, and heard no commercials.

One fellow student named Hulce did have a keen entrepreneurial skill. He managed to acquire French candy and Malabar chewing gum and sell it at a markup on Tuesdays in the basement of the school. How did we fill our time when there was nothing much to buy and little out-side encouragement to think about material goods? We hiked. We went on retreats to mountaintop lakes with just the guys. We explored lemur preserves. We gathered lichee nuts from trees. We read and played soc-cer. These were missionaries, so there was singing and praying. Above all, there was lots of human interaction.

The $26-a-night lakeside conference center provided only simple food on white bread. The bonfire was free, as was the meteor shower. So were the stories, sessions so long and so intense that both my elbows ac-tually blistered from leaning into conversations across the table.

I heard the tale of Joel, my ninth-grade roommate, eating what were known in Madagascar as "hot lemons," prompting within hours an emergency appendectomy. About Nadim's politically incorrect cigarette paper invention and subsequent patent. About Tami lending a dear friend the $10,000 she and her husband saved through back-breaking factory work and never seeing the money again.

These were people shaped in part by the experience of living on an island at the end of the earth and defined very little by their stuff. Per-haps that explains why a group of modern Americans could gather for a weekend at a lake and never once mention their new boats or new kitchens.

A problem arises when life becomes, by and large, a mixture of work, family chores, and shopping. It's a little like the hollow world Clifford Stoll writes of in *Silicon Snake Oil,* his critique of the on-line revolution: "It is an overpromoted, hollow world, devoid of warmth and human kindness." This also applies to shopping. An afternoon dragging your kids through the mall is no substitute for a day tobogganing with them or taking them to see jellyfish in a tidal pool.

I'm learning here at the mall that in many ways one of the big costs of the consuming lifestyle is not just the money but the time. The nov-elist Maxine Hong Kingston is acutely aware of this. Her house was com-pletely destroyed by the firestorm that struck the hills in Oakland and Berkeley, California, in 1991. She permanently lost two hundred pol-ished pages of a manuscript in that fire and everything else she owned. Eventually an insurance settlement arrived, an enormous check, she says, with so many zeros in the number, she had trouble fathoming its worth. But according to the rules, she had to use that money to replace not just her house but all her personal effects. Until the tragedy Kingston and her husband had tried to live simply and made a point to avoid shopping.

"The check forced me to become a shopper," Kingston told me. "It was as if I were on a spree, impelled to turn the money into carts full of merchandise. Lapis jewelry brought to this country from China by my grandmother had to be replaced. I had to go out and shop for new lapis jewelry, but I didn't want new jewelry. I had no use for it. What I missed was the heirloom and its history, which could not be replaced by all the time spent shopping."

"Madonna, safari of four? Your adventure is about to begin," trills the hostess with the headphones at the Rainforest Cafe.

Here? Now? I had heard she shows up at Planet Hollywood openings, but would she appear for a late lunch at the Mall of America's Rainforest Cafe? My pal Jill once sat next to her and Rosie O'Donnell at a sushi bar, so she does go out to eat. But that was at a sushi bar in the real Hollywood. I move in for a closer look.

"Marona safari, please step this way."

Standing outside the perimeter of the Rainforest Cafe, it is easy to feel detached from the knots of merry consumers inside. Perhaps it is my ever-falling blood sugar level, but I am becoming cranky.

The cafe's plastic vines, its soundtrack of bird calls and monkey shrieks, and its simulated thundershowers fuel my repulsion. Dry-ice machines pump a miasma along the edges of the booths, creating the look of a sultry rainforest as patrons ponder offerings like Tortuga Tidbits (chicken nuggets) on their Rainforest Cafe menus. I suppress the urge to toss them a handful of peanuts. What they could use more are my credit cards.

There is something about carrying around a surplus that just loosens up those credit cards. It starts with the simple fact that most of us prefer not to carry great gobs of cash around with us while shopping. It's inconvenient. The automated teller machines are often limited to disbursements of up to $200. There are security concerns about flashing great gobs of cash. So you walk down to the Ritz camera shop in the mall, find that telephoto lens that has been talking to you for six months now, and put down not $700 plus tax, but a credit card with the intention of paying off the bill at the end of the month. The end of the month comes around, the credit card bill arrives, but since you don't have to pay off the whole bill, you don't. If you end up paying $20 a month and there is nothing else on that credit card, that lens at 18 percent interest could take more than four years to pay off and cost about $300 extra in interest. The average American household has four credit cards and runs a balance of about $4,800.

Of course, the owners of this mall would prefer I live more in the moment and spend less time thinking about bills four years from now. But just who are the owners? I sit down next to a grandmother who holds the handle of a stroller containing two blonde toddlers with one hand and a flip phone with the other. I infer that the mother of the two cuties is on another wireless personal communications device relaying intelligence from another of the mall's strategic battlefields. I paw through my satchel looking for my notes. I find a summary of the mall's ownership.

Something looks familiar.

It's the same name as on my quarterly retirement account statements. Part of my pension portfolio is an annuity. I knew this annuity was into everything, including real estate, but who ever thought this very Mall of America would be one of its holdings? The implication takes a moment to find the route into my addled head.

Let's see, the annuity holds a big piece of this mall in its portfolio.

The annuity, then, is a part owner of the mall.

I own a piece of the annuity.

I own the Mall of America.

These lovely, wonderful, ardent consumers I see around me? They are helping my future, my family's future, and the quality of my life after retirement. The more they spend, the better the mall does, and the profits keep my portfolio healthy. What are you waiting for, people? It's time for you to spend!

In fact, it may be time for me to spend. I could get the Ritz Camera here at the mall to order me that Speed Graphic through its antique and collectible catalog. My expenditure wouldn't even have to be in my personal debit column. If Ritz does well, the mall will do well, and I will do well because my retirement savings will be in good stead. It is a wonderful feeling, like metamorphosing into one of those worms with both sets of organs so it can both do and get done at the same time.

I am becoming stupid for lack of nourishment. The Rainforest Cafe denizens laugh gaily as they tuck into their Amazon burgers. One of the toddlers in the adjacent seat is sucking noisily on either a mothball or a yogurt almond. I've got to get out while I can. Is this why the woman seemed to be crying at the mall entrance?

Over at mall location S-108 is a display of my dreaded mall nemesis, the shoe. But a friendly shape catches my eye, a pair of brown Dexters, still manufactured, for the moment at least, in my home state. Dexter had featured in an advertisement targeted, with unerring precision, right at my cerebral cortex. It is easy to take the high road on marketing when an ad shoots wide. I scoff and sneer at the fast food chain that hawks its sloppy burgers with the line "If it doesn't get all over the place, it doesn't belong in your face." But one day leafing through *The New York Times Magazine,* I learned instantly that I was not above the well-crafted pitch. The ad showed a pair of familiar brown shoes with the tag "Worn by Joe Engle, astronaut, as he paced the floor of mission control serving as flight controller to many shuttle missions."

My demographic is said to have few heroes, but the ad caused stirrings, deep preadolescent stirrings, in a guy who was nine when Neil and Buzz did the moon walk. In a moment I switched from having no opinion about shoes to having a desire. My desire to walk in Joe Engle's shoes transcended rationality.

They say skilled Asian street merchants can spot the subtle but telltale dilation of the pupils of customers who are actually interested in their wares and use that knowledge to drive a hard bargain. To believe for a second that they don't have my pupils wired, just because I have a graduate degree and like to watch Italian art films, is to seriously underestimate the power of these messages.

Anyway, even if one has the testicular fortitude to resist defining oneself by purchases, others are happy to do it for you. I used to notice it on the London Underground. One of my jobs was to clip the dozen daily British newspapers and fax the good bits back to headquarters. Depending on which one I had in my hand on the train, people made assumptions about me and reacted accordingly: conservative prat (*Daily Telegraph*), liberal wanker (the *Guardian*), yuppie git (*Financial Times*). The need to place you in your socioeconomic category is famously acute in Britain. Because my accent was no guide, a senior editor at *The Economist* magazine, a man with a fancy double-barreled surname, finally blurted it out one day after I had worked with him for two years.

"I say, David. Are you of the royal Brancaccio line or a peasant Brancaccio?"

A peasant and proud of it, with one little reservation. I am the first-born of a first-born of a first-born of a first-born. Had we been of more aristocratic stock, I might own most of the lower boot of Italy, the rules of primogeniture being what they are. Just the right pair of shoes—say, a $365 pair of Church's bespoke wingtips, for instance—might have saved my editor friend years of wondering. I wish I could say my identity is healthily separate from my patterns of consumption. But I would be kidding myself.

And this runs very, very deep, perhaps as deep as the hunting genes of the species.

The hunt, the search, the chase is actually a pretty decent form of recreation, perhaps more than the actual purchase. I hold an exaggerated notion of myself as a kind of consumer hunter, not a gatherer. Or I used to until Ian Cesa, my neighbor, put me straight. Ian runs a market research business. He says when men shop, they're mostly trying to avoid looking stupid.

Is there a more dreaded condition than buying the wrong thing? The Greek fisherman's cap that makes you look not jaunty, as intended, but in fact like a dweeb. The sports utility vehicle that rolls over easily, according to the consumer magazine that comes out on the day your first payment is due. The VCR that your neighbor finds for $65 less than you did.

But if you have done your homework properly, you can walk into the workplace on Monday with the supreme pride and confidence that come with knowing that no one has or ever will get that Makita circular saw for even a nickel less than you paid for it. You'll never admit to Snyder in the next cubicle that you got the tool at that price because it came without its box, without instructions, without a warranty, and missing the little wrench that you need to change the blades. You got it for 11 percent less than even the cheapest one being sold used in the newspaper classified ads. You are *bad*.

Not looking stupid, it turns out, is a powerful force behind shopping. It was the force that drove me nearly mad the next time I tumbled head over heals in love, this time with the idea of a new computer for the home office.

I read up. I weighed the options. I corroborated. I cross-referenced. I test-drove. I interviewed other owners. I woke up an hour early on Saturdays to get the Sports section with the computer ads. I devised complex spreadsheets to compare competing systems. I snuck away from my son's tennis practice to make calls about computer prices. I lied about my obsession. I frantically and irrationally accused my spouse of deliberately losing track of my computer magazine with the comparison chart of color monitors.

Weeks passed. Competing bids were solicited from computer stores. Last-minute checks of the World Wide Web yielded no better deals. I consulted the graph I had devised predicting the optimum moment when the line describing price and model age, which drives prices down, crosses the line plotting prices and scarcity, as a discontinued model gets harder to find. The chart indicated today was the day to strike.

At home I tried to appear nonchalant. Mary wondered over breakfast what plans we had for the evening.

"Oh, I don't know," I said. "If we are all in the mood, I thought perhaps I might run over and pick up that computer."

Later at the office I promptly blew my cover.

"They're going to get me," I mumbled. "The deal is too good. I've overlooked something; there's got to be a bump in the deal. Why can't I see it?"

Eve, my colleague, shook me.

"Snap out of it, man," I seem to remember her saying. "You're out of control. You've got to focus. You've got a job to do. Your job is to buy a computer without looking stupid. Don't waste time on second thoughts. It's a little early for buyer's remorse, isn't it? Take a deep breath, straighten your shoulders, and go out and buy like a man."

Deborah, the producer, overhearing this exchange, thought it was time for an intervention.

"How about he does his job first and then goes to buy his toy so that our dear listeners aren't treated to a half hour of a postmodern performance-art piece of silence in place of our regularly scheduled program."

It was a tough call, since my normal faculties were, again, clouded by the urge. Foolish men have often been described as thinking with their groins at times. My thinking was now centered just slightly higher, near the location of my wallet.

The sun was setting over the Pacific Ocean as I pulled into the computer store. I poked my head into a back office, as instructed. My contact was kneeling over a radio-controlled miniature race car, tinkering with the battery charger.

"Is your name Arky? It's me, the one with the long Italian last name."

"The seventy-six hundred."

"Right. Let's do it."

It went smoothly. Too smoothly. The machine, as promised, was in stock. So were four other cartons of accessories. There was no battle over an unwanted extended warranty. Arky forced no fancy keyboard on me, just a choice of two reasonably priced ones.

"If you can't tell the difference, buy the cheap one," he advised.

I watched like a hawk when the extra memory chips were added to the bowels of the new machine, to be sure the nice boards I had paid for were not substituted with drek. I paid extra to use my American Express card, and I had been warned about that service charge over the phone, but I wanted the extra buyer's protection that came with the card.

Arky was itching to leave for the night, something about a radio-controlled car race. His moves were brisk.

"Dude, you set? I'm history."

On the way out, the store's guard politely checked my bill of sale against my pile of boxes and helped me pile them into the car. I did one more silent inventory, tipped the gentleman $3, and drove off $3,200 lighter.

I did an emotional inventory to see if I could come up with elation, relief, or pride, but all I found was emptiness, especially in the areas of my stomach and my wallet. I had just run for a sixty-yard touchdown in the computer purchase Superbowl, but all I felt now was disquiet.

"Calm down and drive," I told myself. "You checked everything, and everything checked out."

Still, it was too easy. Why were the folks in that store in such a hurry to see me go? I was sure it was only because it was approaching closing time on a Friday night, that's all.

Five blocks later, nowhere near home, the fear of failure crested and crashed over me. I yanked the car to the curb, hit the trunk release, leaped around the back, and pulled out the dearest of the boxes. Slicing the packing tape with my car key, I dove in and coaxed the computer up from its Styrofoam packing. The street light gave off only a dim orange glow, so for a moment I thought the shadows were playing tricks.

I had just spent a surplus on a 7600. What the box contained was a 7200, a poor cousin to the computer listed on the carton. I had been *stung*.

Or a hideous mistake had occurred, at the very least. Either option made me feel profoundly stupid, which is the opposite of what the art of shopping is supposed to be.

My journey back to the store was a hysterical blur. I grabbed the invoice and my box containing somebody else's cheaper computer and ran to the front door.

It was locked.

A clock somewhere chimed six bells, closing time. A woman at a desk looked up and mimed, "Sorry, we're closed. " That little gratuity I had handed to the guard saved me. I caught his eye, and he smiled and flipped open the lock on the front door.

I put the bill of sale on the counter and pointed to the box. I was inarticulate with a combination of dread and anger, muttering about 7600s and 7200s, but I had no need to explain. It became clear they knew I might be back, only they hadn't banked on my reappearing so quickly. For a moment no one spoke. Eyes narrowed. Teeth were sucked. Shoulders hunched. In the history of high-technology retailing, no one there had ever heard of such a thing occurring.

I regained my balance and my voice.

"Here's how it's going to be. You are going to find me a fresh seventy-six hundred in the next sixty seconds, put in the extra memory, and I'm going to walk out of here nice and friendly-like."

Mr. Big walked over from a back office.

"We have to see if we have one in stock. We may have sold you the last one."

I reminded him that he had not sold me the last 7600, because what he had handed me was a 7200. My plan was to get satisfaction within the next few moments or walk to the pay phone on the corner and block the transaction on the charge card that I had paid extra to use. A few heartbeats passed. Then Mr. Big broke into a smile. For once in my life, the game was mine.

My market researcher neighbor offered me a corollary to his theory about how men shop. Not looking stupid is key. So is coming back with a good story.

Sure, I could have paid $200 extra for the peace of mind of buying from the reputable and tested computer store three blocks from my office. But then I wouldn't have had a story, and why shop if you don't net a story? It's very much like fishing. If a fish is the goal, then you can get one quicker at the market or more elegantly prepared at a restaurant. No, fishing and shopping are very much about the legends they create.

Now to apply this to the big question of my mall trip: Are these new legends worth the time and the money put in? What if the same energy of this hunt was put into not acquiring something but interacting with someone, creating something new, improving, not just using up, the world around me? The hunting doesn't have to end, but the shopping may need to.

The clocks are well hidden at the Mall of America. Not enough natural light trickles in to keep you posted on the passage of the day. But my growling stomach knows the lateness of the hour. At Calido chili traders, the poster screams onions and jalapeños. Even the raw ingredients are starting to sound good to me after a half day of abstinence. I have almost pulled it off. All I have left to do is to get to the exit nearest my parked car. Diagonally across from that Lake Wobegon shop that keeps turning up like bad penny, there is a short queue of customers waiting in a shop that uses a video camera to superimpose one's face on a fake magazine cover. As if my face would have anything to do with *Wrestling Monthly*.

I am about to laugh off the store when number 365 catches my eye. Number 365 would put my face on a white tuxedo at a craps table flanked by two lovelies at the center of a mock cover of *Casino Player Monthly*. It's too perfect. The cover even has fake headlines about "Investing to Win in Gaming Stocks." How much is it?

"Sixteen ninety-five for the eight by ten."

Seventeen bucks? That's ridiculous. That's an eight-dollar laugh, not a penny more. I walk out.

I walk back in. *"Casino Player."* The technician squeezes my face into a blank cardboard cutout.

"OK, Mr. High Roller, lookin' great. Next!"

Two minutes later the color laser printer spits out the result. My little head with no neck sits perched atop the tux like a golfball without a tee. While the craps table and the women in cocktail dresses look like they were photographed in a studio, I look like a photocopy of a TV screen. My complexion is florid. I have a five o'clock shadow. My hair is askew. There is no possible way such a purchase can be justified or, indeed, ever displayed in public.

"That will be twenty-six ninety-five."

I glumly wonder to myself why the bill is ten dollars more than the quoted price. It appears they are throwing in a Lucite frame that I hadn't requested. The mall has won. I have no sugar left in my blood and no will to resist. I hand over my credit card and wordlessly sign on the line.

Tripped up by a pebble. We feel powerful, but we are not in full control. Perhaps that is why the woman seemed to be crying at the mall's doorway. For all my self-conscious musings, I'm still a sucker. It would have been nice to have been able to fly back and report that I had learned in the mall the twelve simple steps to cure compulsive consumerism. But this is the start of the pilgrimage, not the end, and while this examination of the reasons I spend is helping me loosen up the knots around old patterns, I am clearly not on the wagon yet.

My identity is still bound up with what I buy. I cannot completely forsake my love for tracking down and bagging the greatest consumer electronic deals on the planet. I will always cheer when my buddy Chris, a composer, weaves a flawless argument that spending $12,000 on a used Steinway piano is a fine use of money because the instrument will appreciate in value. Or when Walt, the airborne traffic reporter, tells me how the money he spent on a World War One Flying Ace biplane will eventually fund his retirement when it appreciates and he sells it at a presumed big profit.

But I didn't find one thing for sale at the mall that would change my life. I could probably stop my badly considered, compulsive purchases by avoiding burning valuable time somnambulating through shopping situations. I'm learning here at the mall that one of the big costs of the consuming lifestyle is not just the money but the time. It is no secret that while Americans are earning more than ever, they are also working harder. As our down time becomes more scarce, its value rises. We may have more discretionary income, more surplus, but there is less time to enjoy it.

The airport is much closer to the mall than I reckoned, practically around the corner, so I find myself with a generous amount of what could euphemistically be called "time for meditation" in the departure lounge. That image of the woman at the mall entrance stays with me.

The CNN Airport Channel is nattering on from a monitor over my head, and the anchorwoman mentions a local story, which jars me from my glazed reverie. A small tornado touched down in one of the suburbs around here, snatching some roofs and a gas station canopy on its way through.

The woman in front of the mall could have been upset about all sorts of things, her roof, her job, her credit cards. But I will never be sure just what was wrong for a simple reason: Mr. Fine Upstanding Citizen here, I was too self-absorbed to ask. How socially irresponsible. I need to do better than this. I have defined consumption as a very selfish undertaking, and my questions about money have been too inner-directed. Maybe money isn't just about me. Maybe it is about how money connects me with the rest of the world. This pushes me off the fence.

I discovered a mention on the Internet of a pending socially responsible investment conference at a national park high in the Rocky Mountains. Just what the doctor ordered: a trip to the wilderness to dry out. I use the remaining time at the airport to book my next trip.

Souvenirs

An embarrassing picture of my face on a fake magazine cover.

The conviction that I spend way too much trying to entertain myself by shopping.

To do when I get home

Draw up an aggressive program to pay off my credit card debt by the end of these money trips.

File my credit card away in the same folder as my passport. If I really need it, I know where to find it, but it will no longer be allowed to constantly whistle at me suggestively from my back pocket.

Doing the numbers

Cost of buying a Graflex Speed Graphic antique press camera: $425

Credit card interest rate: 18%

Minimum payment: 2% per month

Terms: Pay minimum each month or $5, whichever is more

Time it takes to pay off the debt: More than 16 years

Finance charges: $710

Total cost of purchase: $1,135

Opportunity cost: $425 invested for 16 years at 6% yield: $1,107

$425 invested for 16 years at 10% yield: $2,091

3

Invest Like Your Very Liberal Mother Is Watching

Being socially responsible,
Jackson Hole, Wyoming

From the clipping file: A telephone operator from Manchester, New Hampshire, won $66 million in the lottery. The *Boston Globe* quoted her husband saying, "Everyone has a responsibility to make the world a better place. Maybe now we can do that a little more effectively." December 24, 1997

Could you pass up a chance to visit the splendor of the Wyoming Rockies right at the cusp of autumn if the cost could be written off as a business expense? Neither could I. The business at hand was a gathering of groovies in Grand Teton National Park who believe there is a way to do well and to do good at the same time.

Practitioners of socially responsible investing believe that a surplus can be used to express social, political, religious, or other dearly held values. Among the many variations of this genre of investing is the principle of rewarding companies that behave in ways you like by investing in them and punishing those you do not by culling them from your portfolio. I was attracted to the notion that the treatment of a surplus does not have to be as utterly self-centered as my explorations of consumption in the mall had been. I wondered if the benefits of knowing I was doing good with money were worth the cost. And as a way of probing my own hypocrisy on this subject, I wanted to confront a dark suspicion that this strategy was a sop to folks who feel guilty about selling out after starting out in the world decrying materialism.

I also had a hunch, a correct one as it turned out, that I would meet some folks who have come to terms with many of the uncomfortable contradictions that come with a surplus.

It wasn't another *Challenger* explosion, but word came with the same kind of urgency. Once in a blue moon, news has the capacity to stun. And stun it did at the conference of socially responsible investors and financial advisers. I watched the frisson pass through the crowd like a shock wave in newsreel footage of the Bikini Island tests. The CEO of Ben & Jerry's had just quit.

When it comes to capitalism, Ben & Jerry's Homemade, Inc., is just about the grooviest of the groovy. The company doesn't pollute. It buys milk and cream from local farmers. It has a reputation for treating its employees like human beings. Seven-and-a-half percent of its pretax profits go to charity. A socially responsible mutual fund was giving out Ben & Jerry's gift certificates to those who signed up for its mailing list here at the conference venue, the Jackson Lake Lodge.

Ice cream, however, is not exactly health food, and there was the matter of their outgoing chief executive's salary: he made fourteen-and-a-half times what an ice cream scooper earns, breaking with previous company policy to limit income disparities by capping executive salaries at seven-and-a-half times that of the lowest-paid worker.

The cause of the sudden departure of Ben & Jerry's boss was indeed a mystery. Robert Holland was the outfit's attempt to bring in seasoned professional management. He had been hired nineteen months earlier, after a national search involving an essay contest entitled "Yo! I want to be CEO!" He was brought in by a headhunter, singled out by his impressive résumé. Holland won over Ben and Jerry's with his essay about the roots of his social conscience.

In the Jackson Lake Lodge lobby, a socially responsible banker from Vermont got on the horn to his connections to get to the bottom of the story. Among the conferees a consensus seemed to form around the following scenario: Wall Street wanted Ben & Jerry's to grow and continue growing. Holland, a former McKinsey and Company management consultant, wanted Ben & Jerry's to grow. Is it possible that Ben, Jerry, or both worried about how to sustain such growth? Would it mean buying cream from cheaper, out-of-state sources? Would it mean moving production to some place like China, where labor costs less? I had bumped into a question that I was certain would nag me on this trip: Is going public, that is, transferring ownership of a company to shareholders via the market, a moral compromise? Is corporate responsibility as defined by folks at this conference incompatible with the responsibilities demanded by the market?

Despite the limited information trickling into the remote lodge on the grassy valley floor of Grand Teton National Park, it was possible to draw one conclusion: even the world's grooviest company is a business, not a family, and it may be dangerous to confuse the two. Unlike the typical father or mother, if the person at the helm of a company is not working out or gets a better offer, he's gone. I should have read the omen that unusual news was in store at the conference. On my way there, I had seen a blue moon.

I had visions of observing the last total eclipse of the moon visible in North America in this millennium from a porch at a remote Wyoming lodge. It was even an agenda item at the SRI in the Rockies conference. Instead, I was stuck observing this natural wonder from a cramped airline seat while my Delta flight taxied to the gate at an intermediate stop in Salt Lake City. The image making it through the awful mayonnaise-jar airplane windows was striking, whether or not it bore any resemblance to the reality outside. The remains of the sunset gave the lake a neon glow broken only by an enormous harvest moon with a piece missing, as though someone were already consuming the harvest.

Inside the terminal a man wearing golden epaulets talked on the adjacent pay phone: "The earth is like a basketball, Jim. And the moon is a baseball and the sun is a flashlight," the pilot said.

The earth is like a basketball. Just this morning I had used the same metaphor to explain the eclipse to my seven-year-old during our walk to school. I suspect on this evening, dads all over North America were yielding to a primordial impulse to explain the eclipse to their offspring in mechanical rather than mystical terms.

I hadn't ended my unsolicited lecture about the eclipse with the flashlight and sporting goods model. I did mention to Nicholas that some ancient people were terrified of an eclipse because they believed it meant bad luck.

"Dad?"

"Yeah?"

"What's luck?"

Not another one, so hot on the heels of his "Did the universe begin or was it always there?" on a long road trip a few weeks earlier.

"Luck...luck..." I vamped. "Luck is like when something good just happens to you right out of the blue, something that wasn't planned. Bad luck is when something bad happens that wasn't your fault," I ventured.

"Good luck is when you do something good, and something good happens that you didn't expect. Bad luck is the opposite," Nick told me.

"But you know, you can make your own luck. If you walk down the street with your eyes closed and fall into a sewer, that's not bad luck. If you walk down the street with your eyes open and you get knocked over by a meteorite, that's bad luck. It wasn't your fault."

"Can you make good luck?" Nick asked.

Here we have the central question of both investing and risk management, to which I would very much like to find out the answer as my adventures progress. But it is my son's initial take on luck that has the most resonance for this trip to the Rockies. If you do something good, is good fortune more likely to come your way? That may not be answerable, but it isn't a bad assumption to live by. In Wyoming I would twist this just slightly so the question becomes, does doing something good necessarily have to hurt your bottom line? This question is at the center of the discussion of socially responsible investment, the practice of keeping your money away from enterprises you don't agree with and using it as a reward for enterprises you do agree with. I want to know if SRI is the kind of club that I would join.

It is only September, but the air already smells like snow at Jackson Hole. The airport offers many amenities, but artificial outdoor light is not among them. I spend the next ten minutes groping my way through the parking lot trying to detect the shape of my rental car. Where is moonlight when you need it? It's up there, but dirt in the upper atmosphere is still playing tricks with the waning eclipse. The moon is now a soft blue, as if some shameless ad man figured out a way to take advertising to its last frontier: "The eclipse, sponsored by Indiglo watches."

Seeing a blue moon has the power to shake up one's entire investment outlook. They are a long shot, but walking out to a rental car and seeing one is a cosmic way of goading you into thinking that long shots may actually score. Imagine walking into a casino, sliding a quarter in a slot machine, pulling the handle, and hitting a $150 jackpot. Who cares if you are a statistical aberration? You have just invested a measly 25 cents and gotten a return of $149.75. You have thrown risk analysis and modern portfolio theory to the four winds. Your strategy at that very moment is undeniably effective. Actually, a blue moon is the second full moon in a calendar month, something that happens every 2.7 years. Perhaps luck is quantifiable after all.

Jackson Hole is a long, thin valley with one main road and one parallel secondary road. Lost in all these thoughts of risk and reward, and mesmerized by the New Age space music playing late at night on Wyoming Public Radio, I get really, really lost. Someone up here thoughtfully designed all the highway signs in a faux-rustic style appropriate to the pioneer theme of the national park but illegible at any speed. Fifty-eight miles later I am tired, hungry, and still lost. The alternatives exhausted, I am forced to trigger the last-resort scenario. I open the glove compartment and consult a map. I make a silent deal with myself. If I get out of this alive tonight, I promise never again to allow my male ego to prevent me from using a map on these trips. It is an invitation to open my mind and seek the counsel of others.

As I stand in line for the buffet breakfast included in the socially responsible conference package, I am relieved to see that my dress is up to code. Had I worn the blue blazer I packed just in case, I fear I would have been shunned. But the flannel shirt is right on.

I haven't eaten for eighteen hours. The sausages and Canadian bacon beckon. But what kind of statement will I make if I sit down among socially responsible strangers with a plate loaded with animal carcass? I'm not a huge carnivore, so I opt for more correct fare, scrambled eggs with a side of sliced strawberries. Before I fully settle in my cafeteria seat, I learn it is not correct enough.

"Haven't eaten an egg in nine years," said the man with a midwestern accent on my right.

"I still have an egg in my fridge that my wife bought before our divorce," said a man on my left who looked like Jesus.

I had inadvertently landed on Planet Vegan, where even the consumption of animal-derived products like eggs and cheese carry stiff penalties. I feel like such a fool. Embarrassed but starved, I try a small mouthful. It tastes a little synthetic. They're fake eggs, vegan approved.

"How are those Egg Beaters?" says the man on the left. I manage a muffled "Zesty."

A man of military bearing who looks in charge stands up to make an announcement: "For those requiring soy milk, the hotel has kindly provided it for us." The conference organizers have gone out of their way to idiot-proof socially responsible dining. At the mall, how I used money left me nauseated and I did my darndest to shed the skin of a consumer. But will the new clothes available here fit? If they do, I may have a place to park some money without turning into a creature that I am not.

My bearded tablemate wears a white rectangular badge pinned to his sweater that says, "Hi, my name is" followed by a big UPC bar code.

923337001's earth name is Eric. People don't have much luck guessing his occupation, he says. Night manager for an art film theater in a college town in the Pacific Northwest would have been my guess. Geographically, I am close. In fact, Eric is a certified financial planner from Seattle.

How did you find yourself in the world of money, I want to know. Eric traces it back to his bar mitzvah. An uncle gave him shares in Comsat as a coming-of-age gift. Intrigued, he took some of the other money that came in from friends and relatives and bought more stock: Mattel, just what you would choose if you were thirteen. Then the quarterly statements started coming in. He started picking up the business section to see how his stocks were doing and became intrigued by news of Wall Street printed on adjacent pages. Much later, he became a corporate accountant, and then a socially responsible financial planner after taking time off for reflection in India.

I think back to my thirteenth birthday. Grandpa Hy gave me $200, my cut of the cash he won playing my birthdate in a numbers game run by a local bookie. I had never seen a fifty-dollar bill before, let alone four of them destined for my pocket. I spent weeks carefully considering what I would do with my little windfall. I can safely say that investing it in the stock market never once crossed my mind. If anyone had suggested stocks, it would have been like proposing that I use the money to buy a set of Chinese-language encyclopedias. Why would I want to do that? I confess to Eric that I used my $200 to buy the biggest, fanciest radio I could find, a General Coverage Receiver, with band spread, beat frequency oscillator, and knobs for both audio frequency and radio frequency attenuation. I am acutely embarrassed by Eric's next question: "What do you do now?" Suggested Ph.D. thesis in sociology: "Expenditure of Bar Mitzvah Windfalls as Career Predictors."

Did I mention that Eric doesn't smoke? Neither does Dan, across the table. Nor does anyone at SRI in the Rockies, as far as I can tell. I watch carefully for signs that anyone is faking it: the irritability, the inappropriate wearing of coats indoors, the furtive exits on headings that intercept no restrooms. There is none of that. Maybe I am missing it, but while there must be socially responsible investors who indulge in tobacco, they don't dare show their faces near this lodge on this particular weekend. That's because while SR investors bring many agendas to the table when they discuss their portfolios—from stopping destruc-

tion of the Canadian tundra to encouraging the rights of gay and les-
bian domestic partners to receive company spousal benefits—there is
one issue that has the attendees in lock step, like NRA members tuned
to a G. Gordon Liddy broadcast. Tobacco, they agree, is a social evil.

The premise of socially responsible investing, I learn, is that everyone has a limit, even the most diehard free marketeer, someone who fer-
vently believes that politics have no place in evaluating a corporate
balance sheet. Would you have held a portfolio in the 1930s that owned
a piece of Krups, which made weapons for Adolph Hitler? Krups went
public only in the 1960s, sparing most people this particular ethical
dilemma. But the issue is not just a liberal one. Some fundamentalist
Christians are angry at the Walt Disney Company because of its domestic partners policy, among other things. Many social conservatives do
not want to own shares in a pharmaceutical company that manufactures RU-486, the so-called abortion pill. SRI organizers believe that the
single issue of opposing tobacco can throw a net around the widest possible coalition.

At first glance, tobacco seems a more manageable cause than SRI's
former heat-seeking issue: punishing companies that did business with
South Africa's apartheid government. With tobacco you have a tangible
domestic product, and almost everyone personally knows a victim of
smoking. There are thirteen U.S. tobacco stocks, which makes it relatively easy for investors, or big pension fund managers, to identify
which tobacco shares they hold and run the numbers to see what might
happen if they were to dump them. In other words, the target is big and
carefully delineated. During one plenary session a conference bigwig is
asked why tobacco, above all other important social concerns, has been
thrust to the tip-top of the SRI agenda. Alisa Gravitz from the Co-op
America Foundation replies, "Because it's hot right now."

During a coffee break I overhear whispers of a fiendish plot. Two of
the leading lights of the SRI movement, Tim Smith of the Interfaith
Center on Corporate Responsibility and Jack Brill, author of *Investing
from the Heart,* are hatching a plan to capitalize on the tobacco contro-
versy's current vogue. They are only half serious, but they're spreading
the idea of pushing for the Big Cahuna of tobacco stocks, Philip Morris, to get dumped from the Dow Jones Industrial Average. No stock

has ever been delisted from the Dow for a political or social reason. South Africa getting kicked out of the United Nations is not quite the analogy. It is more akin to, and probably as difficult as, getting a country kicked out of the U.N. Security Council. The SRI folks would love the media coverage such an idea would spawn, with the hope that it would provoke a national wave of soul searching about which stocks are morally acceptable to own and why. If the Dow Jones is a projection of the moment-to-moment zeitgeist of the nation, why should our identity be bound up with tobacco? To the SRI folks it is a little like having the image of a pack of cigarettes sewn into the corner of the American flag where the stars go.

The idea has at least one thing going for it. The Dow Jones Industrial Average has always been a fudge. This index of the mightiest and most influential of American corporations is based on both objective and subjective criteria. Software behemoth Microsoft is not in the Dow. Bethlehem Steel, Woolworth's, and Westinghouse Electric were until they were de-listed in 1997 to make way for more dynamic, modern companies like Hewlett-Packard, Wal-Mart and Johnson & Johnson. Dow Jones and Company, which husbands the index, has been forced to make some fairly subjective adjustments throughout the years as companies in the Dow have gone belly up or, more often, been merged out of existence. Still, the chance that Wall Street would banish Philip Morris from the index for nonfinancial reasons at this stage in our history must be close to absolute zero.

As the representatives of Co-op America work through a presentation that should have been entitled "Tobacco: The Great Satan, and How the Issue Can be Made to Work for SRI While Improving the Health of the World," I scan the room for the spy.

If the tobacco industry had brains, it would have sent a spy, right? If SRI does nothing else, it attempts to cajole companies by pressing a firm's most sensitive button, tampering with the share price. Surely there is enough at stake for the industry to want to pop for the airfare and the $310 conference fee. But who is the spy? I search for the giveaway. I scan the crowd for polyester, but it is a sea of earth-toned cotton. This guy's good. Check the shoes. A CIA fellow I once knew told me that shoes are always the tipoff. If you want to blend in, don't forget your shoes. I drop my pen to the floor as a pretext to check for telltale shoes in the back of the room. Wingtips, that's the ticket. Who would wear wingtips to a rustic lodge in the Grand Tetons? At floor level it's a collage of Rockports, Timberlands, and Bass moccasins, comfortable shoes even too casual for casual Fridays at the office. I have Vibram soles on, so the spy isn't me.

If there had been a spy present, he would have had some questions. Some would be obvious ones particular to the tobacco industry. But others would resonate with more conventional investors both on and off Wall Street. The first question is about risk. Investing in one company is risky. That is why we are told not to put our entire retirement savings into the stock of our own employer. Investing in a rich variety of stocks lowers the risk. The big question then becomes, doesn't banning a whole basketful of stocks because you don't approve of the way they do business limit the universe of stocks you can chose from and therefore raise the risk? Another big question has to do with the fact that there are a lot of what some might regard as naughty companies making a fortune. I have a clipping from the *Washington Post* that suggests that had you invested $50,000 in Philip Morris about the time Ronald Reagan was inaugurated and plowed all the dividends back into the stock, by the time of Bill Clinton's second inauguration the investment would have grown to more than $1.2 million, performance that is about 10 percent higher than the stock market overall. That's a nice little earner and tough to replace. Another problem involves diversification. Companies that make cigarettes also make lots of other products that aren't socially irresponsible. If you throw out the tobacco company, you may lose access to other growth sectors of the market.

How, then, can the folks of SRI claim that "doing good" doesn't have to cost you anything? Here are the arguments: Yes, blacklisting companies for political and social reasons does reduce the universe of stocks from which a portfolio can be chosen. But portfolio managers actually do that all the time. Oh, they say they carefully evaluate which stocks to buy and sell using objective financial criteria, that is, numbers. But we are dealing with human beings here, and people are influenced by all sorts of prejudices. Perhaps they were burned badly in real estate, so they shy away from real estate forever after. Or they fall in love with companies that are currently fashionable because they're getting all the cover space in *Barron's* and *Investor's Business Daily*. Evaluating the risk of a portfolio can be an exercise in almost scientific precision. But actually assembling the portfolio is more an art than most managers ever want to admit. Art involves some dead reckoning. After all, if this undertaking were completely objective, computers could do it. Some classes of stock are trendy, so human managers buy along with the rest of the herd. Some are out because "no one is buying Union Carbide these days." In the real world, no one chooses objectively and precisely from the universe of all possible stocks. Socially responsible investors argue that since there are subjective factors in investing, ones that don't fit easily into a computer spreadsheet, then why not make those subjective factors a force for good?

Another question has to do with losing out on the profits made by companies banned from portfolios. You can find tobacco shares in the portfolios of many of the country's largest mutual funds. If you have a pension fund, more likely than not you're holding tobacco stock. Co-op America calculates that Philip Morris alone represents 1.51 percent of the Standard & Poor's 500 index, the stock market benchmark of serious market professonals. One-and-a-half percent of a portfolio makes a difference. Investing in non-tobacco stocks would probably have earned you less. Some socially responsible investors argue this is a small price to pay for making the world a better, smoke-free place. But that's not the official socially responsible investment pitch.

The main current of SRI argues that doing good does not have to cost anything. In the case of tobacco, the argument is made this way: in the real world, removing Philip Morris from one's portfolio is only half the equation. In practice, the investor would buy another stock or set of stocks to replace it. You could dump RJ Reynolds, for example, and replace it with shares from other food industry giants, like the Campbell Soup Company or Hershey Foods, that don't make cigarettes. A big profit maker like Philip Morris could be replaced with another top earner like Microsoft. If the replacements do well, the tobacco ban doesn't cost a cent.

The movement marshals some credible academic studies that suggest that applying political and social screens to one's portfolio does not help or hinder a portfolio's performance. Pioneer Fund, one of the oldest and most reputable mutual funds, was also one of the first to screen its stocks. Since its inception in 1928, Pioneer has never invested in "sin" stocks (alcohol, tobacco, and gambling) because its founder, a devout Christian, felt supporting these industries was immoral.

Supporters of SRI also warn that the very nature of their businesses leaves the "sin" industry open to lawsuits and political and social attacks—occurrences that can be bad news for shareholders. But detractors say they avoid SRI funds because some have underperformed the market in general.

Take, for instance, the Parnassus Fund, which surprised Wall Street earlier in the 1990s with market-beating results for its socially responsible filters. It had hit a rough patch by the time of the conference. "I told you so," conventional investors say. A year later Parnassus would beat the return of all other mutual funds in the country, socially responsible or not, with a 71 percent return. Later, it lagged again. Volatile but interesting. More generally, the Domini 400 Social Index, a kind of S&P 500 for the granola set, keeps pace with the S&P and actually beat it by five percent in 1998, a great year for the S&P.

The point is that you can buy winning and losing mutual funds whether or not they are conventionally or socially screened. The variable is often the skill of the fund manager, not the social and political filters.

That is the general theory, but as they say, "Your mileage may vary." I have a retirement plan that allows me to switch my 401K money at the touch of a few telephone touchtones from a regular stock fund to an aggressive growth fund to a relatively safe and low-yield money market fund to a socially responsible fund. For whatever reason—the skills of my fund managers or some inherent risk implied by social filters—the simplest SRI fund for me tends to slightly underperform the regular stock fund. So for me the calculation is remarkably straightforward. How much am I willing to pay to send a message to companies that how they do business is more important to me than their results and to know that I'm not supporting some of the worst offenders?

✳   ✳   ✳

What I need, clearly, is some sound advice. Lucky for me, I find myself sitting at a conference dinner with a sound man. Mr. D is a former motion picture audio recordist who left what I consider one of the world's most noble professions to join one that he found had an even higher calling: socially responsible investment adviser.

Although he is perhaps a quarter century older than me, Mr. D is an investment adviser I can relate to: a man who knows which side of a single-edged razor blade to use when editing tape. If a man like Mr. D thinks you can "do well by doing good," then it must be true.

I met quite a few SRI advisers who said they were called to the profession to atone for sins earlier in life. But for the sound man, helping folks cobble together portfolios they aren't ashamed of is the result of a specific episode of soul searching. Mr. D wanted out of the movie business. Whether he had changed or the industry had changed isn't clear. But there came a point where he felt that recording had become an assembly-line job and no longer a craft. The question became, what next?

Some people at this juncture borrow a copy of *What Color Is Your Parachute?* from the library. But Mr. D lives in northern California, where he naturally thought to consult someone he described as "a noted feminist guru." Mr. D and five other men attended the first self-actualization seminar that she conducted for men. Some Ecstasy was offered to the middle-aged bunch. "Didn't hurt," Mr. D volunteers before I have a chance to ask. The guru had asked her participants to bring to the session a box of artifacts from their lives. He was told to arrange the items in a collage and frame the result. The sound man's collage included:

- A photograph of Jean-Luc Godard at an editing console
- A Sharpie indelible marker
- The sash from a kimono
- An Asian purse
- Bits of rice paper
- A pile of foreign coins left over from his travels

"From the back, the Godard shot looks a bit like me," Mr. D explains. The Sharpie is used to mark film and audiotape. The kimono sash and other items from the East symbolized his relationship with his spouse, who is of Japanese ancestry. The coins, Mr. D assumed, were a sign of his love for travel. But the guru saw something else in those coins, which he had arranged in a trail leading to the purse. It was, she announced, a hint of an inner drive to manage money.

If he were going to get into that line, Mr. D figured, then it could not be just any old kind of money-grubbing financial management, that artificially tears people into separate philosophical and financial selves. He would teach people to invest as a "whole person." Mr. D's approach sprang from two indisputable facts: money isn't going to disappear, so it must be addressed one way or another; and some companies have a better track record than others in such areas as the environment, diversity, treatment of employees, or links with nasty foreign governments.

But Mr. D does not have an answer to one question. In fact, although many people I meet during my short stay in the Grand Tetons are willing to address this, no one has fully resolved what I'd like to call the Pandora's Paradox of socially responsible investing: is there or is there not such a thing as a company that is good, through and through? Because once you start scrutinizing a company's performance and get away from immediate bottom-line achievements, then there is a whole lot to worry you about most companies.

The chemical company H. B. Fuller gets attacked for not doing more to prevent the shoe glue it manufactures from ending up in the hands of street urchins in Latin America who use it to get stoned. Fuller is also being pressured by activist shareholders to disclose the extent to which it supplies materials to tobacco-related businesses. Yet H. B. Fuller is in the Domini 400 index of socially responsible companies, based in the Domini folks' expert opinion that Fuller's record is better than most.

Some of this has to do with the nature of a corporation. Although we like to anthropomorphize them, a corporate entity is by definition a hard-nosed thing. It is not warm and cuddly. All companies have to make tough decisions and balance competing needs and goals. Within companies there are winners and losers. They are not, regardless of how whole-wheat the approach, egalitarian systems; there is rank even in the flattest of corporate organizations. Anarcho-syndicalist communes don't get listed on the New York or the American stock exchanges, and probably not even the Nasdaq. Which means that companies that get gold stars for social responsibility in some areas (environment, work-place diversity) might get black marks for labor relations (moving a fac-tory summarily from Michigan to Malaysia).

Trying too diligently to come up with a really groovy portfolio runs the danger of turning you into one of those obsessive-compulsive hand washers. You keep trying to sanitize your holdings, but you keep turn-ing up more dirt.

Once, to escape the burble of noise from an oil and gas conference in London, I was forced to interview a woman with both of us wedged into a phone booth. But the backdrop for my interview with David Berge was distracting in a more dramatic and less intimate way. Just try to focus on a task when confronted by the Grand Teton range at sunset.

Berge did manage to keep the focus on the task at hand: explaining how he works for one very concerned bank. In 1989 Vermont National Bank started a socially responsible savings account that pulls deposits not just from Vermont but from most states in the union. It has taken us a remarkably long time, Berge said, to get our heads around the basic premise of banking, the not-so-earth-shattering idea that when you make deposits into your savings account, the money doesn't stay in the vault. Once you reflect on the fact that the bank ships your money out almost as fast as you put it in, the question becomes, where and how is your money being used?

This is Berge's niche. VNB's socially responsible banking fund lends over $68 million to more than 1,100 small projects in and around Ver-mont—from small-scale affordable housing projects to a foundation supporting sustainable agriculture to a small natural foods bakery. The managers don't take foolish risks, but they do put in the labor necessary to bend conventional rules so loans fund the sort of local enterprises that might get laughed at or, at best, politely turned down at a regular bank. The fund's customers seem to like the idea that their money isn't taking the fast train to money centers such as Boston, New York, or even Tokyo. They like that it stays mostly in Vermont and is used for folks who live further down the food chain. Berge paints a picture of what he calls the Great Cycle of Capital: your deposit goes in and then it loops right back into the farm down the road, neighbor helping neighbor, in theory. VNB's Socially Responsible Banking Fund account pays the same as any old passbook savings account and, Berge likes to cheerily add, "It's FDIC insured."

This isn't about charity. It's about accountability, the reassuring sense that you know where your money goes and how it is working. Not being that much of a control freak, the accountability, to me, is less interesting than the idea that my cash isn't flowing willy-nilly into the anonymous ocean of the capital markets but being used to do something tangible, for people with identifiable names and faces, running enterprises that I would be pleased to patronize.

Berge swears that the risk of these loans is not higher. What is more costly is the investment of time needed to service an oddball loan, the human contact required to make sure that an organic goat farmer going through a rough patch has the kind of business plan that leads to bank payments coming in on time.

Still, Vermont National Bank is not some kind of counter-cultural paradise, like a co-op cheese store with a vault. The 175-year-old institution has plenty of traditional banking functions catering to hard-nosed Yankee customers. As it happened, two weeks after the trip to Wyoming, I would find myself just outside Burlington, Vermont, speaking with a VNB manager. When I told him about the interview with Berge, he looked at his shoes, scowled, and reminded me that his bank has a lot more going for it than just the socially responsible account.

Maybe it was a sign that our man Berge was hogging the spotlight. Or maybe not all VNB managers are hip to the special account's happen'n social mission. Perhaps it's just that all corporations are the sum of a variety of competing and sometimes contradictory interests. My trip to Wyoming is teaching me to live with contradictions.

One such contradiction is that using money in an evolved, socially responsible way can be just as much about changing you as it is about changing the world. In other words, the same person who wants a socially responsible portfolio to make him richer in the most-evolved way may also hope that SRI will help him become more comfortable with the whole idea of accumulating wealth. SRI allows us—to paraphrase the subtitle of Stanley Kubrick's Cold War comic masterpiece—to learn to stop worrying and love the markets. You cannot fix the world until you fix yourself. That is what I learn from the therapist.

Not my therapist, but a genial fellow whom I mistake for a therapist when I enter a room on the lower level of the Jackson Lake Lodge. George Kinder talks like a therapist, only one with perhaps English as his undergraduate degree. He wears tweed and corduroy, and he speaks in parables about the meaning of money. His approach is nothing if not holistic. He would later write the book *The Seven Stages of Money Maturity*. He begins his presentation with a caveat: "I feel uncomfortable talking about socially responsible investing. However, I would be delighted to discuss the socially responsible person."

Managing a person's money is impossible without having a darn good working knowledge of whom you are dealing with. He starts out by asking his clients for a sense of what their personal vision of freedom is. His role as financial adviser, then, becomes a kind of guide for helping people free themselves of their hangups about money.

Normally financial advisers figure you are overwitholding on your W-2 form or you need to stop wasting cash on extravagant restaurant meals. George's more holistic approach would see those as symptoms of other problems that might include "profound guilt about wealth" or, in one case, "old father anger."

Kinder sees his clients coming to terms with money as an expression of their maturity, an indication of the state of their inner growth. As we move from our childish views of wealth, we are first disturbed by a fuller understanding of money as we enter a kind of money adolescence, of wealth's power to divide, to destroy. Eventually we figure out that money is the key to unlocking dreams and we also learn to get a better handle on the mechanics of money. With luck, or perhaps some serious reengineering of the inner self, we gain an understanding, an awareness, that money is nothing if not about relationships. Then comes vigor, when you can swing into action and not be victimized by money. It is a time when you start proactively dealing with your credit cards and the savvy consumer of investment services springs to life. Eventually Kinder tries to get his clients to envision using money to higher ends. At this stage, the socially responsible investment advisers in the audience perk up.

The final stage Kinder calls "Aloha." I gather George is a person who spends a lot of time on Hawaii. Aloha is the stage during which I start to get the creeping suspicion that I am not cool enough for this.

Aloha. The conference room lights are up enough so that I can examine the faces around me and I see no squinting skepticism, just respectful attention. I resolve to pry open my rapidly closing mind and ride the groove. Kinder explains that this final level is about a relaxed state of kindness and empathy that allows us to easily interact with others without money getting in the way. My mind slams shut. Is he saying we should be able to reach a state in which we can hang with the homeless guys on the corner and the differences in socioeconomic status will evaporate and their economic plight cease to be relevant? I am not so sure I want to be so at peace with money that I become blind to the hard and ugly truths that surround it. My annoyance soon turns to self-doubt. What if I am still stuck in an immature, early stage in my understanding of money, if I am some kind of Johnny One-Note playing from only his second *chakra?* How adolescent of me to still be caught up in anger about the tensions that economic status breeds. It strikes me as possible that Kinder's Aloha is probably a stage of enlightenment in which money no long must color all relationships.

He speaks of a woman he once counseled who was not at peace with the world around her. She was active in political causes in her community, but something was profoundly wrong, and her relationships with others suffered. I got an image of a person who was at once politically correct and bitter at the same time, but Kinder's description is gentler.

"After many hours of discussion, it became clear that she had a repressed need," he says.

Further work revealed the nature of that need, apparently a big house. The unhappy client finally admitted that when all was said and done, what she really wanted in life was a substantial piece of real estate.

"I eventually got her to this place."

Her finances in order and her priorities realigned, the woman was able to buy the house of her dreams. She then blossomed as she threw herself into the work of decorating, furnishing, and making a home. Liberated by the house, the woman became a great person to be around.

I am appalled. I begin to extrapolate. Let's see, I can be a nasty cuss on occasion, so clearly something is wrong with me. Maybe I, too, have a deep material need that needs to be coaxed out and satisfied. Perhaps if I am able to purchase that 1964 Volvo P1800 I secretly covet, I will become more centered and a much nicer guy. But Kinder has not finished his story, and the epilogue to his tale possibly changes everything.

The woman, who has finally come to terms with her need for a nice place to call home, doesn't allow the vigor that this new understanding unleashes to stop with material improvements and making everything just so. Her newfound happiness is infectious and becomes a kind of charisma. The big house becomes a salon, an incubator for political action. Liberated from guilt about money, the woman is now working for positive social change. As many a lottery winner has learned, money badly handled can screw you up terribly. Perhaps I should not be surprised, then, that learning to handle money can set you straight.

Another thought occurs to me. Perhaps coming to terms with the need for money is about more than just spending until you're happy. Perhaps it is about understanding how much money you really need to make you happy. Once you've set the parameters, you can free yourself from the money rat race. You no longer have to invest in a distasteful business because you need the exorbitant rate of return. You set reasonable goals and a time frame for achieving them. You can then align your principles with your portfolio because you are financing a reasonable existence rather than an extravagant lifestyle. You mature from the child who wants everything to the adult who understands that having it all isn't about your happiness. It's about making other people unhappily jealous. As a consequence of this realization, the pressure to earn and spend eases, and you turn your back on the life of the unhappy hypocrite. Aloha.

Well, not quite Aloha. Right when I start to groove on this, someone comes along and ruins Aloha for me. Following George Kinder at the same podium is a presentation about targeting SRI to its core constituency, groovy boomers who agree with such statements as "I don't feel good about wealth" and "Social causes come first and profits second." But the market research suggests there is a new area into which SRI can expand. This is a younger group of investors who are involved in community work, who care about the environment, but who eschew "causes" and embrace consumerism. It's a shock of cold reality to witness this discussion as marketing intrudes on what has been a discussion of values. I can't help but wonder if I fit neatly into either of these "target demographics," in much the way that I wasn't sure if I fit in at breakfast. For a fleeting moment I get a flash that I am back in the mall, on the receiving end of a hard sell. If it's a pitch it shoots wide of the mark as one of the presenters holds up a "poster child" for the younger socially responsible customer. It is taken from a full-page ad in the *Wall Street Journal* for another product entirely.

"This is who we are talking about," says the nice woman from a socially responsible mutual fund.

The ad is for a kind of computer peripheral that lets you cram a truckful of data onto a little diskette. The photo shows a Generation X woman wearing funky cotton clothes in oh-so-bohemian surroundings. The copy describes her as a professional with a way-cool job, working on projects in three continents, teaching adult literacy classes, and still finding time for pottery and baking. No doubt she speaks several languages.

"A confidante of four Presidents, this Zip drive user just received the Nobel Peace Prize," I mumble to myself.

"How does she do it? She takes SPEED," grumbles a bearded fellow next to me, quoting the old line from *Saturday Night Live*.

Luckily, Jack Brill shows up to chill me out. I'm in line for the buffet, trying to make socially responsible lunch choices.

"Have a piece of roast beef if you want roast beef," Jack admonishes me.

Jack defines the word "avuncular." A New Yorker transplanted to San Diego, he discovered he was a "closet pacifist" while working as a civil engineer for the navy. He quit the civil service and got a broker's license because he was tired of being "ripped off" by money managers. What he does now is help people devise socially responsible investment portfolios. He and a client wrote, with the help of his son, a book called *Investing from the Heart*.

Jack's son, Hal, is a groovy guy who campaigns for environmental causes and supports co-operative housing projects. While a lot of six-ties hippies slowly devolved into images of their fathers as they went gray, in the Brill family it happened the other way around. As Jack got older, he learned from his son and became more progressive in his out-look.

Jack spends a lot of time worrying about how companies conduct themselves. He worries about what might be considered ill-gotten gains, profiting from companies that exploit people or the earth. But he doesn't spend a lot of time fretting about the compromises inherent in trying to invest responsibly. It does not concern him that there may be no such thing as a pure company with not a single item in the "con-cerns" column of its socially responsible report card. What is important, Jack says, is to use the power of the portfolio to improve the world. That statement in itself is an admission that the world is not a perfect place. The idea is to change for the better what you can and not get stuck in some kind of paralysis that stems from the view that all money is tainted.

If you really believe that all profits are somehow morally bad, your choice is either to become a ridiculous hypocrite or to live as close to the land as possible, cloistered from as many of the corrupting influences of commerce as you can. Gil Crawford, who runs a mutual fund in which profits go to underwrite development projects in Africa and South Amer-ica, calls this a medieval notion bound up in the early Christian concept that all interest is usury. He says there are a lot of investors in Europe who are still influenced by this view, people who provide a logical con-stituency for a charity-cum-mutual fund like his.

But I don't have to "get medieval" to fret about the contradictions presented by many companies labeled socially responsible.

"Look at it this way," says Jack. "Reward the companies doing better than the ones doing worse. You won't find a company that's 99 and 44/100 percent pure, so you look for one that's maybe 92 percent pure."

Money has power, he says, so figure out what you believe in and see if you can leverage some of that power to further ends other than sim-ply feathering your own nest. Pick targets carefully, Brill counsels, and learn to live with ambiguity—like a grownup is his implication.

I think I'm ready to give SRI a try. Park some retirement money in a screened account and see how it does as I investigate the other possibilities. All investments involve risk, and it is now clear to me that the bigger risk lies not with the social screens but with the skill of the person who manages the fund. If at some statistical level SRI might mean not squeezing out every last little bit of profit possible, so be it. We make that decision all the time, when we decide that a stock has had a good run and that the time has come to sell it. If you make a decent profit, be happy, and you shouldn't cry if the stock keeps rising a little more after you've sold it.

All the routes in Jackson Hole are scenic, but I choose a road back to the airport that gets me as close as a car can get to the sheer faces of the Grand Tetons. I am thinking about ambiguity, and at the moment it is hard to accept that nothing is perfect.

I recall meeting a philosopher who hails from these parts. Grateful Dead lyricist and cyber-guru John Perry Barlowe lives on a ranch in Wyoming. He carries a business card with his name and the title "Cognitive Dissident." He explains that he very much wants people to appreciate that contradictory ideas can and should exist side by side in people's heads, with the contradictions rubbing against each other producing a positive, creative friction. But at what point does dissonance become hypocrisy? It's a question I will keep with me on my money pilgrimage as I turn up the heat on myself. If using a windfall to buy pieces of a company or its debt in the form of securities raises these uncomfortable questions, what happens if I actually become a company by starting my own business?

Souvenirs

A North Carolina pine seedling handed out by a socially responsible mutual fund.

The understanding that investments do not have to disappear into faceless capital markets, that I can influence how my money is used.

To do when I get home

Take a solemn vow to read and respond to proxy statements.

Divide the equities portion of my portfolio, leave half in an unfiltered stock fund and the other half in a socially screened fund, and see what happens.

Doing the numbers

In the calendar year that followed the trip to the socially responsible investment conference, the fund offered by my employer that avoids companies with lousy environmental records, companies that make weapons, alcoholic beverages, tobacco, or nuclear energy, and companies that fail to adhere to the McBride Principles in Northern Ireland gained 23 percent. The regular, unscreened stock mutual fund gained 24 percent.

During the year of my visit to the Rockies and the year that followed, responsibly invested assets climbed 85 percent to $1.185 trillion. (Source: Social Investment Forum)

- -

4

Be Your Own Boss

Entrepreneurship in
Pasadena and Universal City, California

From the clipping file: Four years after emigrating from Vietnam, a beauty school student from Canoga Park, California, won $1 million in the lottery. The *Los Angeles Times* reported she planned to visit her parents in Michigan and "perhaps start a business with her winnings." July 29, 1990

I t may be a sign of just how far libertarian philosophy contaminated the drinking water by the time the millennium wrapped up, but I had begun to get the impression that being an employee instead of a business owner was somehow a personal failing. The message seemed to be that folks in their prime earning years are not supposed to still live with mommy. If they are fit, able, and in the possession of a surplus, they should strike out on their own, thumb their noses at the institutions that are holding back their individual talent, and get entrepreneurial. The problem for me was that I wasn't sure if I had this key ingredient and I wanted to find out before dedicating a pile of money to its pursuit.

After the refreshing air of Wyoming, I was ready for another descent into

the maelstrom, which I found behind the doors of a business opportunity fair,
a kind of carnival full of peddlers pitching money-making schemes to people
shopping their surpluses around. It was all there in sharp relief, the promise
and the pitfalls of sinking our money into someone else's idea of a business.
But we all have our own ideas for enterprises that could be funded by a sur-
plus, and before plunging in, I wanted to apprentice at the feet of a group of
masters in the entrepreneurial arts.

"Are you *freelance*?" The accent was Alec Guinness as Obi-Wan Kenobi.

The plummy, velvet caress British business philosopher Charles Handy gave the final vowel of the word "freelance" suggested a very noble condition indeed.

My cheeks began to feel warm because I knew I had to give the wrong answer. I am merely an employee, a functionary within a larger organization, not what Handy sees as a man of the future, otherwise known as a "portfolio man," to use his coinage. He argues that the most successful and consistently employed people in the new millennium will be these portfolio folks who will work outside, not inside, organizations. We will shop our skills, essentially, to the highest bidder. We will all be freelance consultants, working ultimately for ourselves, under our own navigation, getting a proper market value for whatever it is we have to offer.

The visitor to my office has a lot of authority in this regard. Handy left an absolutely secure career as a manager for Shell International, a company that had seized so much control of its employees' lives that he had to get his fiancée vetted by the firm before he was allowed to marry her. He later got tenure at the London Business School, but to the shock of his friends, he eventually quit that too and set out on his own. Handy used to tell his children not to go out looking for a job.

Does he want us to rely on the kindness of the government social safety net, his children wondered?

No, Handy advised, acquire the ability to do something valuable enough that someone will pay you to do it for them. He suggests that this is the essence of freedom.

My embarrassment at having to answer that I am an organization rather than portfolio man leads to another, more productive impulse. Why not use a surplus as seed money to go independent, to start a business, to stop relying on the kindness of managers above me and be master of my own destiny? If I am really looking to invest in businesses that reflect my values, then why not a business inextricably linked with who I am and what I believe, my own business?

On my way back from meeting Handy, a commercial on the all-news radio station shouts about a "Be Your Own Boss" expo. It's a business opportunity fair a few exits up the freeway, one of those places where they peddle franchises and other money-making schemes. It's the sort of place Charles Handy wouldn't be caught dead at. Nor can I readily imagine myself setting up a donut shop or whatever it is you can sign up for at one of these fairs. But is it the donut shop that isn't me or the whole idea of being a proprietor that isn't me? Americans are going to these fairs in droves, often with some severance payment or some other piece of cash they have. I wonder what I might learn about self-employment at such a place. I cannot imagine I would plunk down a surplus there, but it is a starting point, a place where I can confront all the happy talk we hear about the joys of running a business. Anyway, the whole scene sounds unlikely and weird, which is the way I like to travel, even if the destination is just a convention center in the next town.

Statistics on the numbers of businesses that fail vary, depending on how one defines "failure." A 1994 study by Dun & Bradstreet found that 40 percent of businesses failed in the first five years. Some experts have estimated about half of new businesses will not survive the start-up phase. The reasons for failure range from not enough start-up capital to poor management to competition from stronger and better businesses. The high failure rate shows how easy it is to set up shop in America. Succeeding is another matter.

But on this bright Sunday afternoon in Pasadena, city of roses and parades, the threat of failure seemed remote. What seemed more immediate was the opportunity, in the organizer's words, "to make money, to supplement income, to attain financial freedom."

A blond man in a white polo shirt that clung to perfect pecs was one of the expo's organizers. After his pep talk it was time to hit the floor of the expo. I pulled open a heavy double door.

I almost suffocated.

The temperature wasn't the problem. It was the sudden rush of selling, like the late-night infomercials on TV, but without the four- to six-week wait for delivery. The business propositions were live and in person. Paintless dent removal. No-fat snack dispensers. Own your own automated teller machine and earn $1.22 on every transaction. And Tom with his amazing all-in-one, do-it-yourself, can't-make-a-mistake, fold-away fabric printing company.

"It's simple, it's easy, it's clear, it's nice, and it makes money when I want to. Not when anyone else wants to. I make money when I want, I go play when I want, I go fishing when I want," Tom explained.

"I print about three orders a week. Sometimes it's six hundred a week, sometimes it's fifty a week. Most of the time it's about $20,000 a year. Hey, I'm retired! All I want to do is have fun. And this is fun."

Tom was a pro. His pitch was engaging, flawlessly delivered, and he had the locked, unblinking sales gaze down. He was effective because he knew how to connect with his audience.

"You can roll the unit away in a closet. Or you can do what I do, leave it in the living room. Why do I leave it in the living room? Because SHE doesn't live there anymore, all right?" Tom was wearing only a half smile. This was no joke. His cadence was unbroken. It was part of a stunningly well-targeted pitch that seemed to say we all have reasons to be bitter and to spend our days unshaven, on the couch, in our boxers, and that is OK. Tom knew that you were motivated to visit this expo because you were, at some level, disappointed with your life.

Disappointed in love, disappointed with the system. I could hear scattered phrases of a pitch for making it big coming from a seminar-in-a-tent. The subject was taking control of your financial life: "Social Insecurity. . . . You will earn a million in your life, but where does all the money go? Taxes, mortgage interest, credit card interest . . . 87 percent of Americans retire in poverty . . . 30 percent of your income is stolen by creditors."

I recalled the organizer's pitch.

"There is no such thing as job security now," he told me. "Major corporations are laying off people left and right. People who have children, mortgages to pay, car payments. What better job security than owning your own business and creating your own income?

"There are a lot of downsized executives here and people who have heard through the rumor mill that their jobs may be the next to go."

He had picked a good issue. Pressure from investors on Wall Street to show a profit combined with the competitive nature of the global economy meant corporations had cut payrolls to increase the bottom line. Newspapers and magazines filled hundreds of pages with stories of white-collar managers who had lived the good life until they were unexpectedly downsized. Lots of people were losing their jobs, while others were being forced to take dramatic cuts in pay. The unemployment rate was low, but that fact obscured all the churning that goes on in the workforce, people losing jobs balanced by those finding new ones.

On the car radio the pitch for the business opportunity fair had centered on empowerment and the freedom of an entrepreneur to plot his own course. When I showed up at the convention center, someone had flipped that record over to its "B" side, which was playing a relentless chorus about insecurity and powerlessness. It's a song that doesn't appeal to me because I'm lucky enough at this time in my life not to be desperate. I, like many professionals, have tried to leave myself options and construct a portfolio of skills for myself that should give me a professional plan B or plan C if plan A should suddenly founder. The chance this expo has the power to pry a personal lump sum out of savings seems remote. But it is easy for those of us who haven't been surprised lately by a pink slip to mock the idea of trying to earn a living printing corporate logos onto surfaces as tortured as a walnut shell.

But my hunch, from the looks of the place, was that there might be more money to be made selling business opportunities than actually running them.

A heavyset woman flagged me down and beckoned me to her booth.

"Some of these people here aren't playing by the rules," she whispered to me, completely unprompted.

She handed me a card with the phone number for the attorney general of California scrawled on the back. Later I checked with the Federal Trade Commission to see what rules generally apply to the sale of franchises. About a third of the states have their own rules that may also apply.

Most revolve around disclosure—including how many franchisees are having the kind of success that is being advertised. These documents need to be given to a potential buyer ten business days before any money changes hands. For a second I dupe myself into thinking that my college education makes these kinds of reminders unnecessary. I am the king of research. I do nothing without digging deep and amassing great manila files and mega-disks of corroborating evidence. Then how come the one time I did start my own business, an overseas radio news bureau, I conducted no market research of any kind before taking a very expensive plunge?

When it comes to your money, there is no such thing as too much "due diligence." Everybody says it, so why don't we do it, whether we are investing in a fancy real estate investment trust or a concession in expo aisle two? It is easy to be skeptical of a venture that gives off a used-car-sales-lot vibe, but the same wariness should also apply to the ventures we fall in love with.

I pick up another lesson at the expo. I call it the Water Pic, Nordic-Trak, Dayrunner personal organizer problem. These all involve up-front capital outlays for systems that will improve gums, waistline, and life, in that order. But only if, and it is a crushingly big if, we put in a consistent daily effort and don't let the devices gather dust.

I remembered a childhood friend who thought he had caught the entrepreneurial bug after college. He put up some of his savings and got his parents to front the rest of the cash so he could buy a roomful of soap products. Green stuff to wash floors and cars. Upholstery cleaner. Pet shampoo. Cartons and cartons of the stuff because "*everybody* needs soap."

Alas, the soap did not sell itself. Buying huge up-front stock is folly until you have a sense of the pace of business. It is the opposite of the "just in time" inventory system that makes Wal-Mart such a powerhouse. His "way too early" inventory system presented a big challenge for my friend while solving the soap company's problems. They now had cash instead of inventory clogging up expensive warehouse space. My pal had taken on this problem. He was ultimately unable to see his reflection in all those soap bubbles and lost heart. But the real lesson is that even the boss has to take on his share of drudgery.

An oily aroma wafted over from the adjacent aisle. I followed the smell to a big green umbrella, Cafe Express. It was a gourmet coffee franchise on wheels. Bring your business to your market. The profit margins advertised were mesmerizing: Cafe Mocha, your cost, $0.16, retail price, $2.75.

Cool. I could call it Brancaccio's Cappuccino, a name that onomatopoeically evoked the very sound of an imported Gaggia espresso machine steaming a delicate head of *crema.* I could even develop some clever graphic element to share the double *c* in my surname and the word cappuccino. It was another great name in search of a business, but my wife didn't support me in graduate school so that I could squander money for the privilege of wheeling around a coffee cart.

But how many of us, late at night, mutter into the secrecy of our pillows that what we really want to do in life is open a restaurant in (choose one) Cape Cod / the Outer Banks / Texas Hill Country / Big Sur serving (choose one) Italian / French / nonspecific Mediterranean cuisine? Are we ready for the single-minded commitment that this cappuccino cart implies?

The last time I had a surplus I took it to London to start a business running my own overseas news bureau. The stories ranged from the meltdown of the European exchange rate mechanism to the Franco-British war over subsidized lamb, so the work was rarely monotonous. But it was all-consuming, like having sextuplets, with no breaks allowed for nights or weekends. All holidays were ruined by the unremitting need to produce.

The long hours I put in during my days of self-employment were driven as much by my need to make money as they were by my passion for the work. Passion is a tremendous motivator. Nothing at the expo evoked that in me. I felt as though I was wandering around a mall that offered propositions, businesses for the sake of doing something with accumulated capital. But shopping when you are unsure of what you want or need is often a waste of time. If you do buy, you tend to do so on impulse, and those impulsive purchases are the ones we tend to regret.

I left the expo still an employee. If I was to restructure my career more to the liking of Charles Handy, I clearly had much more to learn.

We could all use a mentor, and when chosing one it is helpful to find one who does not work on commission. I had a Rolodex card with the numbers for SCORE, the Service Corps of Retired Executives, a mentoring program sponsored by the Small Business Administration. For the investment of a Saturday, I could get a better sense of whether I have what it takes not to blow a surplus on a business idea with a high likelihood of acquiring the sobriquet "hare-brained" in the fullness of time.

"You know that actress who advertises those diapers for old people? I want you to know, they're very comfortable."

Harry Dictor is warming up the room of would-be entrepreneurs who are here for a reality check on their business prospects. A compact man with a broad Chicago accent, Dictor has been working with SCORE since 1988. A business partner refers to him as "old Midas," a touch that Dictor applied very successfully to construction projects during the southern California real estate boom. Dictor's enthusiasm for business enthralls the room. He asks each of us what our dream business is.

V. J. is a printer who wants to start a home-based graphics business. A pair of soft-spoken women in their forties want to start a new retail concept to market mace and clubs. Ken, with the deep tan and raspy voice of a surfer, wants to sell after-market supplies for boats. A young Filipino American couple would like to sell fresh vegetables. "Everyone has to eat," the man reasons.

I flash on my friend Iffat. She and her husband emigrated from Bangladesh. They are both highly educated. Her husband has a job within a very large institution, an electric utility. Iffat is the owner of two fast food franchises and represents the cutting edge of American entrepreneurship. A recent study found that Asian immigrants started fifteen of the nation's top high-tech businesses, the kind of businesses that have been partially responsible for the great economic boom of the nineties.

Dictor goes around the room getting our entrepreneurial juices flowing. The room's blandness works to his advantage: it is punctuated by only two features, an American flag in the right corner and a Texaco corporate flag in the left. Texaco owns the building where we are sitting. The flags give the room the air of a shrine to our free enterprise system.

Some of the folks have done no advance work on their business ideas, lacking even the rudimentary knowledge that it is illegal to print copyrighted photographs on T-shirts if you do not own the copyright. Others have already done some research on what seem very compelling business ideas, including a combination battered women's shelter and resource center, a mail-order catalog for native specialty foods that immigrants cannot easily find in America, a company that will chronicle the oral history of a family to complement genealogical charts and photo albums. One woman is seeking to subcontract her dancing skills to caterers.

The wave of introductions is heading in my direction. I don't want to say anything about the complete and utter lack of planning that went into my overseas business venture. But I do have a pocketful of inventions, special skills, and ideas for creative projects, just about all of them unformed and unripe. In the interest of both dodging that question and giving full disclosure, I tell the group I am trying my hand at writing. My revelation lights up the face of Kris, two rows behind, who wants to set up her own public relations firm for authors. Harry Dictor points to Kris, then to me, then back to Kris, and then shoots us an encouraging thumbs up.

The program begins with an implied bid for us to leave our employee sensibilities at the door and start thinking about ourselves as businessmen and businesswomen. It is initially grim but important stuff about not stealing anyone else's trademark and protecting yourself from legal liability.

Peter, a well-pressed double-breasted certified public accountant, presents an overview about running a small business in California that should have any Democrats in the audience considering a switch of party affiliation. The course, which should be dubbed "Republican 101," begins with a slide about the huge market in the state, its wealth, and its affinity for innovation. But, Peter continues, it is also a difficult state because of tough job safety and health rules, strong enforcement of equal employment opportunity laws, and complicated environmental regulations. The room snorts in agreement.

It is not that many of my fellow business neophytes who had breakfast thinking as environmentalists would be writing checks to the Heritage Foundation by noon. But the discussion here is enough to create the first seeds of skepticism about the hand of government in the private sector. This is driven by the logic that obeying rules is hard work and often costly for a proprietor. The moment you start a business, regulations become hurdles. It is an irony that this seminar, which cost just fifteen dollars to enroll in, is subsidized by tax dollars and is the kind of government program favored by the Democrat in the White House.

Anyway, if there is proselytizing going on here, it is going beyond a mere political conversion. The push is on to begin mutating from a guy who thinks like an employee to a guy who can think like a corporation. My search for further knowledge is leading me down a dark and dangerous path.

Will I end by transforming into something new and unrecognizable to my kin? I joke, but this is serious business. When it's my capital at risk, my reputation on the line, will I be moved to grind any employees I might have on their health care coverage and other benefits? Will I be able to conduct myself according to the socially responsible principles that I would set for the rest of my investment portfolio? If I can't keep to some basic value principles in my business, there is no use using the money to begin transforming myself into a businessman.

I can see it now. First, there are changes at the cellular level. I keep much of my outward appearance and my own name, but already my accountant knows I am different. I have changed from an employee into a "sole proprietorship." During this stage I can take advantage of the tax deductions for business expenses, but if I get sued for something my business does, the lawyers will come after me, my personal bank account, my car, and even my kids' toys.

In the next stage some merging of identities occurs. I form a "partnership." I am still taxed as an individual and I can still get sued personally, but my partners who have kicked in resources to my business will also share in the proceeds if my enterprise begins to bear fruit. My partners can be sources of both capital and expertise.

Then the really scary changes begin. I go whole hog and transform into a corporation. It is not easy. I now need not only my accountant but a lawyer on retainer. The tax man will be able to dun me twice, by hitting me with both corporate tax and individual tax. But the more than 22 million corporations filing tax returns in America cannot all be wrong. There is one big benefit to turning myself into a corporation: namely, it's a legal bomb shelter.

If a baker sets up as a sole proprietorship and hires a guy to deliver his bread by truck and that truck runs over someone's dog, the dog owner can sue and take the baker's bank account, his house, his car, and possibly his dog. If the baker turns himself into a corporation and hires a negligent truck driver, the worst the dog owner can usually do is sue the corporation out of existence. The baker will be out of business but not personally ruined. Of course, my corporation would protect me against debt collectors. If my business fails, creditors can go after the remaining assets of my corporation, but usually they can't go after my personal fortune or those of my other executives.

I look around the room. The lectures are beginning to sink in: running a business is about drive, innovation, and vision. It is also about paperwork. Some in my group are looking a little seasick as this realization sets in.

The fluttering in my stomach has more to do with how far the pendulum has swung in the late twentieth century. The word "corporate" is shedding its remaining pejorative overtones. The corporate of "corporate hegemony" and "corporate welfare" is changing and taking on a new sexiness, the kind of corporate that fits nicely into phrases like "corporate bonus" or "corporate jet." The man in the adjacent chair leans over and whispers approvingly, "I want to be a corporation, don't you?"

His remark suddenly seems odd, given what I had seen at the Be Your Own Boss Expo. Many of the people pushing in the latter part of this millennium to set out on their own are driven by a powerful countervailing force: the sense of having been betrayed by the very corporations they now are trying to become.

I have higher hopes for small business success for others who seem driven not by bitterness but by an inner vision. At the SCORE seminar, a tall woman named Denise seems driven by an inner vision that sees the world coated in chocolate. Of this auditorium full of aspiring businesspeople, only Denise has the marketing sense to arrange to show off product samples: her handmade chocolate desserts, elaborately crafted, arranged, and packaged. They look and smell wonderful, especially since the seminar has continued right through the lunch hour without a break. It has been a day talking about taking charge of our own lives and taking on the world of American business opportunity with bold foot-in-the-door moves. I can handle that. I invite myself to lunch with the SCORE guys to see if I can get some one-on-one counseling about what to do with the money.

Our little klatch squeezes into Harry's silver Lexus, which is parked in the underground lot. Harry, Harvey, Stan, another Harry, and I head up the two-block hill toward, as it happens, another mall cum amusement park. Universal Citywalk is a retail environment designed to give visitors a controlled Los Angeles shopping experience free of graffiti, traffic, drive-by shootings, and homeless people. The strip is attached to the Universal Cinema complex and leads to the front entrance of the studio's theme park. I worry that I am being led into another virtual experience. But I soon realize this carload of real people will take care of that.

Harry slows at a roadblock at the Citywalk entrance. The parking is a flat-rate six dollars. "Highway robbery," I think to myself, but I keep quiet in this plush car full of guys who have been smiled upon by the business god. "Highway robbery," mutters the other Harry, Harry Spitzer, a retired retail and broadcast sales executive who serves as publicist for the local SCORE chapter. Perhaps I have more in common with this bunch than I think.

We get out of the car into a very odd afternoon for southern California. The air is full of a rare chilly drizzle. Universal Studios is entered from atop Mount Olympus in the Santa Monica Mountains, and on this day the cloud ceiling is hanging low. As we move through the miasma toward Wolfgang Puck's pizza restaurant, I see an apparition.

My blood runs cold at the sight of a live disc jockey in a radio-style booth. He is the prime feature of Wolfgang Puck's competition, KWGB, World's Greatest Burgers, a radio station–themed restaurant. The young man wears authentic broadcast headphones and is spinning Booker T and the MGs off a turntable in full view of the mall. This jock-in-the-box is a fast-food version of my occupation, a radio announcer cum hot-dog-on-a-stick lemon squeezer in a silly costume. Ever since receiving my government-issued radio license just before my sixteenth birthday, I have harbored the illusion that, if all else fails, I will still be able to find work at some modest radio station somewhere. It is my skill, a humble skill, but a skill that brings with it the tiniest shred of dignity. I have persuaded myself that at the very least I will never have to officially ask, "For here or to go?" Yet here is my nightmare, the radio guy turned burger flipper, locked up and performing in a glass go-go cage. Is he a shadow of what could befall me in the future? This may seem farfetched, but experience has shown me that we are never quite as far from this as we like to think. When my enterprise had trouble finding its feet in London and the dollar-pound exchange rate was stacked against me, I found myself scouring want ads, looking for temp work, and generally revisiting that horrible bone-chilling feeling that many of us first had upon college graduation without immediate employment prospects.

This jock-in-the-box is a reminder that my employee attitude puts my fate in the hands of institutional powers larger than I am. I am filled with a strong determination to wrestle back control of my life and use my savings to follow the teachings of the Be Your Own Boss Expo: "Don't be a victim, be a proprietor." What I want is an apprenticeship with some folks who really relish the game. A lunch at Wolfgang Puck's pizzeria with four wisecracking retired executives will do nicely. The formal, organized seminar of the morning cross-fades into something more freewheeling and in many ways more instructive.

"My father had a knack for something, but not for business," Harry Dictor says to disabuse me of the notion that entrepreneurial skills, like language, need to be either genetic or imprinted from an early age. "We always lived behind a store in Chicago. My father was interested in politics. He wasn't interested in business—the store was a front. Unfortunately, the bill collectors didn't know that. He did the best he could. Occasionally there'd be a fire. I remember once we were on a bus and a truck hit us, and two minutes later my father fell. He had one of those elastic bandages he would wear."

I start taking notes: "An entrepreneur is not solely driven by the desire to make money or to make a project a success. He or she is probably someone who hates working for someone else."

"I could not hold a job when I first started out," Dictor says. "I tried it. My first wife, who was not money minded, would only wonder why the color of my paycheck would change week to week."

Stan Liebling is persuaded that his mother, in a different era, would have been a much better entrepreneur than his father. His father was a very nice guy and everybody loved him. "My mother thought the world was a jungle and you get them before they get you."

"Softies need not apply," I write.

Stan seems troubled by the moral implications of this thought, but he has some of his mother in him: he takes the toughest and most no-nonsense positions at the table. Aspiring small business owners come to him with cockamamie business plans full of what one might call "romantic accounting." They leave out transportation costs because "they have their own car." They leave out a salary for themselves and other unavoidable, legitimate expenses. They are often reluctant both to account for these expenses and to pass on the costs. "I can't charge them for that, it's not fair," the nonaggressive folks tell Stan. The aggressive ones try to account for every penny and look for ways to maximize the markup on that.

So I am not in it to be anyone's friend. It is not a charity. "It's a *business*," the other Harry interjects. If I went out on my own and tried to run one, what might it be? he wants to know. Since we are at Universal Studios, I figure I will try the famous Hollywood Pitch.

"OK, OK. You know the way grocery stores print customized coupons on your receipt? A computer reads what you are buying and offers you a deal on another product you might plausibly want. How about a business that would broker some of that cash register tape space for the betterment of society? We have a problem in this country getting parents to bring their infants in for immunizations. The store computer would notice that they're buying size-2 Drypers, and print out a message asking if Junior has had his DPT shots and providing the phone number of local clinics. It's clever, it's doable, it'll improve the world, and I smell government contract here. Either that or we could tap one of the richest groups in America, the pharmaceutical industry. Whaddaya think?"

Harry, Harry, Harvey, and Stan all stop in midchew. There is a pause. One of the Harrys clears his throat. Any other ideas?

"Call it *Falling Down* meets *Speed*. Car alarms—they go off, they make a racket, but are you, the car owner, standing on a balcony like

Juliet, head cocked, listening for your alarm to go off? No, you're inside. You're in your office, at the restaurant, at the movies, *out of earshot.* What the world needs is a car alarm that sets off your pager. Somebody fondles your Acura, off goes your pager, and you're down in the parking lot with your nunchaku sticks. We could get Jackie Chan for the ads."

Harry Dictor puts some Sweet 'n Low into his iced tea. Harvey Austin fiddles with the goat cheese on his personal-size Puck's pizza. "Stan, do you want to start or should I?"

"I find that many times investors are creative and ingenious people but have no idea whatsoever about how to run a business," Stan said. "No idea. None."

"An invention in most cases is really an ego trip," Dictor adds, noting another SCORE workshop on patents and inventions. "We get people at every seminar who have been taken by some scam company, but they are such easy marks. The company says they'll check out the viability of your invention, takes your money, and if they like it, they'll call back. Right."

"There is a difference between entrepreneur and inventor," I scribble in my notes.

They suggest a little market research on either idea might be in order before proceeding. I claim to be the king of all data; this is something I can handle if I just follow through. If I am going to use a surplus on this one, I have to approach the investment with the same manic detective impulse that drives my computer or car purchases. This realization is a thought that I fail to articulate. Feeling I am not getting the message, Stan can take it no longer and begins the cross-examination.

How are you going to get your paging alarm system made? Who will do it and at what price? How much money do you need for all this? Nowhere have you talked about a financial plan. Where's the money for this?

"From your father? No!" he says, answering for all the fathers of the world.

I explain how I am reluctant to take a plunge with it this time because I was so impetuous the last time I had a nest egg of this size. I say that I am approaching the question about what to do with money by spending as much time as possible outside the womb of my office, asking around until I find the course that fits me best. The group takes this in, and what I get in response are two unsettlingly different takes on what it takes to be successful at using money in this way.

Stan Liebling, who sees a lot of people who do not have what it takes during his counseling sessions, once saw a fellow who did. Like all good stories from the old days, this one took place at an Automat, where strangers often shared tables. Stan was listening as someone brought an old friend up to date. It was a long tale of partnerships formed and dissolved and other businesses that didn't ultimately work out. So what was the old friend doing now?

"I am looking for a proposition" came the answer. Stan remembers being struck by this. "*I* look for a job. *He* looks for a proposition. Now that's an entrepreneur."

This is a confounding story. How are any of us going to summon the superhuman emotional and intellectual energy that is necessary to make a business work if it is not something we deeply, viscerally believe in? You would think that walking around with a full billfold looking for the next big entrepreneurial score has to be a recipe for disaster, but some can do it.

The difference we have to account for is the source of our identities. If we define ourselves only by a venture's product and its impact on the market or society, then we become the project and the project had better reflect our vision. But then you get someone like "Chairsaw Al" Dunlap, the fierce corporate turnaround artist who seems to define himself as a person who fixes companies. When he was at Scott Paper, it is unlikely he saw himself as the king of paper, or when he moved to Sunbeam, as king of humidifiers. He looks for a proposition, like the guy in the Automat.

There are also those who are able to work ferociously hard and still define themselves in terms unconnected to their day job. My grandfather owned a bar and grill in a rough section of Brooklyn. His main tales from the business revolved around repeated robberies with occasional shots fired, police corruption, and extortion attempts by local mobsters. The comfortable, middle-class lifestyle Hyman Fleischer provided for his family was proof he was a good manager, but he says it was never anything close to a labor of love and had little, in itself, to do with independence and fullfillment. In the end, my grandfather sold the business for a song because the neighborhood had declined too far. His one bit of advice when I spoke to him about my entrepreneurial fantasy sparked by ideas of a surplus dismissed the notion that a business gives you the freedom to work for yourself.

"You have to have a partner," my grandfather said. "If you don't have a partner, you are going to be working every waking second."

Iffat from Bangladesh works ridiculous hours running her sandwich franchises yet gives the impression that very little of her identity is wrapped up in the specific enterprise she is running. Her business improves the community by creating jobs and contributing to the tax base. But she seems to draw more of her identity from her and her husband's role as activists in the local Bangladeshi community and at the helm of a growing family. She manages her business efficiently and profitably. Not all of us, however, are built that way, and lucky for us, there is an alternate path.

It is Harvey Austin who puts that path on the table with the SCORE counselors.

"What does it take to be an entrepreneur?" Austin begins. "Search your soul for your gift, whatever turns you on, and find a way to turn that into something that sells. Years ago I got into business to get people to stop smoking because that was something I felt strongly about. Some people look at it with a business head, and other people ask what do I feel so strongly about that I want to give to the world?"

This is something short of the *Field of Dreams* approach to a business. Austin isn't saying build a business according to your heart and they, the customers, will come. He is saying find a way to link what is in your heart with something that sells. Even he doesn't want me to lose sight of the customer.

"And if all else fails," Harry Spitzer says by way of parting, "put your salary in the bank and live off the tips."

I think Harry's final take on me is that I am an employee, not a proprietor, which isn't the kind of encouragement I need to shove me in the direction of putting money to work growing a venture.

* * *

The SCORE guys are very convinced that there is a dichotomy not just between employee and entrepreneur but between inventor and entrepreneur. I make a point to explore this further during a conversation with Robert Knotek, a man who is both an entrepreneur and a student of entrepreneurship. I met him during a speaking engagement in St. Paul when he raised his hand from the audience and offered some very sharp observations about the subject.

According to Knotek, an inventor tends to sit in a darkened room dreaming up wonderful solutions to problems that don't exist in the real world. An entrepreneur listens carefully for someone else to utter the magical words "It would sure be nice if someone could figure out a way to solve this problem." When I tell Knotek about my customized immunization reminders printing beside supermarket checkout coupons, he wants me to pinpoint a customer.

"Give me a specific name and telephone number of someone who would be interested in paying for this." His point is, a successful business isn't all about me. It had better be a whole lot about the customer.

This is tough for a creative person to swallow. The reclusive author Robert Pirsig was once asked by a newspaper reporter why it took him sixteen years to produce a sequel to his bestseller, *Zen and the Art of Motorcycle Maintenance*. He replied that he actually welcomed writer's block because it was a clear sign he wasn't giving in to the demands of the marketplace. That is an artist, not an entrepreneur, for you.

And it's not even good enough if customers find your idea fascinating and useful; they have to be willing to shell out money for it. Knotek figured this out early. He loves music but has, by his own admission, no real musical talent. So he went to work for a Minneapolis-based company that was the biggest supplier of musical instruments in the country. People in that business love selling and servicing pianos and trombones, but dealing with the sale of smaller items is considered annoying. The owner of that company once remarked to the young Knotek, "Wouldn't it be great if someone would handle all the guitar strings, clarinet reeds, and tuning forks so we could concentrate on the real business of selling instruments?" Bingo.

Knotek didn't make a fortune selling reeds and strings. But he did make a fortune selling the business after he built it up. He considers the sale a windfall, which he used in part to travel and study entrepreneurship. Although he has taught at the college level for years, when I catch up with him, Knotek is working on his Ph.D. in a program based in Barcelona, looking at entrepreneurship globally. I call him to ask if it is possible to *smell* an entrepreneur the way a dog smells fear.

No, there is no blood test for it, Knotek laughs. Business acumen comes in too many forms for there ever to be some kind of home pregnancy test that turns pink when you have what it takes to begin ripening a venture. Knotek notes that governments the world over always ask a variant of this question, which is, in essence, "How do we identify the winners, because we only want to back them?"

The question gets it backwards. Economist Joseph Schumpeter wrote of the necessity of "creative destruction." The economy grows when new businesses spring up offering product innovations. According to his theory, new products have a strong chance of capturing the largest market share and therefore can offer investors wider margins of profit. Not only does it pay to be the industry leader, but it pays to stay the leader, even if that means that you must pull a perfectly good product (which is still holding strong market share) off the market to replace it with an updated version with newer innovations. Schumpeter would argue that it's not important that hundreds of other businesses fail because they can't keep pace, because the industry leaders will more than make up for their losses by stimulating economic growth. In a sense, the businesses that fail are doing a community service by freeing up capital that then becomes available to entrepreneurs and innovators.

This to me sounds a bit like the argument that unemployed people are doing a community service because they are keeping overall wages down and inflation low, but I ride with it. The principle of creative destruction, however, is cold comfort to the spouse of an entrepreneur who has to watch some wacky idea drive the family into personal bankruptcy.

Knotek also makes a distinction between what he sees as a "small business person," who is by nature conservative, holding onto the status quo, preserving rather than innovating, and the entrepreneur, who starts with the premise that the old way is not the best way. Families and societies are often conservative institutions, and they don't necessarily welcome the chaos that entrepreneurship invites.

Knotek also challenges the common idea that an entrepreneur is someone who cannot stand to work for someone else. "Think it through," he encourages me, ever the good teacher. "You fire the boss, start out on your own, and end up with forty-five different, demanding bosses, otherwise known as your *clients*." The kind of entrepreneur who has no boss is a bit like the Basil Fawlty character, who, like legions of petit bourgeois shopowners the world over, couldn't be more irritated by the insufferable presence of a customer.

Creative destruction, however, doesn't mean self-destructive, and every "great" potentially money-making idea does not have to be put into the marketplace in an effort to ensure we stay vibrant and innovative as a nation. Knotek offers a simple way to do triage on my brilliant business ideas. I should move to the next step only after satisfactorily completing the previous one.

Am I inspired? Does the idea wake me up at night, fill my commuting hours, force me to look out the window and reflect on them during meetings at my current job?

Have I done my research, not just in the library but on foot? What industry does the idea fit into, and what is the rest of the industry's state of the art? Who is the competition? How might the competition react? What prices are charged for similar things?

Where's the written business plan? This can be a weekend task.

Got financing? Line up, but don't actually accept, the money. I take this to mean keep my powder dry on the fuse beneath a surplus. Also, the nest egg may just be the first tranche of the seed money needed to make a go of the enterprise. Relatives? The SCORE executives have already warned me about asking for money from my father. Which banks? How much? Can some be borrowed against an insurance policy? It is this step where all men and women are created equal but are not treated that way. Some come from rich families or communities with a tradition of lending start-up capital from family to family. Banks are bound by law not to discriminate, but when it comes down to a loan officer making a judgment call on the person he sees before him, all sorts of noise may creep into the equation: if it isn't race, it might be class or one's accent, none of which can be correlated in any way with chances for success or failure of the enterprise.

Then test it. If you want to sell a thing, build a prototype and try to sell it, even at a loss. If it is a service you want to provide, try it for real on a paying customer. This is expensive, Knotek warns, but not as expensive as betting the house or the marriage on an untested business proposition.

Finally, step back, consider what you have learned, and make a formal go/no-go decision. Knotek once sank a modest surplus into a book distribution concept he'd worked out that turned out to be before its time. He stopped it the "step back" phase. The idea did come into its own a decade later, when companies opened bookstores on the World Wide Web, but he has no regrets and still believes stopping his losses where he did was a smart decision.

Knotek is able to hear my worried silence. Even with this organized, methodical plan, it is quite a gamble. How about franchising, he suggests. Let someone else make the first mistakes. If I am to use a chunk of money to purchase a franchise, Knotek offers some pointers.

First, you do not need to be an entrepreneur to run a franchise. You need to be a team player who follows directions and takes grievances through proper channels. So, again, don't fool yourself about really being your own boss. Second, you should take care to enter the franchise life cycle at the right time, not too early, not too late. If you are one of the first fifteen or so I've Got the Bleus smelly-cheese-only franchises, the chain will be testing the concept on you, and you might as well have started from scratch with an idea of your own and not pay the training and ongoing franchise fees. Come too late in the franchising cycle, and there is liable to be a Just Hubcaps on every block.

The more I learn about this, however, the less I can visualize personally using a lump sum to do it. I don't want to be a jock-in-the-box, a victimized cog caught within a large organization, but I personally wouldn't thrive owning a KWGB World's Greatest Burgers outlet either. There has got to be a way to merge the inventive/creative and entrepreneurial/business sides. As I would later learn, some do it seamlessly.

It is a chilly early spring morning during a business trip to New York City. I am sitting in the art nouveau Bus Stop Cafe in Greenwich Village, minding my own jet lag over french toast made from challah, when I become aware of an intense conversation going at the table jammed next to my right elbow. A man and a woman perhaps a generation older than me are talking about things better left outside a public place. An affair. Betrayal. Suicide. A tear travels down the woman's face. Did I hear the word "incest"?

Common human decency demands I move out of this couple's space and, shaken, I rise to see if the waitress can move me so these poor folks can be left in peace. As I rise, I notice the man is holding a script. It is Horton Foote's Pulitzer Prize–winning play, *The Young Man from Atlanta,* and the woman is an actress running lines. I clearly was in the presence of greatness to have been fooled sitting just eighteen inches away. Food arrives and the couple's conversation snaps without transition from Foote's world of 1950s Texas into a very contemporary business discussion.

There has been a rave review that morning in the *New York Times* of Christopher Plummer's performance as Barrymore, and the couple work out how this will affect the theater's ticket prices. A rave creates a surge in demand. Higher demand can lead to higher prices, but only if the ticket price is balanced carefully against that of the competition. These are artists and businesspeople wrapped up into one.

Come to think of it, everyone in this trendazoid place has had their body snatched by the entrepreneurial invaders. To my left, in the nine o'clock position, a pair of middle-aged men with earrings are talking very serious business. One appears to run a gallery, and the other owns the building.

"I don't want a situation where you can't meet obligations and you have to be locked out," the property owner says.

"That won't be necessary. We have a plan in place that I think is a good plan that will get us over this cash flow situation."

In my four o'clock position, two women in their twenties are earnestly pitching a screenplay project to a man who, in his thirties, has seen it all. A couple of them are practitioners of the the nonspecific Euroaccent.

"Eets like *Blade RunNEUR,* but from a deeferent place," says the first very earnest-sounding person.

"Yes, a duplicate being, that is the key," says another.

"Wha's eenteresting to me is the dualiTEE," says the recipient of the pitch. "The character landed or she came from a laboratory or whatever, but she is *not one of us*. I think this is an important story that we must tell the world."

I find my breakfast in the cafe a liberating discovery because it allows me to open up my definition of what starting a business with a nest egg might be. The fact that many of us like to think of ourselves as right-brained, creative people does not imply we somehow lack a head for business. There doesn't have to be a dichotomy, or dualiTEE, as the fellow said. You might not see yourself as an owner of a franchise or an antiques dealer, even though you have an eye for quality old pieces. But what about underwriting a theater project or self-publishing a compact disc of original music? I can't see myself shopping for a proposition with a surplus, like that fellow at the Automat, but someday I might find something that fits, and I now feel much more prepared to take advantage of the opportunity, should it present itself.

When you start framing creative enterprises in this way, you begin to see them everywhere. Soon after the breakfast in Greenwich Village, I met a fellow on a stop in Missouri who is in charge of raising money for a public radio station there. He had once found himself with $10,000. He used it to make a nature film about Alaska that aired on the Discovery Channel and won an award. The film was a success, as nature films go. As a business venture, it did better than most—it broke even. It is hard to see that as a bad use of the fellow's surplus, even if the investment in the business did not return market rates and one couldn't live off it. It resulted in a thing of beauty, which is more than can be said of most investments. Since the project broke even, the fellow was stuck trying to figure out what to do with the money all over again. He invested in a second nature film that didn't do nearly as well and his nest egg went away. No regrets, he said.

I kept a souvenir of my day with the retired executives from SCORE. It was a fifteen-point list of attributes entitled "How to Test an Entrepreneur." I met the first five criteria, no problem: oldest child, male, married, first moved to start a company in his thirties, master's degree. One of the points stood out because of its baffling weirdness.

"An entrepreneur takes his or her chair from business to business."

That is a scary thought, the telltale chair talisman. If love of chair is an entrepreneurial litmus test, I am in deep trouble. But another point on the list was more sobering.

"To be successful in an entrepreneurial venture, you need an overabundance of luck."

In the year I visited the business expo, 842,357 new businesses were formed in the United States. But scrolling deeper into the SBA data, I also found there were 849,839 business terminations, 71,811 business failures, and 53,214 bankruptcies. Some of these terminations were happy ones. The original proprietor sold the business but didn't transfer it as a going concern, so statistically it appeared to have gone out of business. Or some folks just wanted to retire and ramp down their businesses elegantly with all bills and shareholders paid. But it is undeniable that contained in those numbers were a lot of broken dreams.

As I fingered the bills in my nest egg, a sure bet like the U.S. government bond market started to look attractive. What's the point of all that risk? I asked myself. Then I learned about the destiny of an old high school chum who, it transpired, had just found a cool million along the entrepreneurial route.

Kevin Ladd and I have birthdays two days apart in the same year. We went to the same public schools. We played with matches together. We both earned money for college by working nightmare jobs in the same wholesale food warehouse, jobs both our fathers credit with instilling in us the diligence that made us what we are today. What I am is a fellow who sings for his supper every day in the nonprofit sector. Kevin is a high-tech tycoon. Why are we so different?

When Kevin came up with an idea for a better mousetrap, he knew he could never realize his dream within the confines of the cubicle he was given as an engineer at one of the world's biggest computer companies. But leaving the warm bosom of an established corporation was a risky step. The in-laws thought he was out of his mind. Everything is at risk with a step like this, not just a nest egg.

Kevin designed software that allows companies to test their blueprints before moving to the expensive step of stamping the circuits into silicon wafers. Engineers already had computer programs to mimic the performance of microchips while their designs were still on the drawing board, but the emulation was painfully slow. Kevin's way is a lot faster.

I phoned to tell him about my pilgrimage, and we got talking about how he pulled off creating a successful company in the tough world of high-tech. What I sensed in him was an intense focus that I have never had. Sixty- and eighty-hour weeks at his old corporate job gave him the reputation that made bankers take him seriously even when he didn't have a demonstrated track record as an entrepreneur. They saw that his whole-body commitment to a project would bring out the same in his engineering team. He didn't get this way; he always was this way.

When we both worked for his father at the food warehouse as teenagers, Kevin approached his fourteen-hour days with almost military precision. His job was a modern-day reenactment of the classic movie *Wages of Fear,* in which four men have to get a truckload of nitroglycerin to an oil field in the rugged Andes. It took a certain grim determination for Kevin to drive a temperamental truck filled with five-gallon glass jars of mayonnaise and twenty-eight-count cartons of graham crackers down crevassed, unmarked roads to deliver the goods to countless lakeside summer camps in Maine. At the bottom of the road, Kevin would have to offload the truck single-handedly, only to learn that back at the warehouse jokers like me had inadvertently fumbled the order in some way.

For me this was the only job at which I ever failed. I just could not summon the precision needed to check the pick list carefully, and I would get ill trying. I know it had something to do with that incessant Barry Manilow blaring from a radio somewhere in the warehouse, music designed by the CIA to break the spirit. Still, there were compensations; $3.35 an hour helped. So did the encouragement from my immediate bosses.

"Hey, college boy. The order here says *pitted* olives. You see any pits in this box of olives?" my supervisor yelled.

"Uh, it says pitted," I replied, exhausted from carrying in the six cases.

"Right, *pitted.* So where the hell are the pits?"

"Doesn't pitted mean no pits?"

"Tell me this, college boy. Now why would they call it PITTED if they DON'T HAVE ANY PITS?!"

I meekly went off to fetch six cases of olives containing pits.

The pin was now pulled from the grenade, and eight hours later, at the end of some winding, desolate camp road, it would explode in the face of my poor buddy Kevin. He would be forced to explain to some irate customer why he was delivering olives *and* pits, even though the customer only ordered olives.

Kevin's poker face helped him then and it helps him now. It is the sign of a fine negotiator who relishes the game of strategy. Bluffing and calling someone else's bluff are part of the game. Kevin has a talent for being completely inscrutable when necessary. Once, after negotiating a killer deal, a colleague asked how he maintained the necessary grim face as the end game was played out.

"I thought about Rwanda," he revealed.

His ability to stay cool has been essential throughout the life of his young company. High-techs attract swarms of predators known as venture capitalists, who wait for companies to bob under the waves two or three times before they throw in the life-preserving cash infusions. Play this wrong and you can end up saving a company that will be owned mostly by the venture capitalists.

By the time Kevin found himself in such a position, his charm and diligence had won over his mother-in-law. She wrote a $50,000 check to keep the company rolling. A brave investor risks his capital. A transcendently courageous player risks his *in-laws'* capital. Kevin was able to pay her back in a week. He showed the venture capitalists that he wasn't so desperate that he would accept a lousy deal from them.

At about the same time I was talking with the SCORE counselors, my old friend Kevin was 350 miles up the road in California's Silicon Valley selling his enterprise to a bigger high-tech company. His surplus had grown by many zeros to the left of the decimal point, but it sounds like we were both in a similar quandary, figuring out what to do with cash. My guess is he will take another risk. I have more traveling to do before I decide if I want the money for starting an enterprise.

I have to confront something that is at the heart of any money decision—risk. I want to know now if I really have the gamble in me or not. Perhaps I have the kind of luck an entrepreneur needs. Time for a test drive. This bankroll is going to Vegas.

Souvenirs

An American flag in the shape of a map of the United States in red and blue ink on white felt, made by Tom at the expo to demonstrate the ease of his portable shirt-printing rig.

The fear that if I had known all this earlier, I might not have had the nerve to take the risk on my one successful business venture.

To do when I get home

Start charging for my cappuccinos.

Doing the numbers

Small businesses account for half the Gross Domestic Product. In the year I visited the business opportunity expo, 842,357 new businesses were formed in the United States. There were 849,839 business terminations, 71,811 business failures, and 53,214 bankruptcies. (Source: Small Business Administration)

5

Learn to Play the Game

Taking risks in
Las Vegas, Nevada

From the clipping file: A part-time cook from Chardon, Ohio, won $12 million in the lottery. The *Cleveland Plain Dealer* quoted her saying that while she is on such a hot streak, "I'm not answering the phone . . . and I'm going to Las Vegas." January 5, 1993

I met a business school professor who takes his students on trips to the battlefield at Gettysburg and the base of Mount Everest for lectures on leadership. If he is ever assigned a course on money and risk, you just know he will have to conduct that lecture along the Strip in Las Vegas.

While some of the destinations on my money trips were the result of painstaking research and deliberation, a trip to the capital of gambling—I'm sorry, gaming—was always a foregone conclusion. I had never been there before, and the pilgrimage presented such a convenient excuse. My destiny had been sealed by that fake Casino Player *magazine cover my image had been grafted onto at the mall.*

Las Vegas is a place scientifically designed to ease us of the burden of our surpluses. I can speculate all day about my attitude to financial risk, but in those casinos I could carry out empirical experiments into this question around the clock. This trip also put me into contact with two former professional gamblers, who passed along some of the wisest counsel I would receive about risking a surplus in the financial markets.

If you want to know whom you are dealing with, ask for a person's car-ownership history. My list of cars over the years would not recommend my induction into an oil-rig fire-control officer training program. Modest and dependable, every one of them, like a fleet of second husbands. New research suggests that first-borns are risk averse, and in my case I am worried the researchers are right.

So for a road trip from Los Angeles to Las Vegas, I have to up the ante. A candy-apple-red Ford Mustang convertible will provide the not-so-modest or dependable horsepower necessary. There is something wrong with the rack-and-pinion steering on this particular rental, which causes the car to switch lanes without provocation from the driver, just the sort of thing for my new life as a risk-taking man.

With the top down, it is easy to throw caution into the slipstream. From the moment I climb into the car, with its long thrust of gleaming sheet metal, everything is out of character. The antitheft device that I have, typically, brought along from my minivan is stowed in the truck. I figure the insouciant effect of leaving the car parked with the top down at the casinos will be lost if I am seen fussily affixing the Club to the steering wheel. The car was presented to me with only a partial tank of gas, sufficient for only about a third of the three-hundred-mile trip across the Mojave Desert. But I shrug off the idea of filling up before striking out onto the freeway. A dice-throwing, roulette-wheel-spinning guy bets that he will find another gasoline station somewhere along the way.

These delusions aside, I am in fact a neophyte headed for Las Vegas, probably to get my wallet laundered and handed back to me starched and folded. But if I want to know about what to do with money, then what better place to visit than the city where cash runs amok, a city where money clips are still in vogue and where the word "bankroll" retains its literal meaning, a wad in the trouser pocket?

I will spend the night ninety miles from Vegas, in Baker, California, a parched town a brief drive from the Nevada border. Baker would be nothing but a gas and refreshment stand for I-15 travelers heading to and from the gambling capital or Death Valley if it were not for two distinguishing features. The first is a thermometer taller than a flagpole, rimmed with neon and visible for twenty miles on a decent day. The digital readouts in Fahrenheit and Celsius rise and fall like the ball in Times Square, only smaller. At first the thermometer seems a little sad, like the old Kliban cartoon depicting an earnest man in western gear proudly posing with his foot on an eight-foot cooked chicken leg, under the sign "World's Biggest." But then on further reflection, you have to hand it to Baker's power elite. They turned a dry lake bed into the town with the world's biggest thermometer—that is to say, a place worth visiting.

It is, and when I do, I know exactly where to stay: Arne's Royal Hawaiian, a cheap motel that features rooms styled in a playful medley of chrome-on-Formica circa 1964. It is a winter night in the high desert, and the readouts on the big thermometer visible from my room are riding low on the staff, 48° Fahrenheit. Like other hopefuls headed for Vegas before me, I paw through my bankroll a few times, checking the bills and folding them into four piles of one hundred dollars each. From my reading on gambling, I have learned to break my bankroll into sessions with win and loss goals. Quit when you are 20 percent ahead was one suggestion, because it is highly unlikely you will improve on that rate of return. Quit when you have lost half your session bankroll. Sounds like a plan. If the gambling environment lends itself to a methodical approach, I should do well.

My wife kindly picked up the new, crisp twenties for me at the bank earlier in the day. It is twice as much cash as I expected. This is either a sweet vote of confidence in my gambling ability or a subtle message that she is taking this thing seriously and expects me to perform and come back with the loot.

The next morning I return my room key to a fragile, translucent woman who probably became eligible for Social Security right around the same time the motel was last redecorated.

"Lived here long?"

She cheerfully nods. I inquire about breakfast.

"Well, the Bun Boy across the way is about the same as the Denny's right across the street. And there is something called the Mad Greek, but I've never tried it." There is something inspiring about meeting someone who has lived in a town with a total of two streets and three sit-down, slow-food restaurants and has never in all these years had occasion to venture into restaurant number three.

I choose the Bun Boy, a Baker institution since 1926. Down home it is not, but the place is spotless. As I wait for my pancakes, a little card set on the counter reminds me of Baker's other distinguishing characteristic. Besides the thermometer, Baker is the lottery capital of the West. More specifically, Baker is home to the Wills Country Store, an establishment that has sold the most jackpot-winning lottery tickets anywhere in the region. The total includes, the little sign on the breakfast counter announces, a jackpot win for one of the Bun Boy's very own waitresses.

"Oh, no. Linda doesn't work here no more," the lady at the cash register tells me. "Moved after she got the $14 million from the lottery. She was driving through Barstow with her sixteen-year-old, who was looking through the paper and told her to pull over. 'Why?' she asked. 'I'll tell you in a minute, just pull over, Mom.' The boy had been reading the lottery numbers and told her the news. She turned around and headed back to the Wills store here to check the numbers.

"Then she called up her husband, who works at the rare earth mine, you know, where they get the red minerals you need to make color TV tubes? Anyway, Linda called her husband to say she'd won, and she had always joked about it, so he didn't believe her. Finally she gave up trying to convince him and told him to hold on because she'd be over to the mine in thirty minutes.

"She bought her son a $20,000 pickup with it. She worked right here at the Bun Boy." All this happened nine months ago.

Linda and her family have since moved to Arizona. Linda had been playing the same number—perhaps her son's birthday—every week without fail since 1988.

It is established that the Wills store has the California record for jackpot tickets. It is presumed, given the size of the California lottery, that this makes it the winningest lottery store this side of Texas. Its track record is posted in two-foot letters on a sign out front:

$14 MILLION
$12 MILLION
$6 MILLION
$5 MILLION
$4 MILLION
LOTTO WON HERE
NEXT DRAWING ____ FOR $15 MILLION.

Although someone has fallen down on their duty to update the sign, the next drawing, it turns out, is that very night. I go inside, introduce myself, and tell Nicole and Mona, the women with the California Lottery polo shirts behind the counter, that I need help because this is my first time. They show me that I can pick any series of six numbers between 1 and 51 at a dollar a play, or I can get the computer to generate a random series.

Alas, I have no numbers. I have known people who remember everyone's phone numbers and birthdays and other numerical oddities and continually cross-reference them and tease out synchronicities. Me, I cannot cope with the clutter that a long series of numbers creates in my memory, so I don't carry them around. But I need a system for my first big lottery play.

My brother-in-law Michael, who has a very good head for numbers, once observed that the best way to increase your chances at winning a lottery is to buy your first ticket. You can't win if you don't play, as the ad goes. But the second ticket hardly raises your chances of winning at all: the curve stays so close to zero that the second, third, and fourth don't raise your chances in any practical way. But this is a romantic purchase, not a practical one. So I resolve to buy twenty entries. I'll let the computer pick half of them randomly. Five more are based on a cockamamie system of the frequencies of radio stations where I have worked. Then in a nod to convention, I choose three sets of numbers based on my children's birthdays. The strategy had worked for Linda, the Bun Boy waitress, after all. I also let my right brain take over for one. I fill in six numbers that appear in a neat, vertical line down the face of the ticket: 6, 15, 24, 33, 42, 51. Finally I choose 1, 2, 3, 4, 5, and 6. I want to confront the grim fact that these numbers have the same chance of turning up during the drawing tonight as any other six numbers, as amazing a coincidence as that may seem.

I turn over the first $20 bill of my gambling bankroll. Twenty sets of six numbers, 120 numbers, so many numbers that I feel I have at least a fighting chance at winning. Adding this to the proven good karma of the Wills Country Store, I begin to see the possibilities of a happy ending. I write in my notebook: *Score: California Lottery, $20—Me, To be announced at 8 p.m.*

A charter bus returning from Vegas pulls in. The people get off to stretch their legs as the driver fills up the tanks across the way at the Texaco station. Groggy, pale, and still wearing their fine casino duds and gambling jewelry, most of the passengers file in to buy lottery tickets, which Mona and Nicole supply with the practiced hands of baccarat dealers. Is it like this all the time? Mona nods.

It is clear what is going on here. The Wills store does a huge volume of lottery business, picking off the last-chance gamblers returning humbled from Vegas or those, like me, looking for a head start on a hot streak. Shooting fish in a barrel is the marketing metaphor. The main luck here has to do with owning a lottery shop in this bounteous spot. Location and its cousin, foot traffic, are at work. Once you factor in the volume of business, luck at the Wills store is probably about the same as at other stores.

Still, Ron Barr is looking to get lucky. A genial blue-eyed trucker with a sandy blond mustache, he is ambling toward the store to get a ticket. He says he has two sets of twins at home in Colorado. His wife has ordered him to buy a lottery ticket in every state where the jackpot climbs above $10 million. He says he has bought in every one of the Lower 48 that has a lottery.

"I've never won anything, but you still try, right? It's temptation," Barr says. "You see all that money there, and you have to do it." His strategy isn't bad. If you want to increase your chances by buying more than one lottery ticket, the best thing you can do is buy each of them in a different state lottery so you have a very small chance of winning in a

lot of places. The trick is to keep track of all the drawings. The year before the trip, $44.1 million worth of winning lottery prizes went un-
claimed in Florida alone. The problem of unclaimed winnings is so
common that the majority of states with lotteries have laws on the
books that either plow the money back into the lottery's pot or into special funds for education or public works.

Barr says he will not stop working if he wins but will instead find
work closer to home so he can spend more time with his twins. He figures if he won and quit, he would probably die after a couple of years of
sitting around. He recalls a lady who won $28 million in the Colorado
lottery and later killed herself because she became overwhelmed with all
the cash.

"Money is not the answer. It's what you put your money into and
what you put your life into, that's the main thing," Barr says. "You've
just got to set your goals and say, 'Yeah, I've got a lot of money, and I'm
going to have a couple of nice things, but I'm not going to overexert myself.'

"Yes, I'm going to take that Alaska cruise," he says with gusto, "but
that's it." Ron Barr is a rare man who has done the accounting on just
what it would take to make him content, a vision with a quantifiable upper limit.

A whoop of joy erupts from the store. Unfortunately, while I was out
front chatting with Barr, I was not inside investing $2 in an instant-win
lottery scratcher. A man named Aquino has just scratched and won
$100. If this is his first and only attempt at the lottery, it is a handy re-
turn on investment. "No, I play all the time," he says as he climbs into
his black Chevy pickup with his son. I am pleased that he is happy and
rationalize that now is not the time for me to win cash. Any windfall at
this moment will just be more cash I will have to find a place for in Las
Vegas.

I turn onto the highway and the wind shifts. As I hit the curve, the
pattern of turbulence courses over the windshield and into the Mustang's cockpit. The burbling sounds like thousands of tiny voices
screaming with joy, very much like the sound you hear between tracks
on early live Beatles recordings. Sirens are luring me onto the rocks.

I begin to feel a kinship with a fellow who came to our office earlier in the day. As we were chatting in preparation for a formal interview on a different subject, I mentioned Vegas. He told the story of how he had studied blackjack for a year but could not afford the airfare to Las Vegas from Montreal, where he was living at the time. A business associate recommended him as a professional gambler, and the MGM Grand Casino agreed to fly him out and put him up free with two conditions: he had to play at blackjack tables where each hand costs $25 or more, and he had to play at the table for at least three hours a day for the three-day weekend. Imagine being trapped at a table with no exit, with every minute that goes by having the potential to suck away $25. The fellow traded away his one major ally in the competition against the casinos—the time element, the ability to quit while he was ahead. If I quit right now on the road to Las Vegas, I will be ahead the $380 I still have left in my bankroll. A turn north into Death Valley and I can hike for free (except for the modest park entrance fee) and stay at the Stove Pipe Wells Village motel for $50 a night, single occupancy. But there is no exit. The entrance ramp from Baker to the interstate reflects little of the American ideal of freedom of choice: "Las Vegas ONLY," the sign says, even though the city is still eighty-nine miles away. I am committed.

My first glimpse of the Strip, the business end of Las Vegas Boulevard, is at Sahara Avenue. An old guidebook identifies the southwest corner of this big intersection as one of the last undeveloped stretches of the Strip, making this plot of ground perhaps one of the most valuable pieces of real estate on earth. I am curious to see what it has become.

Nothing, yet. The desert floor has been raked by backhoes, and there are some construction trailers, but there is nothing close to taking shape. Frank Sinatra is widely quoted about his trip to Vegas in 1946, when he and a friend looked at a plot of land across the street from the Hotel Tropicana that was then selling for a dollar an acre. At the time he couldn't imagine such a plot would be good for anything, an assessment he ruefully admits was probably the worst play ever made in the history of real estate. Yet here was another stretch of the Strip, one that should have been a sure bet for some developer, lying fallow still. Especially in Vegas, there are no sure bets.

I park and follow the pedestrian flow south along the Strip. Some pause to catch the Treasure Island tableaux, but most press on. The hot spot on this temperate winter morning is the New York, New York casino. The exterior is impressive, for a stage set. It looks like an electronic rendering of the New York skyline: more squat, compact, color saturated, and two-dimensional than the original. The Statue of Liberty seems a bit short. It stands next to a modernized Coney Island roller-coaster, next to the Empire State Building, which stands on the same block as the Chrysler Building.

A young couple works their way down the sidewalk toward the travel-sized Brooklyn Bridge. Each is tapping smoothly and deliberately with a white cane.

"We're looking for New York, New York," the man says. I tell him he is right on track and try to render the bridge for him in words.

"Are we on the bridge now?" he asks. We are parallel to it, at the entrance to the casino. Can I help direct them further? No, they are fine. I tag along enough to learn they are from San Diego, and they listen to AM talk radio.

We pass together through a set of double doors into the full-blown casino experience, starting with layer upon layer upon layer of sound. There is Jewel's voice singing about heartbreak; there is carousel music and that big crowd rumble. Alarms buzz, bells chime, the irregular clatter of heavy $1 coins being put into the big slots overlaps the occasional storm of quarters gushing into holding trays. The tempo seems to be 7/4, and if someone has brought a guitar, we could live the opening bit of Pink Floyd's "Money."

The couple from San Diego breezes into this whitewater rapids of cacophony, their sticks guiding them around knots of gamblers and gawkers and the hodgepodge of slot and video poker machines, change carts, and waitresses carrying full trays of cocktails. I offer no assistance since none is required, say nothing, and walk respectfully behind. Finally the pair stops at an unoccupied slot machine. Here the man does need help.

"Does this take fifty cents or just a quarter?" is his only question.

I set off on my own, confused about where to start, as if I have parachuted into a forest-size apple orchard holding only a bushel basket. A row of very serious older women wearing fanny packs filled with coins sit at the machines grinding through their stashes with the grim faces of seamstresses in a sweatshop. This is not recreation; it is work. The bank of quarter slots melts into more imposing dollar slots. My boss told me that he had a relative he took to Vegas who won $3,000 in these machines. I get a tightly wrapped tube of special casino-issue dollar coins at the change booth and begin feeding the machine. In one minute and forty-two seconds, I come up with cherries, bars, sevens, diamonds, but never all in a row. My roll of coins, $20, is gone. I have already forgotten the stop-when-you've-lost-half-your-session-bankroll rule.

I know I have to get out of here to regroup. But how? Giant illuminated signs point to restaurants, shops, the rollercoaster. But I can't for the life of me find an exit sign. I wander around and find myself tracing a loop that ends right where it begins, near my unlucky dollar slots. I have read that casinos, like shopping malls, have few clocks and no windows, so that time stands still. But I never read there would be no way out. The Nathan's Hot Dog place is over here, the fake Times Square photo place is over there, but where did I come in? Just then I notice a familiar pair of faces. It is the visually impaired couple from San Diego, styling through the crowd sticks first.

"Hi, it's me again," I announce. "Where are you headed?"

"Back out," they reply, to my relief. I tag along, and they pilot me safely back to the sidewalk by the bridge. Before we part company for good, the man asks how I did in there.

"Not bad for a first-timer," I lie. He and his wife won $21. Well, at least my money went to someone I knew, if only for a short time. *Score: New York, New York Casino, $20—Me, $0.*

What I need is a fresh start. I cross a catwalk at the other side of the intersection and walk to the venerable Tropicana. It has a casino that looks like a casino, with an illuminated stained-glass ceiling and a mezzanine from which you can view the action at the tables from above, as though living your very own movie crane shot. The friendly, quieter atmosphere calms me down, and I descend onto the casino floor to change a $10 bill into quarters.

When I find a machine that agrees with me—some casino machines are rigged to change colors, redder to attract you, bluer to keep you at it—I pop in a pair of quarters and yank the handle. Seven, blank, bar.

Nothing. I put in another quarter and yank the handle. The reels turn to some arcane combination that produces a win of two quarters. I have won, sort of. The casino is still up net one quarter. I put in two quarters and by this time realize I can gently tap the handy illuminated button instead of expending excess energy pulling the lever. Around the reels go and land on diamond, diamond, wild card. The machine erupts with ringing and clicking. The digital counter starts racing upward, 8, 15, 21, 50 . . . when will it stop? At 60. I have won 60! Sixty thousand dollars? Sixty dollars? No, 60 quarters, otherwise known as $15. I try three more single-quarter spins and lose three times in a row. The second rule of casinos is, quit if you lose three in a row. I still have $9 of my original $10 in coins in my plastic cup. Triumphantly, I go to the change window, hand back all my quarters, and get $24 back in bills. *Tropicana Score: Investment, $1—Return, $14.*

The only problem is, the whole process took only about five minutes. I am richer, but it can hardly be said that I have enjoyed a jam-packed day of gaming recreation. This is a choice that I need to make here and now. Am I here to pass the time or am I here to make my money grow? What is in order is some expert advice.

If the idea is to turn down the color saturation and talk turkey about Las Vegas, Anthony Curtis has picked the right spot. The concrete courtyard behind his small publishing company is the opposite of a casino. It is spare, more like a parking area than a yard, and very real, lit by white desert sunshine and nothing else. The hill to the west of this industrial corner of Las Vegas is dominated by the purple and red hues of the Rio hotel and casino, but the courtyard itself would photograph identically whether one used color or black-and-white film. The courtyard contains just five features: a table, two lawn chairs, Curtis, and what appears to be a pile of paper just short of a ream, containing the galleys of a book. Curtis, a former collegiate wrestler, options trader, professional card player, and now columnist and entrepreneur has agreed to set me straight about gambling. He is about my age and is dressed in cutoffs and an armless T-shirt. Watch him shuffle and you know you are in a heap of trouble. But Curtis's real skills are not about manual dexterity.

"Vegas is a microcosm of the whole animal of capitalism," Curtis says. "It is competition at its most heated. The savvy consumer can take advantage of everything this free market has to offer. In gambling, as in most capital markets in general, the public is not sophisticated, and they get suckered into losing games that subsidize the market for the rest of us, and the whole thing works."

As a teenager, Curtis was very smart in both math and the card game hearts, and he wanted very much to get to Vegas to try his hand. His intellect and skill as a wrestler got him from Georgia Tech to the University of Nevada–Las Vegas by way of UCLA and Duke. A textbook entitled *Grim Moments in Parenting* would have to include a chapter devoted to the moment when Curtis told his father, an academic, that he wished to drop out of college to become a professional gambler. The elder Curtis played his cards right, listened carefully to his son's pitch, expressed doubts, but did not hit the ceiling. Curtis said the professional gambling gig could help him toward his longer-range goal, becoming a publisher of gambling books. That won him his father's blessing.

As soon as he turned twenty-one, the legal age for gambling, and armed with the ability to count cards, Curtis headed for the casino. Card counting is a mental feat involving the acquired ability to track 312 cards as they come out of the "shoe" at a six-deck blackjack table. Knowing which cards have already been played gives the player a sense of the cards that remain, which provides the counter with a slight edge over the casino. It's legal, but casinos hate it, and they tend to frog-march practitioners out the back door as soon as they are identified. Curtis was wonderful at counting cards in his basement in Michigan. But a Las Vegas casino is not somebody's basement.

"To count cards in the real world with pit bosses on your trail, kicking you out, is a different animal," Curtis says. "I realized I was just a rank amateur."

His folks delicately inquired about the chances of Anthony finding a real job. So he went to the Vegas office of Merrill Lynch and became an options trader. And had worse luck than at the blackjack table.

"I felt completely behind the eight ball at the options game. Everything seemed discounted by the time it got to me. I was too far down the food chain to make money. As the saying goes, if you write options, you make money, but if you are buying or selling, you probably won't."

Curtis quickly reckoned he could do much better in what he called the gambling markets.

"While you are at the brokerage, if you are going to speculate, you don't know when you have the edge. I wasn't that good at it, and I was never sure when I had the edge. I would find what looked like good bets, but there was no way of telling. In blackjack you absolutely know when you have the edge; it's all mathematical. A good card-counting system will tell you. You are putting your money down in situations where you know you have an advantage. At blackjack those situations might come up a hundred times a night."

The other thing is that blackjack tables accepting as little as five dollars a hand are easy to find. Curtis had just a few thousand dollars, a bankroll that could be eaten up in a single options play via Merrill Lynch and Wall Street. He became a professional gambler and says he has the tax returns listing that as his occupation to prove it.

Slowly, inexorably, over hours of play, Curtis was able to get the less than one percent advantage that card counters have over the casinos to augment his nest egg. It involved exhausting work, a lot of beer, and a lot of all-nighters at the table. In the end it was barely a living. He tallied up the hours invested versus the return.

"Plying this trade, this art, was earning me $2.35 an hour on average. It became evident to me very quickly that I could make twice as much working at Burger King."

What about the high rollers who make a killing at blackjack? There's the tale of Australian media magnate Kerry Packer's big win in Vegas over the 1996 Christmas holiday, so big that it had to be listed in the Hilton Hotel Corporation's annual report to shareholders (the report soberly stated that the casino sustained $22 million in losses, most of it to Packer), causing an 11 percent fall in the casino's share price. Packer had already been banned from further play at the MGM Grand after taking it for $20 million over two years. Big bankrolls can beget big returns in absolute terms. As a percentage, it is possible Anthony Curtis was winning more than Kerry Packer at the blackjack table. But high rollers in the Packer mold do not just win at the table. Curtis even has questions about the astuteness of players like Packer.

"I'll tell you what these whales are doing. The high rollers get a percentage of their losses rebated to them. If a casino won't play ball, they take their millions of dollars to a casino that will."

The high rollers also get a ton of their expected losses back in comps: complimentary first-class airline tickets to Vegas, fancy suites, blocks of tickets to the shows or boxing matches. There are even whispers, never confirmed, Curtis says, that some clever high rollers arrange to profit on the fall of the casino's stock that can occur when the financial market hears about a whale winning a huge jackpot. Far-fetched? Perhaps.

I can just see me walking into the Mirage tonight and demanding a rebate on some of my expected losses. They'd nail me with a cattle prod, like they do with one of the blackjack cheats in the movie *Casino*. Curtis says what I might do is sign up at the casino tonight, use the electronic card they will provide to track my prodigious expected losses, and if the losses mount high enough, I might be able to score a comp buffet dinner. So I came here in a linen jacket and a Mustang to win Swedish meatballs, side of rice, and a bowl of raspberry Jell-O? My newfound mentor here, Mr. Sharp Practices, may not have a big bankroll, but surely he would not settle for a comp buffet.

But it turns out that Anthony Curtis is a coupon man. Not the coupon on a U.S. Treasury bond or the coupon you slice out of the Sunday paper for 35 cents off mayonnaise, but closer to the latter than the former. His secret is to look for mistakes that casinos make on special-offer coupons and other promotions, little temporary changes to the rules designed to lure customers. These can be a gold mine for the professional, who can profit nicely from what are, essentially, loopholes.

One Friday the thirteenth, a casino on the Morongo Band of Mission Indians' reservation offered such a deal. Instead of just paying out automatically on natural 21s in blackjack (scoring 21 on your first two cards), the casino agreed also to pay one-and-a-half times a player's bet when his or her first two cards totaled 13. Curtis did not need pencil and paper to calculate that this could be a $600-an-hour proposition for a gambler in the know.

"Where else can you go, play blackjack, sit and have a beer because you don't even have to count cards, and win that kind of money?"

When he arrived three hours later at the casino, it was immediately clear that others of his ilk had read the same tip on the Internet.

"Oh. My. God. Every guy I had ever known in my life was there— one came all the way from Hawaii. I had to buy my seat at the table. Gave fifty dollars to a pair of tourists to hit the road."

But no one won a thing. All those sharks sitting there rubbing their pectoral fins in anticipation had set off alarms.

"The casino spooked big time."

Down went the promotion one hour before it was scheduled to start, all because the Internet had spread the news too widely.

Why would a casino offer to pay automatically on 13s? Sounding very much like a Wall Street analyst giving me the straight poop on an undervalued stock, ripe for the buying, Curtis reminds me that Casino Morongo is in California, not Nevada. Under California law, casinos are not allowed to profit from blackjack. They can charge players a fee to enter the game, but all wins and losses go into a pool, and from time to time the casino is required to "give back" the money in the pool to players in the form of special promotions.

"Let all the suckers lose fifty weeks out of the year, and then guys like me show up for these fabulous promotions, promotions that let me put money down in situations with *positive expectations.*"

Positive expectations. Curtis does not mind losing money on a bet if the odds are stacked just slightly in his favor. What he always avoids as a point of honor are payoffs that don't reward the level of risk involved and games in which, statistically and over time, he will lose. Roulette is one of these. So are the slots.

Unless you are playing in a tournament.

In a roulette tournament or baccarat tournament, you are not playing against the casino. You are playing against other players.

"If you know the mathematics of tournament play, you can kick some major butt."

It is time to ask my big question. What did he do with the jackpot, his windfall?

Curtis doesn't answer directly. He speaks of the tragedy of professional poker players, guys who really have the *gamble* in them. They clean up at poker, but what do they do with the resulting surplus?

"Well, they can't tie it up in mutual funds or real estate. Liquidity is everything to a poker player. Cash is the tool of the trade. They don't stick it under the mattress, but they do the financial equivalent. They stick it in a safe-deposit box so they can get at it fast."

Those are the smart ones. More common, Curtis says, are the sharpies who clean up playing poker at tournaments and then, during leisure moments, throw their money away at other card games they are no good at or in negative-expectation gambles like horse racing. It is a great gambling and market conundrum: when do you get out? Some of the best poker players in the world have failed to answer that question.

Curtis got out when a bunch of his hard-core gambling buddies wanted to go for broke, setting up what Curtis describes as "a high-level, high-profile system designed as an attack on legal sports betting." You couldn't get in without a big investment, so the choice came down to keeping his fledgling publishing company or going for the big score. He stuck with his small business.

"My buddies are knocking 'em dead. Millions a year. Millions."

But Curtis isn't doing bad either. His publishing house employs eleven people, and he claims he has already turned down a purchase offer that would have put him in a league with his sports-betting pals. He runs the business with the same kind of mathematically driven game strategy that worked for him at the casinos.

"I came to the conclusion that my enterprise has a much higher upside than gambling. The upside at the casinos has to be limited in some way; it has to stop at some point. Eventually the pit boss puts his hand on your shoulders and says you just can't do this to us anymore."

Curtis also remembers the promise he made to his father when he broke the news that he wanted to drop out of school. Vegas is booming, he had argued; there will be ancillary opportunities. It was at this point that the senior Curtis had smiled and said his son's plan might actually make sense. Leaving professional gambling was a way to honor the promise, but it was more than that. Curtis, in putting his parents back into his story at this juncture, is hinting about the respectability that the job of CEO of a publishing enterprise brings. Gambling can be a vocation, but it's not a serious career.

That's what the great Edward O. Thorp did, after all. Professor Thorp is a mathematician who is credited with inventing modern card counting, a man who later dispensed with gambling to shepherd a big-time hedge fund to even greater riches.

"Thorp," Curtis repeats in a whisper, in the way one imagines Neil Armstrong would repeat the name of Chuck Yeager. "I don't want to put myself in the same category as Thorp, but like him, I want to do something really big in business."

I want to do something really big at the casinos.

"What is the best bet in this town for a loser like me just off the turnip wagon?" I ask. Curtis is at a loss. If I am in it for the cash, not the comps, then my options are limited. Find a busy blackjack table, where everyone is yakking and yucking it up, he says. That will slow down the number of hands per hour the dealer can do, and it will slow your losses.

"The casino edge, which can be affected by your skill, multiplied by how much you bet, times how long you play—these are the three things that determine what it costs you to play."

Costs me to play? I thought I was here to win.

Grasping at straws, I wonder if my reporter's skills might be of any use. I know that the new Stratosphere hotel-casino-scenic-overlook is currently in bankruptcy protection. Might that make it especially eager to attract gambling customers?

Curtis perks up. The Stratosphere does have a bunch of good promotions going on, a certified deal in which slot machines pay back 98 percent of dollars invested.

"Now, that is negative expectations. That doesn't jazz me, I wouldn't play it, but it is the best deal you are going to find." They are also supposed to have one of the best blackjack games in the city. And, of course, lightning may strike. That is what keeps people coming.

"Something incredible can happen," Curtis laughs, doubtfully. "It is sort of a form of religion, isn't it? I mean, you can't see it, but it is hope."

Back at the hotel, I turn myself into Gambling Guy. Mousse. Pointy shoes. Black linen trousers, a white turtleneck under a white linen jacket. Actually, the preparation began weeks ago when I taught myself blackjack from scratch. The so-called basic strategy is not particularly hard. Among the rules: If your two cards total 12 through 16 and the dealer's exposed card is on the high side, then ask for another card. If the dealer's card is low, then stick with what you have. There are a few other basic strategy rules that even my sad, non-card-playing brain was able to grasp. What I was not able to grasp is the basic, first-grade math, that is to say, adding three or four cards quickly. That I had to practice. And practice. We all were given talents in this world, and I can do all sorts of party tricks, like reciting entire Washington, D.C., airborne traffic reports from memory. But if you hand me a 6, a 9, a 4, and a 2, I have to work very hard not to use my fingers or to keep my lips from moving. This is a handicap in blackjack. On this earth of 4.5 billion people, it probably makes me the 4,499,999,999th most likely candidate for a job card counting. There are people who are so facile with numbers that they can actually run a tally on all those cards. But in the time it would take me to learn proper card counting, I could acquire an entirely new, more socially acceptable skill, like veterinary medicine or particle physics. Basic blackjack strategy is enough for me. Jazzed and looking about as marvelous as I get, I head out into the night.

The Stratosphere is an attempt to bring the CN Tower in Toronto or the Seattle Space Needle concept to Las Vegas: a hotel, casino, and restaurant for the Jetsons. By the time I get there, its visionary founder, gambler Robert Stupak, is no longer with the enterprise and investors are hearing differing stories about whether or not there are actually circumstances under which the place could pay back its debt. This makes it one hungry casino, which is why it has set up its systems to give a little less of an edge to the house in favor of attracting and keeping customers.

As I enter the Stratosphere, I know I have what it takes. There, on a high platform above the first bank of slots, is a sibling of my very own rent-a-car, a red Mustang convertible. I am going to fit right in.

This is confirmed when I register for the Stratosphere's Players' Club, an electronic credit card system that tracks the size, quality, and rate of your bets and makes you eligible for a graduated scale of complimentary goodies based on how serious a gambler you are. At the registration cage the young woman is about to offer me something, some kind of key chain thing, but then catches herself and says, with a blush, that she doesn't think I am the key chain type. I don't know what the chain is for, but I am not going to burst her bubble. The chain, I soon determine, allows me to wear the electronic card around my neck, to free up both hands for common slot players. I, on the other hand, give the appearance not of a mere slot man but of a man of the tables, a fellow who knows his way around the green felt and who probably knows the croupiers and dealers by name.

Emboldened, I go to scope out the cheapest blackjack table I can find. Five dollars per hand sounds like my speed. I buy $40 worth of $5 chips and sit down next to a man who is still basking in the glow of a $1,000 keno win a few minutes earlier. To his right, a young Armenian American couple tell the dealer, Katrin, that they are new to the game. I tell Katrin to be gentle because this is my first time.

I bet one chip. The first hands are dealt. I have a 7 and a 5. The dealer's up card is a 10. I hit by pointing to my pile. An 8, which equals . . . I take a breath . . . 20. I wave my hand in the cutoff motion over my pile, stand. The dealer turns over cards totaling 22. Anything over 21 is a bust. I win another $5 chip. This isn't all that bad.

Katrin has a nice habit of running her hand in a gentle arc over the table to reset the table after a hand. I notice that I have some kind of muscle memory of the "hit" and "stand" motions. The choreographed hand dance is a bit like radio hand signals: the first is a downwardly inflected variation of "You're on," and the other is an inverse version of "Cut!" with the fingers pointed out over the cards instead of across one's throat.

As we progress, it is clear that the couple with the Armenian surname are only feigning naïveté. They are good and pass along some nice advice to help break a losing streak that brings me down to my last $5 chip. I fight back, get on a winning streak as the dealer repeatedly busts her hand. I try to count my little pile of chips in the few nanoseconds between hands. There are fifteen of them. I have accumulated a net chip worth of $75, an 87 percent profit for just fifteen minutes of work. That is way over the cutoff point of 20 percent profit that I had set for myself. But quitting implies a betrayal of our little impromptu team. I know that if I stay another moment at the table, I will start to lose. I need an exit strategy, something agent 007 would use to charmingly extricate himself from a game of chemin-de-fer in Monaco, but all I can come up with is some awkward mumbled apology about needing a bathroom.

I have won in a game that, like horse racing and poker, benefits from skill, unlike roulette or the lottery, in which the god of chance totally rules. I cannot control much in this place, but I can control my time spent playing.

I try the roulette wheel. The dealer is nasty and withdrawn; I should know better, but I start putting down $5 chips on my favorite numbers, my kids' birthdays, of course. Loser, loser, loser. Then I try a chip that overlaps four numbers and score on 17, my birthday. The dealer sneers and rakes a pile of chips my way. But they are soon gone. On the spin that precedes my intention to play my spouse's birthday, the number hits. It doesn't do me any good, and $40 gurgle down the roulette drain.

I try some dollar slots and my bleak mood continues. A waitress *en plein décolleté* appears to offer to fetch me a free drink, but I decline. My betting is that the drink will take a while to arrive, chaining me to the dollar slot machine until the law of averages takes over and I am forced to lose more, making that drink the most expensive one of my life. I pull the slot handle once more, and this time the icons on the reels display a theme. The ringing begins and heavy dollar coins begin falling, twenty in all. I still have four coins left from my original $20 roll. I quit right there, with a slots profit of $4.

I rejoin my blackjack table and play another twenty-five hands or so. With $40 down, I lose $30 of it, consider punting, but then fight back to break even. Time to go. No, I haven't won big, but I still have my California lottery tickets for that.

I calculate my final Stratosphere score: blackjack, +$35; slots, +$4; roulette, -$40, for a total of minus $1. For an hour and a half of action, it cost me a dollar and the parking was free. And the chance to not feel like an "electronic card chain kind of a guy" was worth it. I was not drinking tonight, and I do not seem to be afflicted with an uncontrollable gambling compulsion, as some do who require treatment. So I kept a measure of control over the situation, which might not have been possible for others. It's a skill I want to hold on to: the ability to quit and not throw good money after bad in casinos or in the stock, real estate, or even used car markets. The night out was like being charged a dollar to live in a movie instead of paying $16 plus popcorn to take a date to one.

I drive to the hotel with the top down. For the first time, prowling southbound on the Strip, I start to get it. The clutter and incongruity of the daytime Vegas skyline are put into order by the tracings of neon and the fill of blinking lights. What seemed a hodgepodge in daylight now looks centrally planned, as if we were meant to see the huge Stardust sign layered with the shimmering, hopped-up McDonald's arch, backed by the slower notes of the alternating vertical sign announcing, "Circus. Circus." What do you do with money? Ultimately, you bring it here and use it to build big signs so that people will come and build piles of coins on your green tables. Thank goodness the feds built Hoover Dam up the road in the 1930s to help power all this, private enterprise and government in partnership.

The disc jockey on 97.1 The Point cross-fades from Lynyrd Skynyrd to a drop-in, one of those snippets from a TV show or a movie apropos of nothing or everything, depending on how well it is chosen. The guy doing the night shift in Vegas is attempting to capture the zeitgeist by dropping in a bit from some comedy stand-up. The tone is vicious.

"These panhandlers, don't you just love 'em," the comedian sneers. " 'COULD YOU SPARE A QUARTER?' A quarter? Hey, buddy. All I carry are HUNDREDS!" The audience roars with approval. "And why should I help YOU out? I'm the one who put a boot in your eye when you were sleeping on the corner, you low-life, no-good loser, you BUM." Applause.

Screw you, Vegas. It's not good enough that I am throwing money away in the casino? I have to flaunt it in the face of less fortunate people too? On this note of good Christian charity, I close the car's roof and head in to flop in my hotel. The homeless guys in my neighborhood don't ask for anything as heavy or as grand as a dollar coin when they put their hands out. What am I going to say next time—"Sorry, bub, I have to save my spare change so I can give it to ITT Corporation on my next gambling trip"? The foul comedy on the radio works at some subversive level. It will be the only sermon I get this weekend.

It is 5:20 the next morning, if I am to believe my watch, and I am about to enter the lion's mouth, the big, cubist MGM lion's mouth that serves as the entrance to the MGM Grand. The neon kept creeping through the drapes into my seventh-floor suite at the Jockey Club, and I figure I am not here to sleep anyway.

I have heard stories about casinos in the wee hours, of wives pleading vainly for dealers to cut off their compulsive, drunken husbands. What I see at the craps table is crankiness, a moment of bickering between a pit boss and a gambler on some point of honor. A look from the pit boss shuts the gambler down. At the newsstand a dolled-up gambler in an antique dress expresses some mock shock when she is told they do not sell Zig Zag rolling papers. A security guard promptly appears to ascertain the exact nature of the customer "disturbance." This is a casino on yellow alert.

My main mission is not to gamble. I am here to pick up the morning paper, and sure enough, the *Las Vegas Review-Journal–Las Vegas Sun* combined Sunday edition has the California lottery numbers from the night before. I carry the paper to the marble ringed bench in the center of the MGM's spectacular lobby. The video wall grinds away with exhortations to gamble. There are stars of gold in the floor, stars of gold in the ceiling, and nothing of gold in the paper: 23, 27, 28, 32, 35, 46. Out of twenty Super Lotto tries, fourteen are total goose eggs. On five I match just one out of six numbers. On one, my best score, I match two, also making me eligible for nothing. The lottery was my crutch, my backstop. It gave me the ability to be detached and to approach the casinos with reckless abandon—I didn't have to win in the casinos; I was going to score in the lottery. Vegas was play; the lottery was work. On that night my odds of winning were 1 in 18 million for each set of numbers I played. Twenty plays put my chances at one in a million. I hadn't defied the gods, and I got the return that was to be expected. Nothing.

By way of consolation, I buy a roll of dollar slot coins and lose them all in the time it takes to order a cappuccino. *Score: MGM Grand, $20—David, 0.*

At this stage a rational investor would pack up and go home. Know when to fold 'em. Cut your losses. Don't throw good money after bad. Write it off. But this is Vegas and I have a reputation to uphold. When a risk-taking man-who-needs-no-card-chain has a problem, he takes it right to the emperor.

The emperor wouldn't actually see me. But Caesars Palace is

quaintly charming. That is, quaint in the sense of Taj Mahal. Long, arc-ing, moving sidewalks that shame the puny ones at Chicago's O'Hare airport pull me in from the street. Gold inlay and other not always Ro-man details do not disappoint, not even close up. When you go to the real Roman Forum, you have to spend the whole time squinting and conjuring, trying to imagine what it might have looked like in its prime. At Caesars Palace in Las Vegas, only the widest eyes are necessary. The only thing that isn't quite up to snuff—and this is the smallest of quib-bles but the only thing that seems just a little beneath the standards of a top bacchanalia—are the headliners posted prominently on the mar-quee, Crosby, Stills and Nash. Young would have been a different story.

It has been a full thirty-six hours since I have been to a mall, so I first cut through the convention center–sized casino to search out what are billed as the Forum Shops. A giant penis guides the way. It is the lower half of a replica of Michelangelo's *David,* framed by a doorway with the apex of the arch visually obscuring everything above the statue's waist. Naked David has only sporadically brought me luck in life, so I should have known. I quickly roar through several buckets of quarters as I scramble also to keep a log. The list of wins looks impressive: 10 on two occasions; 15 on eight occasions; a 30; a 20; lots more 2s and 5s. But wins make better memories and there are loads of losses, and each time my cup begins to runneth over, I hit a bad patch. If the bad patch starts to get uncomfortably long, there are wins. In a contest with the odds, I cannot win—if my universe begins to warp, a tractor beam will pull me back to the mean. There is a theory of stock investing that plays to this. Buy stocks with disappointing price-to-earnings ratios because they will tend to go up in search of the mean. Buy stocks on a roll, with high P/Es, and they will tend to underperform, to statistically "make up" for their earlier achievements. The norm rules, and casinos would not have slot machines if, on average, the machines did not take in a lot more than they paid out. My forty-five-minute run comes to an end with my last losing quarter.

Almost the end. I cannot help but notice a stray $10 bill tangled with my keys in one pocket. So I buy ten $1 coins, not enough to im-press the disdainful change lady. Coins one through four are sucked away in two pulls of a standard dollar machine. But what I really want is one chance at the big Cahuna, a slot machine that does for Caesars Palace what the big thermometer does for the desert town of Baker, a massive battle-ax of a slot machine with a crooked handle that gives the effect of a towering headmistress staring down reproachfully with her hand on her hip. A crowd is gathered. This is gambling as spectator sport. I put in the maximum of five coins and pull the lever, an act as futile as trying to snap, rather than saw, a tree. The goal is four busts of Nefertiti lined up in a row. A supportive man with an Indian accent begins a chant of "You got it, man/You got it, man/You got it, man."

I don't got it. In shame, I bolt.

In the sunlight of the sidewalk out front, I do inventory. Caesars Palace, $28—me, just two last hefty metal coins with the embossed Caesars symbol eroded with age. One would be a nice, cheap souvenir, but that leaves one more. Was the desert playing tricks, or did that sewer at the curb really look like a giant slot? Ceremoniously, I pinch the dollar coin, raise it over my head . . . and let it drop. It disappears into the maw of the sewer without a clink. An elderly woman in an electric wheelchair takes in the scene, then demands to know what I am up to. "About the same chance of winning here as inside," I reply, resigned.

She rattles a fanny pack lashed to her waist, evidently filled with a dense mass of coinage. "You just got to make your own luck," she cackles as she locks in a course back toward the casino.

They say you used to be able to see the flash of the nuclear tests from Las Vegas and the Atomic Energy Commission used to circulate a cartoon showing a happy couple standing on a ridge viewing a test the "proper" way with sunglasses, with the caption "Your best action is not to be worried about fallout."

But I am. Not being a gambler is not a character flaw that I hoped this trip would repair, but what if some of this rubbed off? Next thing you know I might be acting on long-odds stock tips or at the very least switching my family's nest egg into aggressive, cutting-edge, higher-risk mutual funds. I might take up flying ultralights or ordering with abandon from menus in languages I don't understand with no prices listed. We love risk takers, but only if they succeed.

One last stop, a graveyard in an industrial park off Tropicana Avenue, is the kind of place that would cause a semiologist's head to explode. It is the last resting place for Las Vegas's neon and bulbage, the YESCO Electric Sign Company's back lot. Cemeteries make for strange bedfellows. The saucy, bulb-filled letters that spell out BINION'S casino nestle against the brawny, blue-collar Denny's. The Flame Steak–Prime Rib plays footsie with a chipped and faded motel with a perpetual VACANCY. A giant three-dimensional magic slipper pocked with screw-in sockets for lights stands separate and lonely. Even L'Amour Wedding Chapel is having trouble finding takers. Next to Joe's Longhorn Casino lies a marquee with slip-in letters that will forever read "Closed." In the middle of the heap sits a mustard and red neon-ringed Kodak sign. This one looks pristine, and it crosses my mind that it is just possible the photo company may have paid to sponsor the scene, a Kodak moment to beat all Kodak moments.

I have been told they do not welcome gawkers here, and the antipersonnel fence surrounding the island of misfit signs looks foreboding. I am sure I hear a guard dog or maybe a guard coyote. This is the part you never see at Disneyland, the proof that what you have been experiencing is an illusion. Without hope, the hope of winning and winning big, the Las Vegas Strip is just this, a heap of neon littering the desert floor.

With the top down, engine off, I press a cassette into the car's tape player. The tape is a recording of a conversation I had before the trip with *the* Dr. Thorp, Edward O. Thorp, breaker of the blackjack code, mathematician, hedge fund manager.

I wanted to know if he was a gambler.

"No, just the opposite. What I try to find are situations where I am likely to win and pursue those. If the situation is against me, I just avoid it."

Based on hunch?

No, based on scientific reasoning, analysis, thinking. "I have to be able to prove to myself that I have an edge, or I won't do it." It was only when he was able to devise a way to count cards and refine the system with a computer, a method that produced a systematic edge over the House, that he was willing to play.

Thorp is a trim man with a thatch of salt and a pepper hair who entered college the same year as my father. An elaborate pager hanging awkwardly off his trousers pocket and two pencils in the breast pocket of his shirt said "engineer" or, indeed, "mathematician." If he had grown up in the East, his shirt would have been white, but his office overlooked an upscale southern California marina, and he was wearing a striking op-art print that matched his hair color.

The stock market is a little different from gambling but not completely, Thorp said. He didn't advocate taking much risk with either. He started with the example of a portfolio of stocks that mimicked a major stock index, a so-called indexed fund. If a person had bought all the stocks in the Standard & Poor's 500 in 1926 and sat on them until 1995, he would have averaged about 11 percent a year, Thorp said. (That is, with reinvesting dividends and not counting taxes.)

"So the average person in the stock market is a winner if he does not trade a lot and spend all his profits on broker commissions."

I recounted some homework I had done to corroborate the claim that if you had purchased a very broad index, consisting of every stock on the New York Stock Exchange, in 1952 and put in the same amount of money each year until 1972, the return would have been a negative point-65 percent, without chopping it down even further by calculating in taxes and inflation. You would have been in the market for quite a long time, twenty years, and still *lost money.* Thorp considered this and replied that each of us has to decide what our tolerance for risk is and what our time horizon is. The ability to wait a long time allows a lot of risk to iron itself out.

"If you are basically on the right horse," Thorp added. The right horse? Right when it started to look simple, it was not simple at all.

I recalled Thorp mentioning his daughter had new triplets. What does he, the Fancy Hedge Fund Manager, the man who had to don clever disguises to fool Vegas pit bosses who might cotton onto his card-counting ways—what might he recommend for his daughter's portfolio? A plodding, boring approach, the approach that would not make a good movie. His big advice? She should put any surplus into one of these indexed mutual funds.

Thorp seemed to sense that I was looking for more excitement, and he developed his argument. If I buy an indexed fund, I have essentially bought the market. If the market goes up, my return goes up, and vice versa. The other approach is to have a fund manager make informed decisions about the portfolio. Buy things that look good and sell things that look lousy. Add up all these active fund managers, and what do you get? Essentially, the market, Thorp said. Some will do better than the market. Others will lag. When you include the effect of fees, which are higher in a traditional mutual fund to pay for all that clever active management, the return can be less than that yielded by the boring, passive approach.

"A fundamental truth of the market is that unless you know you have an edge and know exactly why, then you are better off buying an index and sitting back and letting it run," Thorp said.

And are there ways to know you have an edge?

Not many, according to Thorp. The folks with the real edge run hedge funds, if he did say so himself. Hedge funds are, by law, private limited partnerships, with no more than ninety-nine investors allowed. With membership in this club so exclusive, only the big shots can play, with a typical minimum set at around a million dollars. Why can't I get in on the hedge fund? Because the funds will take the richest ninety-nine investors they can find, and that is not going to include me.

"If the great hedge fund manager George Soros wants to run a billion dollars with ninety-nine people, each person's got to put up slightly over ten million on average. So that dictates the fact that a hedge fund will rarely take someone in for less a quarter of a million, and many have limits of five or ten million dollars."

Would Thorp like to "run" my nest egg? I got a polite smile. Just trying.

Tired of the smoky, boozy casino tables, Thorp in the early sixties scrutinized a kind of hedge using something called a warrant with the same intensity that he had applied to blackjack. A warrant is an option to buy a certain number of stocks at a certain price for a certain time. If the price of the stock on the market is cheaper than your warrant, then the warrant is worthless. Once Thorp proved to himself that warrants were amenable to mathematical analysis and could, in his view, supply a predictable, quantifiable edge, he tried his hand at other instruments, convertible bonds, interest rate futures. The hedge fund business was very good to Thorp, and he could also run the hedge fund and teach mathematics at places like the University of California–Irvine and MIT. On Thorp's evolutionary scale, it is the hedge fund folks who are the best, followed by the institutional investors, followed—down the scale—by the mutual fund managers.

"The logical concept and the analysis of both investing and gambling are very much the same," Thorp said. "A lot of the really good people in the stock market have been involved in gambling and games at one time or another."

There are two sides to this. I once met a San Francisco psychologist trained in the treatment of gambling addiction who has devoted an increasing part of his practice to treating what he calls "market addiction," a similar pathology involving compulsive, self-destructive securities trading. Brokers busted for fraud often trickle down to him.

But Thorp's focus on numbers is more of a gift than an addiction. There is the famous story of Albert Einstein, who, it is said, had trouble with simple arithmetic. Dr. Thorp doesn't have that problem.

"I won't call them phenomenal computational skills, but mine are unusually good, better than the skills of anybody you would normally run into but not better than those of the Great Calculators, the phenoms, those people."

Thorp operates on two levels: exact calculation and approximate calculation. If someone asks the weight of the earth and you say six times ten to the twenty-first power tons, it really does not matter if it is 6.1 times ten to the twenty-first or 5.9 times ten to the twenty-first.

"And if you can get six times ten to the twenty-first right away, then you can save a lot of time."

When he uttered those words, I was overwhelmed with the nausea-producing prospect that I'll never work easily with a surplus. For whatever reason, too many Cheetos as a child or secondhand smoke, I just cannot think his way. A few weeks later, with the benefit of a tape recording, a rewind button, and a pen and scrap of paper, sitting there in front of the dead Las Vegas neon, I can finally visualize a six with twenty-one zeros to the right. But it all comes so slowly.

I told Thorp that I didn't want to shock him but I have been practicing blackjack at home and am having trouble adding the sum of just three cards. He chose to be kind.

"Well, if you asked me to draw a sketch of your face, it would be very difficult for me. Others could work it right out." *Work* it out was the phrase he picked, like the drawing was a math problem.

So the great Thorp sees himself as a talented rationalist and not a gambler. But could he rule out luck?

"If we are flipping coins together and you call 'tails' and we flip a hundred times and seventy times it comes up 'tails,' I would say you were lucky because you beat the expected number of fifty. But I do not believe that any mysterious force brought luck to you or that you had any control over the outcome or that you would repeat the pattern if we flipped again."

But what about people in Vegas who say they are on a roll?

"I would say to them, 'You have *been* on a roll,' but their future is not better or worse than anyone else's in the casino."

On the long drive home, that vile taped bit I heard late the previous night on the radio keeps turning over in my head. Does the greed that drives you to keep playing in Las Vegas breed a contempt for those whom good fortune has abandoned? Do you begin hating them because they are proof that you can lose and keep losing? Oh, it's cute spending a $400 bankroll trying to be a risk-taking man, but when was the last time I used $400 to help someone? It is clear the next money trip is going to have to help me reclaim what is left of my charitable self.

I give back the Mustang and return to one of those domestic dramas. I have been partying in Vegas and my toddler has just swallowed a coin. I race her to the urgent care clinic in my minivan. Normally it is tough for a layman to read the hazy, translucent jumble on an X ray, but there it is, floating just above the image of her pelvis, a penny.

"Is it heads or tails?" I ask the doctor.

"You tell me when it comes out. If you don't spot it in a week, come back and we'll do another film to be sure it is gone."

So we monitor the situation as best we can. I wonder if I will, indeed, see the penny. Could this be the coin I tossed into the sewer outside Caesars Palace coming back around so soon?

We spot nothing, but by the next X ray the coin has mysteriously disappeared. Now I am keeping my eyes open for the return of the *two* coins we have invested.

Souvenirs

One last silver coin with the Caesars Palace motif nearly worn smooth.

The realization that I was confusing the fear of the unknown with being risk averse.

To do when I get home

Try to keep my money out of situations where there are negative expectations, where the math is against me, where any profit is a fluke and over time it is highly probable that I will lose.

Doing the numbers

My odds of winning the lottery with one ticket were about one in 18 million. By purchasing twenty tickets, I increased my chances to the same odds as being struck by lightning, roughly one in a million.

6

Give It Away

Charity in Hawthorne, Nevada

From the clipping file: A schoolteacher from Oak Park, Illinois, won $17.3 million in the lottery. The *Chicago Sun-Times* reported he pledged to donate $50,000 a year to a fund for the needy providing anything from "milk to shoes." January 30, 1993

*O*ne of the horrors of the lottery is that winners are not allowed to keep it secret. It is there in the fine print: "Thou shalt appear at a news conference holding an oversized check so that anyone who ever so much as brushed up against you in a crowded subway car feels entitled to demand a piece of your bounty." Others are fortunate enough to acquire their surplus in much more private ways, but that doesn't relieve us of what I think is our duty to share.

The last shred of my self-respect in tatters following the indulgences of Las Vegas, I felt the need to atone. If I could start on the long road toward moral recovery in the same state, Nevada, so much the better.

The town of Hawthorne was not looking for charity from outsiders. It was trying to dig itself out of a terrible economic rut with an endearingly improbable bid to win a national contest honoring civic virtue. Even more improbable was the notion of me as philanthropist. But the town clearly needed help, and

I was able to examine for myself that uncomfortable interplay between altru-ism and self-interest that goes into a decision to give surplus away. Among my teachers on this trip was one of Hawthorne's town fathers, as well as a drifter named Wayne whom I met on a desert road at the edge of the town.

"It's not like you killed a man outside Reno just to see him die." The phrase jumped out at me from the radio one day when I was surfing the wrong end of the dial. The cast of fools on some morning show was us-ing this slight variation on a chilling phrase from Johnny Cash's "Fol-som Prison Blues" to mean "what you did was not all that bad," especially in comparison to one of the most heinous acts imaginable. The choice of Reno was genius. Mineola or Palo Alto would have fallen flat. Bad things happen in the desert outside Reno. But so, I am told, can good things, like charity.

It is not just that I wanted to scrape the Vegas off my heels or take the notion of socially responsible investment to its logical conclusion. It is that charity, whether it be giving all or part of a nest egg away or its corollary, donating one's time or expertise, is supposed to be selfless. And I have a problem with selfless. Selfless seems irrational. At some level, noble or base, there has got to be something in it for you, and if you do get something back, then it is fair to examine philanthropy's re-turn on investment. I figure if you can look at it this way, charity would fit much more seamlessly into a portfolio—stocks, bonds, mad money, charity. And truth be told, I have not been very good at this in the past. There is no grand pavilion built in my name at either my college or grad-uate school. There's not even a tile with my name on it anywhere.

Anyway, I'd better get a grip on my relationship to giving. After all, I am the fellow who, with the persistence of a telephone solicitor at din-nertime, comes on to beseech listeners, out of the kindness of their hearts, to send in their $65 to keep the public in public broadcasting. I'm stingy, but I'm not a complete hypocrite.

The moussed snob behind the car rental counter in Reno is unimpressed with my final destination today.

"Oh, you'll love Hawthorne," he sneered. "I hear they have their first McDonald's and everything."

Pretty rich coming from a man playing in the sand of the 119th media market, but I keep my mouth shut because my business here is, after all, charity.

My eyes must have narrowed, though. Slick tries to make it up to me.

"For just $9.95 extra a day, I can get you into a Lincoln Continental."

"Thanks, but no."

"Has Mr. Bran . . ." He stares desperately at the name on my credit card. "Has Mr. Brantoshito ever *driven* a Lincoln Continental?"

Slick isn't just trying to upgrade me. He is trying to elevate me to a whole new class that the likes of me, destination Hawthorne, presumably has never experienced.

"Boulevard ride," Slick says with enthusiasm.

"And what boulevard would I use it on?" I reply. "They have a Champs Elysées to go with their McDonald's, do they?" I am tumbling to Slick's level. I pick up the keys to a Ford Contour and leave.

Highway 80 rises up and passes through a notch. The sign says Mustang, a reminder that somewhere around here is the state's most famous legal brothel. On the way out the door very early this morning, my wife cast a protective spell around me. "If you run across a place called the Mustang Ranch," she said matter-of-factly from her pillow, her eyes still closed, "keep in mind those women wear stretch pants and fuzzy slippers in their off hours." If that were not enough to take the gloss off what was already a preposterous concept, the vista is doing the rest. All I can see behind the Mustang sign is a junkyard stacked high with rusting car parts.

On the radio a personal finance smoothie talks in an unbroken, metered stream about a package of cash-flow strategies to build income, which he offers for $44.95. If I am listening to an infomercial, it isn't labeled as such during the few minutes I tune in.

"The absolute dumbest thing our listeners could ever do is say no to this," the fellow says.

He then explains what he suggests is an underappreciated financial tool known as "writing a covered call." Try this at home is his message. Writing a covered call means you sell an option on a stock you own. Say you buy Buttafuoco Enterprises at $30 a share. You sell an option to

someone for a dollar, giving that someone the right, but not the obliga-
tion, to buy your share at $32. If the value of that stock rises higher than
$32, the option holder will exercise his option and buy the stock from
you at $32. It's a beautiful thing: you've already pocketed the original
dollar the guy paid you for the option, and you get the two dollars in
profit from the stock rising on the market from $30 to $32. What the
guy on the radio doesn't make clear, however, is that if Buttafuoco Enterprises rises to $40 or $50, tough Tootsie Roll. The other guy still gets
to buy it at $32. Selling a covered call limits the upside profit potential
of a stock, but as long as the investor understands this and it fits into his
or her strategy, where's the problem?

The problem is that a listener who, like me, needs the sort of basic
explanation of what an option is and how a covered call works may not
be the best person to take a jump off the high dive into the world of options. It's not much of a leap to get from covered calls to regular calls,
selling an option for a stock you don't own on the hunch that its price
will drop. If that price rises, the option buyer will exercise the option
and will have to run out and buy that expensive stock at the market
price and sell it for a loss. If you know the risks and have the money and
the skill to do it right, it's a useful instrument. If you don't, just remember to ask yourself, "Do I feel lucky?"

As I climb down into a wide, arid lowland, another AM station resolves from the blur of static. They are also talking markets, but markets
of the more down-to-earth kind. KVLD's *Trading Post* is on, with listeners calling with asks and bids on a set of Bicentennial Avon dishes, a
Sunbeam humidifier, a 16-cubic-foot Kenmore freezer, and a 389-cubic-
inch engine, transmission, and rear end for a 1977 Oldsmobile.

If this were Wall Street, not a radio station out of Fallon, Nevada, it
would be possible the middle man, in this case the host of *Trading Post*,
might try his hand at a little arbitrage. He could ask on the phone, but
not on the air, how much the woman wants for her Bicentennial dishes.
Answer $60, but he would keep the asking price under his hat and just
mention the dishes on the air. Then the host might take some calls
from other listeners interested in buying. How much do they want to
spend for those dishes? $85? Sure, he can get them for $85. The middle
man then buys the dishes from the seller for $60, sells them to the

buyer for $85, and pockets the $25 difference, the spread, as profit.

There's another possibility as well. The host of the *Trading Post* might take his cue from stockbrokers and charge a 3 percent commission on every item sold or bought through his show. From what I can tell, KVLD is taking the more traditional approach: allowing folks to buy and sell for free but charging advertisers for the privilege of presenting their messages during the program.

Alternate 95 enters Mineral County at the northern, Walker River Indian Reservation end. I can see a lot of low-desert creosote. Gravel is in good supply. A dusting of copper highlights a distant ridge with a harsh, fluorescent green, not the green of photosynthesis.

Here is no water but only rock
Rock and no water and the sandy road.

So much for my meticulous planning. I had thought to bring the T. S. Eliot; I came loaded with information about Mineral County and the town of Hawthorne specifically. I had half a ream on Hawthorne's underdog bid to win a national contest for America's best cities. But I have just entered one of the most hostile deserts on earth without a drop of water.

Actually, there is water. Just after a sharp bend, I come upon Walker Lake, one of the Northern Hemisphere's two desert terminal lakes. There is no transition zone—the landscape goes from beige rock to water, like a sapphire dropped into a sandbox. A few hundred more miles down this road lies Lake Havasu, a man-made thing created by Colorado River water backed up behind Parker Dam. The developers of Lake Havasu know how to wring cash out of a pool in the desert. There are time-share condos. Souvenirs. Ice cream shops. Fishing boat rentals. And London Bridge, the real one, shipped block by block from its original spot along the Thames between the Southwark and Tower bridges.

Around Walker Lake there is none of this, save a few picnic tables with billowing sunshades like something Christo might have left behind. Even if you were hard-pressed to buy a souvenir, there is none to be had. This is the lake that some local visionaries hoped would eventually bring tourism and therefore wealth. As it stands now, a third of all households in this county make less than $15,000 a year, and the number of folks living below the government poverty line is among the highest in the state. Teen pregnancy in Mineral County is the highest in Nevada, and Nevada is vying with Georgia for the tragic distinction of having the worst teen pregnancy rate in the country. Most of the old mining jobs here are gone, and the biggest employer, the army's huge ammunition depot, has radically downsized since the end of the Cold War.

Despite these challenges, the good folks of Hawthorne think they have what it takes to win recognition as what is known as an All-America City. What they have to offer is some charitable dollars and a lot of donated time and energy, *social capital.*

Social scientist Robert Putnam was noted in academic circles for his study of civic organizations in Italy. But a burst of wider fame came after he applied some of his wisdom gleaned in Italy to the American experience. Putnam's essay "Bowling Alone" got noticed by towns across the country and by the White House. In it Putnam argues that one of the problems with late-twentieth-century America is that we no longer do things with the rest of our community. Individualism has triumphed. We stay in our TV rooms and backyards. We don't get out to the Jaycees, Kiwanis Club, or Knights of Columbus the way we used to. We go bowling, Putnam argues, but we no longer bowl in leagues; we bowl alone. When you bowl alone, you don't crack jokes with your pals. You don't talk about the news. You don't talk about the mayor or raising money for a new community swimming pool, the stuff of social capital.

For a town in the middle of nowhere, Hawthorne has a fine bowling alley. The Silver State Bowl is just south of the spot where tracks cross the highway, near the point where you hit the brakes at the sight of a black-and-white police cruiser poised to snag speeders. At the moment you are sure you are toast, it becomes apparent that the police car is (a) empty, (b) circa 1984, and therefore (c) a decoy.

Circa 1955 is the aquamarine Chevy Bel-Air parked under a lone tree outside the Silver State Bowl. The alley's owner, Vern Holloway, prefers the term "bowling *center.*" Holloway is lean, silver-haired, and tanned from cigarette smoke, not the desert sun. He is friendly but does not give the impression he is a fellow who eats much tofu or would cotton much to concepts like community self-esteem. The connection between bowling and social capital, however, he buys.

"They'll be out on the lanes discussing what was happening at a county commissioners' meeting. They talk about their families. They talk about the town, the way things are going, the way they think things should be going. Yeah, they do a lot of that in bowling," Vern says.

The Silver State, originally built for the soldiers handling all the ammunition stored around here, is divided into two rooms of six bowling lanes each. In the old, segregated military, one set of lanes was for blacks, the other for whites. At this moment two preadolescent boys and their dad are using three lanes in one room; in the other a noisy bunch of folks from the mining town of Tonopah have driven a hundred miles to get in a few cracks at the pins.

Vern used to go out on bowling's senior pro circuit. He says he shot most of his high scores and made most of his money from 1986 until the early 1990s. He ran a bowling pro shop in Reno but then took his bowling winnings, his windfall, and moved to Hawthorne when the county gave him a good deal on the Silver State.

Business is quite good. So clearly the good citizens of this area bowl. But do they bowl in leagues, in the way that would befit a town trying to make a national claim about the high reserves of social capital? Oh yeah, Vern says.

"I want to know another town of this size that sends eight to ten teams to bowl in the national tournament. It just doesn't happen, but it happens here."

You can invest in New York, Tokyo, and London. I want to know what kind of return you get if you invest in your own community.

A heck of a lot is Chuck Gardner's answer.

Chuck Gardner is a lightning rod. He is also the former Mineral County economic development coordinator, now retired. Chuck considers "lightning rod" a term of praise. He used it in all the invitations he sent out to the great and the good of Hawthorne to explain why their presence was requested at a final meeting before the All-America City application was sent to the judges. "You are a lightning rod, sometimes attacked for your positions." That's Chuck's way of buttering you up. He knows that it takes a certain kind of personality, the love-him or hate-him kind, to shake people into action. Chuck is this town's agitator-in-chief.

Grizzled with a beard that could use another two week's growth, carrying the extra weight around the middle that a man of retirement age is allowed, Chuck Gardner is an imposing character. It's his voice that does it, the voice of God: pear-shaped, measured syllables in a baritone rich with traces of his native Oklahoma, the kind of voice with the power to sound high-fidelity even when squeezed through the archaic technology of a 1930s radio. Next to this Broadway voice, mine sounds like a high school production. I really hate that. But I had to like Chuck.

We're on the Hawthorne tour. First there is the new firehouse with a special community meeting room made possible by a donation from a local benefactor. It's a garden in which to grow social capital, a place where folks can come out of their individual dens and yards and do something with others in the community, be it arguing about the relative merits of a dump versus a sanitary landfill or reviewing the offerings of a sixth-grade science fair. There's the small but modern library, also made possible by one of the few around here of some means. Surrounding the library is what Chuck describes as a tourist attraction, a carpet of rose bushes with the name of a deceased local resident planted by each one.

Thomas Spilett, Virgil Kinney, Elsie Duncan, Agnes Wallace . . .

A memorial rose garden all tended by local volunteers.

"When these roses are all in bloom, it is absolutely breathtaking," Chuck says, rattling nearby windows with the sonic boom of his voice.

At the moment the garden isn't breathtaking. It is poignant in a stark way. It is mid-March, the sky is leaden, and even though we are in the desert, Hawthorne is 4,000 feet above sea level and it's chilly, and the denuded, prickly stalks of the rose bushes rustle in the breeze. But it is something most towns don't have.

I get to see other sights. The public golf course bequeathed to the town by the ammunition depot offers nine holes of golf, plus cart, for $14, and you will never need a tee time. The army depot remains the county's main employer, despite being radically downsized. Regular concrete warehouses stretch across miles of desert like vast, buff-colored Monopoly hotels. A disastrous munitions explosion in the East in 1926 persuaded the military to move the facility to what Washington must have seen as the middle of nowhere with a railway link. The sign just before entering town warns ominously, "All commercial and explosive-laden vehicles, LEFT." My suggestion for a town slogan would be "Don't Mess with Hawthorne: We've Got Way More Ammo Than You Do." But I had missed the slogan competition. In the run-up to the All-America City competition, the town put their heads together and came up with "Hawthorne: Jewel of the Desert."

It's Nevada, so there is a casino. The cheap and cheerful El Capitan motor lodge and casino is hardly the MGM Grand in Vegas, but if you want to lose money on slots, it gets the job done efficiently and with the simple flare of a Grange Hall traced in neon.

Chuck is a man with grand visions. Why not an amphitheater blasted out of rock where a history of Nevada dramatic production might be staged each summer? An upgraded rodeo? A bigger fishing derby on Walker Lake? Hawthorne, alas, doesn't have the money for any of this. What it does have are citizens working together on community problems, an attempt to harness social capital when the more ordinary kind of capital is scarce. But to get a job done you need deadline goals. That is where the All-America City competition comes in.

"It's the Greatest Show on Earth, the World Series, and the Super-bowl of community development all rolled up into one," in Chuck's words. The annual contest is sponsored by the National Civic League in Denver. First a panel of judges wades through the applications to identify thirty finalists. These go on to a big national weekend at which ten winners are chosen after two days of speeches and razzmatazz rather like a political convention. There's a $10,000 prize sponsored by Allstate insurance. And a set of signposts for placing at the entry points to town. The previous year one of the winners was New Orleans. No Nevada town has made it to the finals in the contest's forty-eight-year history.

"We will put up the signs with the red, white, and blue shield and we can put it on our promotional material. Even people internationally know what it is to be an All-America City. If you're going to come to Nevada and are looking for a place to invest, you probably ought to come here."

Chuck chokes up.

"It has to be a magnet at least of interest. At least we might get to talk to you and try to put together a package for you that's competitive."

Chuck can taste it.

"We're an All-America City, the only one in the state." But first the town has to finish its application.

The Consolidated Agencies for Human Services looks like it might once have been someone's house. A small group of people are sitting around a conference table, united in their belief that Hawthorne can reach the big time. There is Evelyn, the social worker and mother of four. There is Ken, a powerful local businessman. Also Tiffany and Brad, a local pair of young entrepreneurs, and Bob, the county commissioner. The part of the Wizard is played by Chuck.

Ellen has created an image of the National League of Cities contest application on the computer, and pending a final typographical test run, she plans to send it out the following Monday.

"We are not picket fences and neat green lawns," Evelyn says. "We are a group of people willing to put our shoulders to the wheel and invest an awful lot of time to make this a community that we can feel proud of and want to be a part of for a long time."

It wasn't always this way. The town hit bottom a couple of years ago, drowning in the self-doubt that came after the ammo depot was downsized. Civic life had foundered. The aging population fought to keep their tax bills as low as possible. Someone noticed that no major new business had relocated to the area for twenty years. Some folks looked around and realized that the community would have to look inward for its resources. "We are like a desert island," one resident observed. "Only instead of ocean, we are surrounded by miles and miles of *nothing*. We used to just see each other at Safeway, see each other at the post office. We used to converse sometimes, but we didn't communicate."

It was at this nadir that Hawthorne's Civic Roundtable was born—a group of folks, some represented around the table with me, who refused to succumb to the sense of futility. First, the town needed a plan, a blueprint for the next century. Something had to be done to improve education. There needed to be efforts to attract new dollars by charming new businesses and tourists. And folks had better start speaking up about all the teenagers who were becoming mothers around here. The All-America City contest would be a way to focus these energies and to set a deadline.

The Civic Roundtable recognizes the challenges the town is up against, but everyone expects victory. Why? Because they have a stockpile of social capital big enough to fill some of the ammunition warehouses over on the base. And social capital is not play money. As proof, I am offered this spreadsheet of what social capital bought.

The Sign

Every town needs a sense of identity. London has Big Ben. Baker, California, has its tallest thermometer. Hawthorne had nothing until someone noticed that a nifty sign was about to be demolished with the rest of the old Hawthorne Club. A group of concerned citizens rallied to save it and have been digging into their pockets to pay back the county for the $24,000 necessary to refurbish it and stick it up on the northern entrance to the town. Now nighttime travelers surveying the desert for an oasis can pick out the illuminated vertical letters spelling Hawthorne, with a neat little neon art deco flourish gracing the sign's upper edge. It is not the St. Louis Arch, but it's Hawthorne.

The New School

Hawthorne's crumbling school is not up to earthquake code, but voters were in the habit of defeating bond measures to raise cash to replace it. But the surge in civic involvement created a legion of education evangelists who successfully crusaded for a tax hike needed for a new school.

Teen Pregnancy

Folks responded when the hat was passed around to raise $2,500 for a motivational speaker to visit and talk tough with junior high and high schoolers about how sex leads to babies. Social worker Evelyn Allen says there is no one in the county who does not now at least acknowledge the problem.

Social capital can also be an investment. This doesn't mean a ploy to simply make money, a thought that seemed to prompt a California oil company executive once to ask how donating money to the arts would help the company at its gas pumps. It's more about how what goes 'round, comes 'round. The folks in the Consolidated Agencies of Human Services board of directors room provide this concrete example.

Tiffany and Brad Ammussen are a young couple who moved to Hawthorne from Sparks two years ago with "little more than youthful exuberance," Chuck recalls. They quickly surfaced, he said, like good cream to the top. Brad is a big fellow with longish dark hair and a mustache. Tiffany is lean but not at all fragile. They divide the work evenly for their young business, B.L.T. Ready Mix, but forceful and articulate Tiffany gives off the aura of CEO. Both have forfeited many hours that could have been devoted to their business in order to attend community meetings, work on community projects, and generally lend a hand when a hand or their front-loader is needed.

Tiffany says she doesn't have a lot of spare cash to give to Hawthorne, but they try to help build its social capital. For Tiffany this happens on the second Thursday of the month, which starts with a 7 A.M. Civic Roundtable board meeting, an 11 A.M. community conference, a different board meeting at noon, and a 7 P.M. Civic Pride gathering. These meetings can be tedious, and she has second Thursdays when she comes home and drafts a series of resignation letters. But after some rest she sees them as an investment with benefits that can accrue to the town. And to her business.

"I get something back. I get a community that wants to look a little better. They want to get the dirt cleaned up; they want to put in sidewalks; they want to put curbs down the streets; they want planters, garbage receptacles."

Now, as they say, to a carpenter every community problem looks like a nail, and to a woman in the concrete business, many community problems can be solved with concrete: sidewalks, curbs, planters. Even regarding the place to toss litter, Tiffany says garbage *receptacles,* not garbage cans, which might imply metal. She is not being cynical. She is just like a convenience store owner donating books to her local library: she does it because she wants to support the library, not because a better library stands a better chance of capturing the imagination of kids, who will then be less likely to turn into the kind of alienated delinquent who will steal from her. It is the right thing to do and possibly good business too. Tiffany and Brad just happen to be in a line of work in which the benefits of community involvement come back around in this most tangible, concrete way.

But do these good people really think they can win this contest? I mean, there are a lot of towns in America with sidewalks, curbs, trash receptacles, and a school that is up to code. The Wizard fields this one with a note of finality that suggests the benediction will be next.

"Yes, I think we can win, but I think we already *have*, because doing the things we have to do to even become a candidate brings people together in a collaborative effort, working in the best interest of the community. Even if we lose, we can never put that genie back in the bottle."

Reporters are leeches. We show up, suck people dry, then give nothing back. We are observers and pay nothing for the privilege of being allowed to profit from other people's lives and experiences. The journalism world convulsed with outrage a few years ago when a newspaper reporter "paid" for an interview with a homeless person by taking him for a burger and fries. It is a one-way street, dammit. Some reporters give absolutely nothing back. They say one of the many talents of the great reporter Bob Woodward is that he doesn't fill in the blanks during an interview. He waits with his mouth shut for an interminable period after a subject finishes a statement until the subject becomes so suffocated by the silence that he blurts out something more. Even conversation is giving too much.

Chuck Gardner is having none of that. I am going to have to sing for my supper.

The singing will occur in a cinder-block room with four long folding tables inside Hawthorne's small but modern library. The library itself was built through a grant from the owner of the El Capitan Lodge and Casino. The library's board room, a windowless box with no decor to speak of, is the public forum in a town without a central public square. All those folks dropping quarters into the slots at the El Capitan probably thought the money was going into a sewer, but a little bit of it came here, to Hawthorne's version of Hyde Park Corner.

A young man is mounting a video camera on a tripod, and Chuck and I sit down at a table opposite. Chuck is interviewing me for local TV.

KWI Channel 13 donates time so that Chuck can talk about community affairs. The station even broadcasts the program during a time folks are likely to watch it, at 5 P.M. on the first and second Sundays of the month. The video camera is a VHS consumer model. The only lights are the flickering fluorescent bulbs above. No one is about to say, "From Television City in Hollywood." I relax, ready to wing it.

Chuck does one last preflight check of his twin hearing aids, smooths his beard, and looks into the lens. Everything goes quiet for fifteen seconds. Suddenly I'm sitting next to Walter Cronkite himself.

"Good evening and welcome to *The Civic Roundtable,* the program that brings you the information you need to know to enhance your quality of life. I'm your host, Chuck Gardner, and normally we talk about upcoming events and activities here in the community. But tonight we have a very special treat . . ."

Chuck is smoother than I'll ever be. The cadence is perfect. The little camera-friendly nods and mock gravitas would make Peter Jennings weep. This guy is very, very good. I'm beginning to feel like a deer in the headlights.

We talk social capital. We talk about civic pride. Then Chuck reaches for the pepper spray.

"Why should the government pay for public broadcasting?"

"Uh . . ."

"If the public really wanted that elitist stuff, there would be a commercial market for it, right?"

"Well, uh, Chuck, uh, first of all, public broadcasting isn't just government money. It's a private-public partnership. The system gets some money from the government, and it gets some from corporations and foundations and some regular folk, our listeners."

"But your listeners aren't regular folk. Are they not elites trying to tell the rest of us what is and is not important?" Chuck shoots back.

"Well, Chuck, if you did a referendum today on whether this place could use an art museum, folks might say no. But you have to agree an art museum might be a nice addition, and folks might start coming if you had one and grow to appreciate it."

"Are you saying we ought to build an art museum before we figure out how to pay for better education and all our other social challenges?"

OK, we're not fooling around anymore. Do I hit him with a petulant "If it weren't for public broadcasting no one outside this valley would ever hear about this fine town"? Or "If more commercial stations would make a commitment to high-quality public affairs programming like this unusually generous Channel 13 in Hawthorne, then perhaps we wouldn't need public broadcasting"?

Chuck senses I am ready to pounce, and in the nanosecond it is taking to form my thoughts, he makes a preemptive strike, wheeling to face the camera. "We'll be back to talk about the benefits of tourism with our guest right after this message."

The venerable jump-to-the-commercial-break-before-the-guest-can-respond trap, and I tumble in headlong. Old Chuck has crushed me like a sour grape.

There is no waiting in line for a table at Maggie's. Even though I rented the Contour, not the Lincoln, I must be giving off the erroneous vibe that I require cloth napkins, and Maggie's has those, so it was recommended. It also has a menu with a warning. At the bottom of the list of entrees, it says in italics: *"Management Not Responsible for the taste and texture of Prime Rib ordered well-done."* I imagine the ugly scenes that had led to this.

It is a fine warning, though, a turn on the Burger King pledge, to the effect of "We'll do it your way, but management would like you to know that your way is stupid." It says a lot about Maggie and her operation. Lean out the window of the speeding train if you want, dear customer, but if you lose a piece of your head, don't come crying to us.

"I'll have prime rib, please."

"How would you like it cooked?"

"Medium-rare is fine."

"All our prime rib is well-done tonight. A mistake was made."

Never buy without a warranty. I order the chicken.

Whether or not the editors of the *Columbia Journalism Review* would approve, I am already violating the prime directive not to interfere. The $19.62 I am spending on dinner at a steak place called Maggie's is an indirect subsidy of the subject of my inquiries, the people of Hawthorne. The tax is flowing out into official coffers. Maggie's profit will get injected into the veins of the community if she spends it or saves it locally. The highest multiplier effect is in the hospitality industry; every dollar you spend on a hotel room will be spent and spent again as it ripples outward into a community. Sticking money into the El Capitan slots has the same effect. But if Maggie the restaurateur sends the profit on my dinner to a distant mutual fund or buys a polo shirt by mail order, what started as my money will not have this multiplier effect.

It is a pleasant thought that I am not only taking from these people but leaving a little behind. But it is all a little vague, like the Endangered Species store at the Mall of America, helping the environment through spending. It hard to account for your contribution. Who exactly gets your money, what is their reputation, and how will it be put to use?

This is where philanthropy comes in. I can designate who gets the money and for what purpose. I can focus it right smack where I want it, no discussion, no committee, no act of parliament. That is power.

It is the power to show Chuck a thing or two about the role of art in a community. I could take a cash accumulation, explain the plight of this town to perhaps the Museum Loan Network, and get matching money. Then I could get a space built onto the quaint Hawthorne Historical Museum. With a little charm and some phone time, we could arrange to borrow famous works of art from a major museum back East.

It's a nice thought and arrogant all the same. A fellow like me shows up for a couple of days, has a look around, and then gets it in his head unilaterally what this town needs. If you come with money, you have to be heard. Money buys you a place on agenda, and you can use that platform as you see fit. Unfortunately, that is the kind of thinking that has caused many a development project to come crashing down in the third world. The white guys appear with a vision of saving the western Samoan rain forest. They initially work with local people to come up with alternative ways to provide income to them so they will not give over their land to logging. But the money comes from the West, and Western attitudes take hold. Then one day the nongovernmental organization established to protect the rain forest is dictating to the local people how they must behave and denigrates their time-honored rituals. Hard feelings abound, and the conservation campaign begins to crumble.

Am I willing to put aside my arrogance and allow the recipients of my charity to have a hand in its dispensation? Hawthorne is already on record with one of its most pressing needs, doing something about all the kids having babies. So am I willing to call up Evelyn Allen at the Consolidated Agency of Human Services, check their nonprofit status, and write a big check with the blanket wish that "the money be used as folks there see fit"? Charity is about those in need. But it is also very much about the donor, and it's very hard to completely cede control. I try to imagine my reaction to some of the possible letters back:

"On behalf of the citizens of Hawthorne, thank you. We have used your generous gift to establish the David A. and Mary V. Brancaccio Foundation for Economic Opportunity for Young Women Job Counseling Center. "

Or . . .

"On behalf of the citizens of Hawthorne, thank you. We have used your generous gift to establish the David A. and Mary V. Brancaccio Foundation for Sexual Abstinence."

Or . . .

"On behalf of the citizens of Hawthorne, thank you. We have used your generous gift to imprint the words 'Courtesy of the David A. and Mary V. Brancaccio Foundation' longitudinally onto every free condom we give out."

No, I don't want to micro-manage a gift. I am willing to allow someone else to define the need. But I have to feel that the act of giving, in one way or another, expresses my values.

On the other hand, this whole line of thinking is giving me such a sickening overdose of sanctimony that I might not be able to keep Maggie's entree down. If I have a surplus, I should consider myself lucky and give a piece to someone who needs it more than me, and do it quietly so that only the recipient and the Internal Revenue Service know for sure.

*   *   *

The next morning the Hawthorne sky betrays me. Living in southern California, I have forgotten what March is supposed to look like: glum and chilly. I drive south from town, looking for a place where the road rises into the hills and offers a vantage point from which to photograph the way the irregular buildings of Hawthorne mingle with the highly regimented warehouses of the ammunition depot. Such a spot is not easy to find. There is no quirky underground documentation about how to do so.

A friend had once shown me an underground guidebook to another lonely stretch of road a few hours' drive from here. Published on a photocopy machine, it specified the exact latitude and longitude of spots where one can catch illicit glimpses of a secret military installation along Nevada 375, the so-called Alien Highway. It was a viewer's guide to Area 51, where either secret military stuff is going on or there is a base for studying flying saucers. Or both.

But no one seems to care about me stealing snapshots of Hawthorne or its depot. I turn right off Nevada Route 359 and go seventy-five yards up the unpaved road to a sign that says, "Road Closed, November–April." It is one of the incongruities of the high desert, the sort of thing that tripped up the Donner party: the land can rise suddenly from hot desert to a place where snow blocks your way for six months of the year.

Out of habit, I park on the side of the road, even though leaving the car in the middle of the dirt track would have been fine: no one else would have any need to pass any time this month. Gravel, wind, and some electrical poles—that is about it. And a sound. It is a sound of skittering sibilants as the wind strokes the electrical wires, a kind of murmuring mixed with the torsional rattle of a Slinky. I toss the camera and grab the tape recorder and stand holding the microphone toward the wires, hoping that electrical storms are not features of this season in these parts. In this Statue of Liberty pose, I get a new angle on the Road Closed sign and notice that it obscures another lined up behind it. "Bodie, 39 miles," it reads.

The road to Bodie is a bad place to be.

Bodie lies on the California side of the border and did not appear on my Nevada map. It is one of the West's great ghost towns. The last resident left in the 1930s when the mining jobs finally dried up. It is a whole, empty town, right down to the dusty Methodist church pews and the chipped antique coffee machine inside the window of what used to be the general store. It is a place full of curses and graves; we hear a ghost of its name each time we utter the word "foreboding." The place stands as reminder that if a town doesn't get it together in a land as hostile as this, it can dry up and blow away. Bodie could have used a bowling alley and some good people committed enough to put up the social capital and other resources to keep the place vital. The threat of Bodie is a big reason we give. I'll consider myself lucky that on this day, at least, this road happens to be closed.

So we have the threat of extinction behind what is usually described as a charitable impulse. It can also be a self-interested investment in one's surroundings. It is also about power to control the destiny of your money. But one of the sweetest benefits of them all has to be mentioned.

The Tax Deduction

At least, giving money or merchandise is a deduction. You can't deduct time spent volunteering. Americans, as I have just learned in this town, are wonderful givers of their time. So generous are we that it would destroy the federal budget if we could write off every hour spent cleaning up a park or serving as a Brownie den mother. Still, it is one of the great ironies of the tax code that volunteering at an AIDS hospice is not tax-deductible, but money lost at the craps table in Atlantic City is. It is right there on the Schedule A itemized deductions tax form. A few more places where the IRS will not allow you to deduct your contributions: political organizations, chambers of commerce, foreign organizations, business leagues, sports clubs, and country clubs.

But you can deduct the cash you give the hospice. Or the used underwear you donate to the St. Vincent de Paul Society thrift shop. Charity is a very popular deduction, the second most common item behind the one for state and local taxes and more common than the home-mortgage interest deduction, according to the Internal Revenue Service. It takes a big amount of charity to top the mortgage deduction. Americans deduct an average of $2,400 a year in charitable contributions. Just try to get up to $2,400, even with $20 a week to a mosque, temple, church, or New Age healer, even with that $100 to your college and $50 each to a nonprofit community theater and hurricane relief in Bangladesh. The seventeen handfuls of spare change to various deinstitutionalized people who put out their hands in a year don't count; donations to individuals are not tax-deductible.

The tax write-off can be very seductive in practice, especially when it comes to the world of moonlighting and freelance gigs. The pottery class you are teaching or that two-weekend grant-writing project you took on seemed like a nice little chunk of extra income when it was offered. But after federal and state income tax and federal self-employment tax are paid, what are you left with? Perhaps enough to buy yourself a nice meal somewhere or to pay for that transmission work that needs to be done. In high-tax areas middle-class people can see half their moonlighting income disappear. "It's hardly worth the effort." Ever say that phrase after calculating a quarterly estimated tax payment to the government? Given this reality, you can make either of two conclusions. First, even though you can keep only $500 of the $1,000 check someone gives you for writing their grant, $500 is better than nothing. Or you could conclude that the most powerful way to use that one grand check is for philanthropy.

When my friend Marcia, who leads an exhausting life making three small businesses work in the northern Arizona desert, got work teaching part-time at a community college, she looked at the $1,000 honorarium and realized it would be reduced to $500 by taxes if she kept it as income. So she donated the money to a science program at her old public high school 2,500 miles away, the school that once employed a biology teacher who recognized Marcia's promise. The $1,000 she earned was worth the full $1,000 as an act of charity.

What else would make a top ten list of reasons to give money when I don't have to?

You Don't Want to Go to Hell

That is a dicey one. Rehearse the pearly gates pitch: "Yes, I was a sphincter-head for most of my professional life, but right at the end, my next of kin threatened to turn off my respirator if I didn't give a lot of money to nonprofits." What is that argument going to buy you? There is a variation on this that serves as a justification for acquisitiveness. It sounds something like this: "I want to be able to give lots of money to projects I support, but I first have to ruthlessly make the money needed to give away."

You Feel Guilty

You don't have to be rich to feel guilty about not being in a desperate financial situation. Lots of people go around with the unswerving conviction that every penny they have ever earned has been earned through their own sweat. But not all. Remember, the magazine is called *Fortune*, not *Diligence*, and many see charity as a kind of insurance policy to prime the pump should fate ever frown on our lives and we need help from others. Late-twentieth-century people like to think they are guided by rationality, but I am among the many who walk around completely convinced that a blast of karmic blowback will smite me if I don't do a better job directing my efforts outward rather than inward. Once, at an airport during a tense preflight moment when my children were being particularly fractious, a middle-aged woman approached me with a notebook full of pictures of children being oppressed in Iran. A donation would help. It probably wasn't the best time for the pitch, given the fact that my normally charming child number two was at that instant sinking a neat row of milk teeth into my ankle. I barked in annoyance at the solicitor of the charity, and I just know right in the pit of my stomach that I will pay for that uncharitable moment one way or another.

There's a Problem That Needs Solving

This is a very practical motive. Sometimes a little cash from us is the shortest route to fix something.

Immortality

This is a big one. Lots of the charitable money that gets the national average up to $2,400 a year comes from people endowing money to institutions, in large part to help but at least a little to get their name forever engraved on the front of a campus or hospital building. In one intriguing example an anonymous donor gave UCLA's medical school $45 million to build the Gonda (Goldschmeid) Neuroscience and Genetic Research facility. The donor did not wish UCLA to explain why the name of the building would be partially in parentheses. But creating immortality doesn't have to be monumental. Hawthorne's memorial rose bushes near the library, each one labeled with the name of a late member of the community, are part of this theme.

Your Kids Will Be Spoiled If You Don't Give It Away

We all worry about transferring our values about money, wealth, and hard work to our children, but wealthy folks really are preoccupied with this one. If the money comes too easily, the fear is, the offspring will become dissolute. Business news tycoon Michael Bloomberg was very specific about this when I broached the subject with him one day. Bloomberg has two teenage daughters whom he sees as smart and well adjusted. But he still worries at some abstract level that his wealth may hurt them more than it helps.

"My great fear is that these kids will not have any self-esteem. That they will think that their parents bought everything, and they will take the money and ruin their lives. In that case everything I've done will have been for naught."

What Bloomberg has done is, first, make sure his daughters will "never go hungry." But the bulk of his many millions is set up to flow to a family foundation in which the daughters will be voting members of the board but together will not have majority control. They will have to learn to consult with and build coalitions with the rest of the board, which will be made up of Bloomberg's ex-wife and other mentors. He is very clear that among the advantages of having his daughters become

involved in his philanthropic foundation is the social standing and influence it will bring them.

"I can give my kids the greatest gift, which is the ability to do good,"
Bloomberg said. "But maybe from a little selfish point of view, from the
kids' side, it may raise their profile, and people will certainly be nice to
them because they can steer money around. Mainly they will be able to
do an enormous amount of good. But the fact that they can't go and
ruin it all on a bunch of bad marriages or not have to work I think is to
their benefit."

I'm with Bloomberg on this. We all want responsible children with
drive who know the value of a nickel.

"I think Warren Buffett's got the problem and Gates has the problem
and Bloomberg's got the problem," he said. "And the problem doesn't
just have to be at our level; it can be with people who have just a couple
of million bucks."

It was the "just" in that sentence that made tears well up in my eyes.

Paying for What You Use Even If You Don't Have To

This is the Metropolitan Museum of Art in New York conundrum.
The suggested $6 entry fee ($3 for students) is described as a "contribution," but you get the *malocchio* big time if you choose not to "contribute." There is a much more positive variant of this, usually described
as "giving something back." You give money unsolicited to improve a
park that has brought you pleasure.

Passing back through Hawthorne, I drive along the western perimeter of
town, past corrals for the public works department's backhoes and trailers of congealed tar. I pause for a moment along a street surrounded by
several mobile homes parked at a right angle to the entrance to a closed
fairgrounds. There is one splash of color, a wide, thin, hand-painted
"RODEO" sign punctuated on either side of the yellow letters with two
red circles. I walk over to examine a vintage car parked next to one of the
trailers. It is a fifties Studebaker, so regular in the lines of its design that

it is tough to tell if the car is coming or going. It has an original white-over-gray two-toned paint job and, in this bone-dry climate, no rust to speak of. It is a pretty fine specimen, with tires that still hold air. To my eyes it is an object of beauty and value.

But not to someone else's eyes. From the left quarter panel, across the driver's door, and onto the rear door, someone has taken white paint and sprayed the letters "REWARD." On the driver's window and again on the rear left window, the same paint has been used to write "$100." A reward for what? For the return of such a nice car? No, that's backwards. A reward for the kind soul who tows away something regarded as an eyesore? But this is the desert. People don't pay $100 to tow away junk cars in the desert; they push them behind boulders for free. If the reward is somehow related to the car, then why desecrate it with spray paint? Is it possible that this car has sat on this spot so long that it has come to be seen by some local resident as a fine medium to display a message, as if it were plywood hoarding? If so, maybe the $100 reward is for something completely unrelated to the Studebaker, like the return of a lost hunting rifle or a beloved cat. My explanations are getting increasingly desperate. I wonder if some local teenagers stole the car, then painted the words onto the gem out of spite after the owners offered $100 for its safe return? Reward. The word has a Norman root very close to "regard," to stare at, to consider, or to esteem, to value. It is a mystery that will require further consideration.

On my way back to Walker Lake, I stop at the city limit, the spot that may someday sport the coveted red, white, and blue All-America City sign, purchased with social capital. Actually what I find is a number of signs that have already been bought in just this way. The orange deco Hawthorne sign rescued from the wrecking ball is there. So is a kind of horizontal picket fence of reminders about the power of community interaction. Care and Share, meets 7 P.M. Mineral County Eagle Forum, "God, Home, Country." Operating Engineers, Local Union 3. Disabled American Veterans, Mineral County Chapter, meets third Monday.

Contributions to a number of these organizations may be tax-deductible. Others might go down as an appropriate business expense.

There is a lot of potential horsepower in this roster if it can be harnessed.

People who think about charity for a living are starting to take social capital more seriously. The traditional model of charity involves either the donor or an outside expert identifying a problem or a need, then fixing the problem with charity. One of the difficulties with this approach is that those on the outside looking in might not know what they are looking at. It also can be demeaning to treat the recipients of charity as "problems" in need of solutions. An emerging way of structuring charity attempts to play to the existing assets of even the most disadvantaged community. Instead of outsiders making the decisions, communities identify their own needs and approaches. People from within the community marshal their own strengths that can be put into action with charity from outside.

"We all have gifts, and it's the gifts that grow under nurturing, not the needs," John Davies once told me. Davies runs the Baton Rouge Area Foundation in Louisiana, a group that tries to partner with poor communities. He argues that letting communities decide what to do with the money makes charity much more self-sustaining. When people with passion emerge from within a place that could use outside resources, they can live a project the way the folks of Hawthorne are living their All-America City bid. The trick is not for me to give money to a problem but to invest in the people with the drive to sustain things that will improve their own situation. Davies doesn't have much use for charities that encourage well-intentioned folks from nice neighborhoods to go into poor neighborhoods for one evening or one weekend to paint and plaster dilapidated buildings.

"As soon as you stop playing the game, the game is over," Davies says. "Then we go home and pour our pleasantly chilled bottle of chardonnay and feel sanctimonious. We have done our bit and now we feel good. But is it sustainable?"

The social capital that is stockpiled in Hawthorne is just the sort of fuel that can be ignited by charitable donors with the optimism to just give and trust, letting the people affected run with it. People like Davies would argue that the whole exercise of charity is pointless without the sort of initiative from within that the townsfolk here have already mustered.

* * *

"What *are* you doing?" a voice calls out.

Oh, man. That Area 51 booklet is right. The sheriff is going to bust me for trying to observe a restricted government installation or something. What was the booklet's advice? Tell the truth, but don't let him search you without a warrant? I slowly turn, expecting either a lawman in mirrored glasses or perhaps Leonard Nimoy in twentieth-century disguise. But there is no one.

"What are you, from the government or something?" the voice says. It is coming from a telephone pole across the highway. At the base of the pole, there is a fellow crouched with his knees up and an Atlanta Olympics hat pulled low. I have the mirrored sunglasses right, but that's it. He has white hair, white beard, and an Eagles T-shirt under his navy blue windbreaker. I cross the road to introduce myself. His name is Wayne. I explain that what I am doing is copying down the names of all the clubs in Hawthorne listed on the sign, which seems to make sense to Wayne.

"Where you headed, Wayne?"

"To the end of a month," he replies. Wayne is a drifter.

"What are you doing here?"

"My net worth was $133,000" a few years ago, Wayne volunteers. How did we get there so fast? I hadn't even gotten to the subject of my quest yet.

Wayne and I definitely need to talk.

He wants to know if I have any money. I tell him the *Columbia Journalism Review* won't approve if I pay for an interview, but the specter of a CJR inspector doesn't seem to carry much weight in the dust alongside this desert highway. I come up with a jesuitical solution. If Wayne will allow me to interview him on tape for free so I won't violate any professional standards, I will pay him $10 for the right to take his picture. Photography is my avocation, I rationalize, and not subject to the same rigorous rules as my profession. This is strike two for me in this town. I have already violated the prime directive about not interfering in the local culture with my TV appearance.

Wayne looks like an aging Jerry Garcia, and the youthful California surfer cadence in his voice belies his forty-eight years. He is clean, highly articulate, and drinking from a Big Gulp–sized cup filled with vodka and soda. He confirms he is from California, a Vietnam vet, and an alcoholic.

In the 1980s, Wayne says, he built up a window-cleaning business in what was then California's boom town, Lancaster. There was a flood of military defense work washing through the area, the northern edge of the Los Angeles sprawl. Wayne at first specialized in the windows of commercial property, but on a hunch one day he trolled his business card through a neighborhood of single-family homes and soon converted the whole business to residential work.

He and his third wife paid $57,000 for a fixer-upper in Lancaster, and thus began a series of tragic money traps that turned Wayne into a perpetual nomad. In 1990 the couple sold their home for $135,000. Even factoring in the money they spent on improvements, the sale generated a sweet profit, and $55,000 went into the bank. As far as the real estate market went, the timing was perfect. The Cold War was just ending, and soon defense dollars in the region would dry up, touching off one of the West's worst property busts. But at every other level, the timing of the sale was horrible. Wayne volunteers matter-of-factly that alcoholism killed his wife three months after the real estate windfall. He had his wife's life insurance policy, of which he was the beneficiary, and there were also some bonds.

Although the rules have changed since, back then the IRS specified that you had two years to buy another house or pay tax on the capital gains. But when his wife died, there was no way Wayne could stomach buying another house.

"So I just blew it. I spent the money."

Spending a windfall is one thing, but not paying the IRS the capital gains tax one owes is another. The way Wayne has it figured, he still owes Uncle Sam $30,000 in back taxes and penalties, something that would dog him for the rest of his life if he were to come in from the cold and end his midlife "retirement." A tax attorney might tell Wayne that if he really wanted to re-enter the real economy, a good bet would be for him to find a lawyer who would work on his case pro bono, then approach the IRS and come clean. If the IRS realizes there is no hope of recovering, it is possible Wayne could get off paying a manageable sum per month for the rest of his life. But he would have to be working steadily to be able to pull this off.

Wayne says after his wife's death, he let his business go to hell and began drinking just to catch up with her. Wife number four, a bartender who was not an alcoholic, pulled him out of it, saving his life, he believes.

She was also a woman, by Wayne's account, with expensive tastes. There was a $2,000 limo ride from Lancaster, California, to Las Vegas to get married. His new wife didn't want to drive back and demanded an airline ticket for the 250-mile ride. The limo driver would not give him a break on the forfeited return trip.

"She showed me how to spend $130,000 in a short time. She walked away from a six-month marriage with a new car. She had to have things like this Rainbow vacuum cleaner, which cost me a thousand, and stereo surround sound. I took the rest of my money, went to the Pacific Northwest, and bought a motor home and lived in it for four years until I couldn't keep up with it."

He now lives off monthly checks from his military retirement and the surviving spouse portion of his third wife's retirement. When I ask how much money he would need to get back on his feet, he smiles and says, "To be perfectly honest with you, I like this lifestyle."

I'm not sure I believe him. Wayne, it turns out, had a retirement plan a lot earlier than most of us. When he joined the marines after quitting high school, his idea was to work twenty years until retirement, then get a job with the same defense contractor as his father, work another twenty years, and retire at age fifty-seven with two pension plans going and Social Security payments to come.

"I would have been set for life, but it didn't happen that way."

What did happen was that he learned to smoke dope in Vietnam, which led to a dishonorable administrative discharge after a sheriff in San Diego caught him with some marijuana. That and the fact that his peripatetic aerospace engineer father had the kind of job that moved them into eighteen different houses by the time Wayne was sixteen. But what he blames the most is his drinking.

"And yet at forty-one, because my wife died, I became retired. My goal had been to retire early, before my life was over. And it happened one way or another. It wasn't my design, but it was someone's.

"And that's the thing about retirement. These snowbirds come down here, and they've got their motor homes and their money every month. They look like they enjoy it, but do they? When was the last time they really climbed a big mountain or a hill? They're too old for that. Shoot, they're too old for anything; they're living the last days of life."

Make no mistake, Wayne's is a tough lifestyle. I'm looking at everything he owns. A backpack, a rolled sleeping bag. His blue winter jacket that seems a bit much for desert wear until you sleep in it. His official Atlanta Olympics hat, his plastic cup of the hard stuff.

"I tell people a lot, 'What more does a man need than what he can carry?' I mean, we strive for things. When my wife died, I sat there at the dining room table looking at our hutch where she used to keep crystal, and I thought, Rita, what's it all for? You are gone and here's all this crystal. What good was it to collect it? It did give her pleasure during life, but at the same time, what exactly are we striving for? The Bible says 'Where your treasures lie, so your heart shall remain there.' " Wayne's second wife was a Jehovah's Witness, and he has a good ear for verse.

"Where are our treasures? Are they in the love in the brotherhood of man or in our own personal possessions, which we treasure so much?"

For a drifter, Wayne knows how to sit. The gravel-strewn median strip and concrete utility pole fall short of the kind of loving attention provided by his old Barca lounger in Lancaster, yet Wayne makes no effort to unwind his lotus position, adjust his sunglasses, or remove his winter coat, even as the sun begins to burn away the morning pall. I, however, am extremely uncomfortable, not just from the unforgiving ground or the dust kicked up by the passing trucks. I am itching to put as much distance as I can between me and Wayne's kind of fate, no home, no job, no family. Money is supposed to make the difference. A modest small business, insurance, a home purchased low and sold high are the tickets to security. If you get there, you have matriculated into the middle class, where I had presumed you were protected. That this all began to unravel for this seemingly sincere soul at about the time my wife and I willfully abandoned the security of jobs within big institutions and set out to conquer the world with our own modest savings, I find a chilling reverse synchronicity. I want the distance of knowing that Wayne is stupid, incoherent, and foul. He is none of these things.

Even the fact that he is a drunk doesn't fully explain away his situation, given his level of self-awareness.

Oh, it does get a little weird when Wayne mentions that he is preparing for a kind of imminent Second Coming in which the industrialized world will simply shut down and that the last time that happened was thirty thousand years ago and it is about to happen again. But the convenient distance that this revelation produces is quickly dissolved when Wayne mentions the call letters of the radio station where he once worked writing commercials and selling ad time. From lower middle class to almost invisible in seven years.

I wonder how you stay alive when this combination of substance abuse, bad decisions, and bad luck drives you into a nomadic life wandering the desert. Wayne isn't a jovial fellow, but he doesn't seem embittered either, even when his tales are about the robberies and confrontations that come with his life. Wayne is able to keep going because, he says, people are, by and large, charitable. When he offers to clean the bathrooms or pull the weeds at gas stations, more often than not people take him up on the proposition or just hand him five dollars. When some sleaze rode off with all of Wayne's modest belongings during a pit stop while he was hitchhiking from Santa Barbara to San Luis Obispo, there was another fellow who picked him up a few minutes later and then remarked that his passenger "looked like he could use some help." The man reached into his wallet and pulled out $100, then drove Wayne to the Kmart in Santa Maria so he could buy a new sleeping bag, backpack, and set of clothes. This man waited outside as Wayne shopped and gave him the rest of the ride. The folks here in Hawthorne, he remarks, are pretty good to him when he passes through.

It becomes clear. You give because people need you to give, and you give because you yourself may need someone else's charity more quickly than you ever thought.

I shake Wayne's hand and wish him luck. He doesn't look up. I never do see his eyes behind the mirrored glasses. For some unconscionable reason, the $10 bill I gave him earlier seems enough and he asks for no more. It seems enough until I start spending money elsewhere later that day. The $112 for the rental car with the snob at the counter in Reno. The $15 I put into the slots at the Reno airport, known derisively as the CasinoPort. The $31 plus tip I give to the cab driver who takes me home from the airport. Guilt that I didn't follow through with more is actually a useful guilt. It's not that I waste my own money. It's that I waste money that could be in someone else's hands, someone who's stuck in a jam.

Driving back north of Walker Lake, I pass through the tiny town of Schurz in the middle of land owned by the Paiute tribe. There is a little grove of trees that has sprung up around the Walker River, serving as a canopy to some houses straight out of a Walker Evans photograph. At a fork in the road, someone has set up a kind of tableau to sobriety, a pair of compact cars made even more compact by some horrendous crash long ago. "Drinking and Driving Don't Mix," reads the rough, hand-painted sign. It gives the impression of being a permanent installation, a feature of the town, like Hawthorne's restored deco masterpiece. It also suggests there is a tradition in these parts of using old cars to convey public service messages. Maybe that is what the old Studebaker parked near the rodeo grounds was all about. When I later develop the film of my trip to Hawthorne, the image of Wayne does appear on the frames, so presumably he was no ghost. And that Studebaker shows up too, with the word "REWARD" glowing as vividly on the side as I remember. But as I examine the frame using a magnifying loupe, I notice a detail that escaped me when I originally surveyed the scene. There is what appears to be a rectangular piece of plywood lying face down at the foot of the car's front bumper, a scrap big enough on which to paint the first part of a public service message. I have no doubt that if I could reach into the photo and lift the corner of the plywood, it would read, "Charity is its own . . ."

And thus would end the Hollywood version of my trip into the desert to confront my tightfisted self. The real version ends with me on a day off, stuck in Los Angeles traffic with the first sundown of Passover approaching. My colleague Sarah is on the radio talking about the All-America City contest. There is a disappointed note in her voice that foreshadows the outcome of her copy. The list of finalists for the contest has just been released, and the contest organizers have failed to include the good folks of Hawthorne. I offer a gesture to the radio that should be avoided when traveling in Mediterranean countries, a gesture that is gravely misinterpreted by the occupants of a lowered Impala SS driving adjacent. Charity, it makes you feel so wonderful inside.

There I was, hoping the folks in Hawthorne would win the lottery, even after everything I had learned to the south in Vegas. That would have been nice: they win, they solve all their problems, and I'm off the hook. It would have been yet another one of my baroque excuses to avoid giving away money, but now I have no excuses. It is time to act with my checkbook.

Souvenirs

A letter for my tax records from the Consolidated Agencies of Human Services in Mineral County Nevada listing a modest contribution.

A renewed understanding that the barrier between people with a surplus and people in need is very permeable.

To do when I get home

Add charity to all our tax-planning, portfolio, and personal finance discussions.

Start thinking in terms of percentage of disposable income, not dollars donated.

Doing the numbers

The amount given to charity is about 2 percent of the personal income in America. Of those who give to charity, the average annual amount is about $1,000 a year. Households in which there was at least one person doing volunteer work donated 2.6 percent of their income. In households where no one volunteered, contributions totaled 1.4 percent of income. (Source: National Commission on Philanthropy and Civic Renewal)

7

Invest Like a Grown-up

Buying a fat hen on Wall Street

From the clipping file: A retired Defense Department employee from Fairfax County, Virginia, picked up a lottery check for $4,534,749 after taxes. The *Washington Post* reported the money is all in the stock market. June 19, 1998

*A*s the insidious advertising line for the computer company goes, no one ever got fired for choosing IBM. When it comes to a surplus, no one by the turn of the century ever got ridiculed for putting it where the culture had deemed the obvious choice, the stock market. Sure, the market could turn sour and you could lose it all. But it might also turn out very well and the message—loud and clear—was that only a fool wouldn't be in there playing.

It was time, already, to visit Wall Street. Time to see if there was actually asphalt or cobblestones behind the metaphor. Time to watch that circus in action to see if I could discern some rules to prevent a surplus from disappearing in the market the way my lottery investment had disappeared.

I didn't meet a Reeve, a Miller, or the Wife of Bath on this section of the pilgrimage. But I did come across, among others, a trader, a cobbler, a beekeeper, a chief, a parson, and a boatman who shared their wisdom about a surplus.

*The markets were, as promised, mesmerizing theater. The payoffs and the
heartbreak drew me in. But a little cautious distance is good for a portfolio. Get
too close and emotions begin to guide investment decisions, which can turn the
enterprise into an expensive, time-consuming hobby. I have other hobbies, and
as I was to be reminded by the boatman, I would rather be woodworking.*

The Trader's Tale

Welcome to the center of the universe.

The court of the T'ang Dynasty, China, seventh century B.C. Queen
Elizabeth's court, 1588. The Bastille, 1789.

I have just stumbled backward onto the trading floor of the New
York Stock Exchange during one of the peaks of the great bull market of
the late twentieth century. The play is already in motion, the crowd is
primed, there is no chance to pause to regain my balance. Two-dollar
broker Ed Rode is ready to rock 'n' roll.

Ed is stylish, Ed is fluid, Ed has mastered the ability to surf backward
through the chaos on the floor with the ease of a realtor who has given
this house tour two hundred times. He is a few inches taller than me,
and in order to communicate in this stadium without shouting, Ed leans
down and locks his face in at a slightly uncomfortable proximity to
mine. It is as though we are on a moving sidewalk in an airport or sliding through an extended Steadycam shot as my guide plows a furrow
through the high grass of clerks, brokers, runners, and security folks,
turning sharp corners and negotiating obstacles without varying the
pace. Before this, my only insight into what hallucinogens might be like
was an occasional fever-inspired delirium as a kid.

Ed and I descend into the Jovian atmosphere together, a three-dimensional space of green flashing "ask" and "bid" prices, CNBC television feeds, and flat panel screens on goosenecks. An emergency cabinet
marked "Defibrillator" in urgent letters flies by. Drifts of used order slips
make the wooden floor unreliable, so I look up to get my bearings from
the heavens, only to find a gently spinning kaleidoscope: a traditional
gold leaf ceiling of carved rectangles superimposed with a postmodern
burnished aluminum web of pipes from which dangle cables that sup-

port the stock trading kiosks. I want to reach out and trace trails, but Ed grabs both my shoulders and gets me to focus on his rap without breaking his backward stride as we roll through one of the ancillary trading floors, the Blue Room.

Ed doesn't like the acoustics in here; they are too controlled. Compared to the main floor, it is almost quiet. Too quiet.

"It's hard to feel the market in here," Ed says with a couple of snaps of his fingers. "You gotta *hear* when it's heating up or cooling down."

My eyes finally line up on a landmark, a bid readout of the numbers. The Dow is down just a percent.

"No big deal," comes the real-time analysis.

This is New York and Ed talks fast. There are three kinds of people in this world, he explains. "House brokers" work for specific investment houses, such as Paine Webber or Smith Barney–Dean Witter; "two-dollar brokers" are freelancers, such as Ed. If you want a share of Archer Daniels Midland or something, the word gets through to Ed's people, Richard Rosenblatt and Company, who pass the word to Ed's clerks, who shout or radio to Ed how much you want to buy and at what price. Ed is like your personal shopper at the mall of stocks, and it is his job to take your order over to the third kind of broker on the floor, "the specialist," and bid for you.

Some client somewhere does want some Archer Daniels, ticker symbol ADM, according to Ed's headset.

"Time to rock 'em and sock 'em."

So Ed makes the first and only stop of our cruise at the specialist who handles pieces of the Decatur, Illinois–based agricultural products giant. Ed's bid is recorded with a specialist. The specialist handles a specific group of stocks. He matches the supply with the demand for those stocks. But he also has to sell to the first buyer whose bid comes in at the sell price. If several bids of equal price come in, he fills those on a first-come, first-served basis. So the specialist is the record keeper and auctioneer, if need be. He is also a "market maker" and is supposed to use his own money to buy a stock temporarily if no buyers show up to make a bid on an offered pile of shares. He also looks, in his little framed kiosk, like Lucy in a high-tech lemonade stand.

A specialist is allowed to buy and sell a stock using his own money under limited circumstances, that is, to "maintain a fair and orderly market." Since the specialist knows how much folks are willing to pay for a stock and how much folks are willing to charge for the stocks they are selling, the specialist is the ultimate insider. There is a theory of investing that intensely scrutinizes the activities of the specialist for insight into which way a stock is going.

The area near the specialist's post has been likened to a swap meet, where brokers representing buyers and sellers mingle and haggle to come up with a price. On the rival Nasdaq stock market, the all-electronic system is closer to that of a used car lot, not a swap meet. The dealer buys cars from folks trying to get rid of their old vehicles. When an interested buyer comes along looking to purchase a used car, he buys from the dealer, not the original owner, at the price set by the dealer. Nasdaq and New York Stock Exchange officials argue endlessly about which system provides the best price for investors.

Ed's already moved on with a slip filled with an ADM order. It is stamped GTC, "Good Till Close," meaning the bid will stand until either a seller is found at that price or until the market closes at four o'clock. It is three hours and forty-five minutes until the final bell, and at the moment the mood is busy, but genial. It is Maundy Thursday, and a lot of folks are looking forward to the three-day Easter weekend. Ed and a woman moving in opposite directions recognize each other. At the same moment their cheeks touch in an affectionate greeting.

"Emma!"

"Ed!"

Neither has stopped moving or even broken stride.

"Lovely person," Ed says before banking hard left.

We are on course to a hot spot. The spot on the New York Stock Exchange floor where the glib and charming Maria Barteromo stands as she delivers her live updates to CNBC viewers. There is no Maria here at the moment, only the spot.

"Cool, huh?" Ed says.

One story up, through a wide window, the back of the head of a CNN man can be seen bobbing and shaking in that anchorman way, the cord from his ear piece snaking through his slick 'do and into his collar. It is like looking at the rough, unfinished side of a movie set. Ed points out the business end of this reporter visible live on a nearby monitor.

"Cool, huh?"

We are still moving.

"Hi, Joey."

Ed high-fives a broker coming in on a tangential trajectory.

"I love to feel the pump of adrenaline as things get cranking in here. It's unbelievable."

I note that Ed walks briskly in his black sneakers, but he does not run. There is no running. Once, long ago, Ed ran. He was hurrying to execute a trade in an auxiliary trading room known as the Garage. One of the governors who vigilantly polices the floor snagged him.

"He ripped my face off," Ed recalls.

It isn't clear if this is a metaphor or not. He was warned the next time there would be a major fine. There was no next time.

Ed's official Rosenblatt and Company black smock with ventilated shoulders is one of the awkward traditions of his business. It makes him look like a stock man in a grocery store, but Ed, of course, is a very different kind of stock man. As if to offset the silly smock, Ed is wearing a metallic necktie and metal-rimmed glasses that are more hipster than Brooks Brothers. He has been at this for twenty-seven years, first as a messenger, then as a "chalk boy" who toted up the latest prices on a chalkboard before the coming of automation. If he failed to get the data up fast enough, there was trouble.

"They'd absolutely kill you dead."

Ed kicks open a set of doors. Somehow we have landed in the brilliant daylight outside the 11 Wall Street entrance. The music stops. If there were a safe rock, I would have clung to it. A cigarette materializes. I have never smoked, but at that moment I understand why people do.

"You picked a good, mellow day to stop by, Dave. A good, mellow day."

Despite Ed's patient and affable efforts, I feel my training is just beginning. If someone had handed me a headset into which a clerk was barking "A thousand shares of Boeing at 55 3/4," maybe with a map I could have found the specialist on the floor who handles Boeing. But I sincerely have doubts I would have any idea about how to get a good price. Auctions are intimidating. Intense, in-your-face auctions are tougher still. Auctions in which the denominations are in terrifying fractions are even worse. Repeat after me, five-eighths is a smidgen smaller than three quarters.

It isn't the haggling itself that worries me. After many failed attempts, I had finally savaged a car dealer on my last negotiation. It involved lots of prior research and actually memorizing the wholesale prices on a myriad of options available for the vehicle. The real power in the negotiation came from keeping open the option of walking out of the deal right up to the end. But what if I had been faced with a cluster of competitive bidders? I offer the dealer $22,700, and some other bidder raises his hand and offers $22,800. And what if the time allowed for the bidding process were compressed to under a minute? Perhaps this floor-broker stuff will have to be for me just one of those things, like English cricket, for which I seem to be missing a gene.

It is this insight that has kept me from being seduced by the home version of Ed Rode's game, daytrading, in which stock market meets video arcade. Daytraders use special computer screens that show lists of just who is stacking up to buy and sell a stock at what price, then try to gauge a stock's momentum and make lightning-quick bets. Daytrading requires nimble reflexes: at one training course for daytraders, students actually practice hitting the "buy" and "sell" keys on their keyboards to develop the required dexterity. I saw one daytrader rack up more than two thousand transactions in a single day, paying a commission on each and every one of them. By the time the market closed, the trader was left glumly muttering that he had lost $20,000 that day. It isn't about the type of business a stock represents or how that company makes a profit. It is about selling the instant a stock price tics downward. It is about getting out of the market entirely at the end of each day.

Whatever a daytrader does, he must never, ever, hold onto a stock overnight, when the market is closed. Daytrading is less than short-term; there is no time horizon whatsoever. "Next thing you know, you are *studying* the company," a daytrader said with mock disgust. "Next thing you know, you are attending annual meetings." It is a tough game, and one daytrading company even admits that its practitioners tend to lose money in their first months at it. While there is no independent study, the same company claims that 65 percent make money after three to five months of practice. I do have one thing in common with a number of daytraders: my aforementioned problem with fractions. Tacked on along the bottom of a bunch of the computer screens at the daytrading room I visited were cheat sheets that allow these daytrading cowboys to quickly check to see if 5/8 is bigger or smaller than 3/4. It is chilling to think about someone putting real money on the line without a firm grasp on this basic skill.

A horrible irony about investing is taking shape. The markets are good sport. It is not much of a leap to switch from the twenty-four-hour financial news on CNBC to the twenty-four-hour sports news on ESPN. It cannot be denied that hanging with Ed Rode is exhilarating, and it is the drama of the markets that lures many investors in. But once we are there, this dynamism and volatility can impel us to play more often than is prudent, encouraging the kind of short-term thinking and churning of a portfolio that costs money. A study by a pair of economists at the University of California at Davis strongly suggests that the more one trades, the worse one does. Stocks are supposed to be a fine place for a surplus if the portfolio is not constantly worried and tweaked, but amid all this hurly-burly, how can one resist? Falling in love with a stock and holding on to it for dear life through thick and thin can be a problem. Stocks, a broker once told me, do not care if you sell them; they never knew you owned them. But developing an infatuation with the thrill of buying and selling, so that we trade stocks with the casualness of trading marbles, can equally cloud our investment judgment.

Outside the New York Stock Exchange, it isn't exactly the Grand Canyon, but it is a concrete canyon and sure beats the Camp Snoopy vista at the Mall of America. I have just climbed the steps of the Federal Hall National Monument at 26 Wall Street. I am perched atop an abutment that projects from a pediment supporting the building's Doric columns. The eponymous rickety wall put up to protect the Dutch town from the Brits has been gone for three centuries, but this stubby Greek Revival marble wall will do. I am getting leery glances from some gray coats marching solemnly down the sidewalk to their Bloomberg, Dow Jones, and Reuter terminals as they spot me sitting on the wall, my loafers dangling, like

Humpty-Dumpty in pinstripes. But I get a momentary rush from feeling taller than the famous green-and-white Wall Street–Broad Street sign. From here I am able to angle my gaze from high ground down to the battlements of the New York Stock Exchange. I am enjoying the illusion of power over the markets that this vantage point provides.

I am up barely one story, but the air under my shoes is a little dizzying. It occurs to me that I am catching the last glimpse one would see if things went terribly wrong on the markets and one were moved to take the fastest route down from the upper floors of one of the great financial houses. Humpty-Dumpty had a great fall.

How many times have I had the occasion to say "Wall Street," meaning the securities industry or the investment community? Wall Street, before my eyes, is being reduced to an address as I spot a DHL delivery truck crawling along the sloping narrow street that runs between Broadway and the East River. Wall Street is a lot shorter in person.

A workman is stacking electric blue police barricades in a pile in preparation for carting them away on a flatbed truck that is backing down Nassau. Yesterday demonstrators from ACT-UP! caused pandemonium on this street, using capitalism's ground zero to protest the high cost of anti-AIDS drugs.

"We die, they make money," they chanted.

Drug companies countered that the $20,000-a-year cost for the most modern treatments is the result of the high cost of developing increasingly effective products. The protest was a bid to march the Wall Street crowd, both literally and figuratively, toward the basic principle of socially responsible investment: politicizing the portfolio. The heavy police presence limited ACT-UP!'s movements, but not its voice.

The voices I am hearing are more fatalistic. Perhaps it is my demonstrated ability to consistently choose the slowest line at the grocery store. Perhaps it is that insecurity growling again, the one that impelled me on this odyssey: what if I just don't have the knack to properly parlay a surplus? Just watch what happens the day I show up on Wall Street, I tell myself. Inevitably, this baby is going to tank.

Some folks, of course, do have the knack. A friend from Texas seems to have the magic touch.

David Johnson is a stockbroker, not a handicapper, but on a lark, I once dragged him out to the races. At the track Johnson balanced the racing form in his hands as if trying to identify the most formidable horse by weight, then he mumbled something plausible about "good in the stretch." And which horse did this successful broker pick, of all those running in twelve races? A horse named Freehouse, a 16-to-1 shot in the big race of the afternoon, the Santa Anita Derby. Naturally, because it was David Johnson making the pick, Freehouse won. Since I followed his lead, I turned a $5 bet on Freehouse into $41.50. I am sure Johnson also picks the fastest grocery line. I am left, however, with the sense that this bit of luck is an aberration and that it will take more to flip a polarity that was reversed long ago by some negative charge.

A good way to banish negative thoughts in a great metropolis like New York is to engage in one of the many decadent perversions for which the city is renowned. I have a sudden craving for scripophily.

Just what the doctor ordered is available on the sidewalk at the corner of Wall Street and Broadway. A woman wearing elaborate earrings presides over a wooden table. This is how the Lombards started the first banks in medieval London, using wooden tables like this, called banques, topped with coins for money changing. The woman on the corner is displaying not coins but old, ornate stock certificates for anyone suddenly struck with an impulse toward scripophily: the collecting of antique stock and bond certificates.

The certificates are magnificent, about the size of a diploma, engraved in several colors on heavy rag paper with a precision usually associated with banknotes. The vintage railroad stocks on display today are wonderful, evocative renderings of locomotives with plumes of steam roaring out of their tanks. Judging from the hand-lettered sign, the stocks are usually available at five for $25 but today have been marked down to just a dollar apiece. Other antique stocks, those signed by financial notables like John D. Rockefeller or tied to historic events like the *Titanic* or those from Russia's czarist era, are worth hundreds, even thousands of dollars. Even in their dotage, these stocks are forced to continue their exhausting market dance. Three bells ring from the church at the top of the street. I will have to remember to confess my scripophily to the priest of Trinity Wall Street when I consult him about the contradictions of a surplus later in this trip.

The Cobbler's Tale

As I learned in the Nevada desert, seek the truth from guys you meet on the street named Wayne. The Wayne in Hawthorne was white, unemployed, bearded, and stocky. This Wayne isn't.

"Good pair of leather, but you haven't shined them for a while," Wayne says.

It's the next afternoon, a cold one back in the financial district. For eight months a year, Wayne works as a custodian in the New York City public school system. From January through April every year, he runs a small business shining shoes along the wrought-iron fence that surrounds Trinity Church at the top of Wall Street. I wonder if he gets any tips.

He replies that he is always happy to accept a gratuity.

The financier Bernard Mannes Baruch said he knew the stock market had reached a crest in 1929 when he received a stock tip from the guy shining his shoes. The class snobbery implied by his statement is intolerable, but there is an almost mechanical logic to the notion that at the point when everyone who can invest is invested, the market has no place to go but down. For the later half of the 1990s, stock market indices have grown by double-digit percentage gains every year. A hot sport now is looking for signs that the market has crested and it is therefore time to pull the surplus out.

As for the insider information kind of tips, Wayne says his customers keep it to themselves.

"Why? Is the stock market getting good, or something?"

Wayne has eight children, two of whom are about to enter high school. I ask if he expects them to help him in his retirement.

"They just have to come out good; they don't need to support me. One is interested in basketball, the other football. They say they are going to the NBA or the NFL and will buy me a nice house. I tell them, "Hold the thought!" I'm not going to say they are and I'm not going to say they ain't. It's about determination, and if they have that, I say they could buy *themselves* a nice house because they achieved it."

From April to December, the custodian job provides a take-home pay of $800 and change every two weeks. Most important, it is a job that provides medical benefits for the family and a contribution to Social Security.

"Shine 'em up. Shine 'em up."

Wayne's cousin stops by. Donnell is older and works as a runner at one of the houses of finance here. Donnell says he owns a little stock himself. I want to know if you can tell from the collective attitude of the four o'clock throngs whether the market has closed up or down. Donnell has no doubt. It's 3:59 P.M.

"Anybody you see rushing for the PATH train, they had a bad day. If you see them taking their time, you see them *strolling,* you see they got just a little smile, not a big one, then you know it's been good.

"You see them running down the sidewalk doing this"—Donnell pantomimes a wild man—"then you know they had such a wonderful day they went out and had a drink."

A carefully coiffed woman walks by.

"Come on, baby. Put a smile on that face. The stock market's that bad?"

Down?

Both Wayne and Donnell solemnly agree, the Dow has closed down. A chilly wind blows up through the Wall Street canyon, takes a sharp right, and smacks us in the face.

"When it gets warmer, that's when the stock market picks up," Wayne observes.

I take it as a sign some kind of top of the market has been reached when I see that, on the very night of a live Academy Awards telecast, the entire eighth floor of the Fashion Institute of Technology in New York is filled with eager folks taking a seminar on how to pick individual stocks.

There is Vivian, a recent retiree, who started down this path when she picked up the Beardstown Ladies' investment guide during a vacation in Nantucket. There is the steel salesman whose kids just graduated from college. He is looking for something to do with the bump upward in income that comes with the end of tuition payments. Jose, a high school teacher from the Bronx, is tired of wasting money pooling cash for the New York lottery with his co-workers.

"At one time twenty of us were putting in three dollars each a week for Lotto," Jose says. "I looked at all that money and figured we could probably get a better rate of return in the stock market."

Rita, an African American homemaker and former computer programmer, is part of Jose's investment group. She says she enrolled in this course provided by the nonprofit investment club umbrella organization, the National Association of Investors Corporation (NAIC), to get her feet wet with this investment stuff. Both Jose and Rita assure me that they have other retirement savings in tax-deferred 401K plans and that their individual stock picking doesn't involve huge risk.

"This is for fun," Jose says. "For education and hopefully for making some money. It's not like we are throwing our rent money into this."

Avi, a certified public accountant and one of the seminar leaders, weighs in. "You're employed, right? You have cash reserves equal to three months' living expenses?"

Six months if you are self-employed is the traditional wisdom. It sounds like Avi is the kind of prudent soul who would not countenance taking out a cash advance on a credit card in order to invest the proceeds in the market.

I recount the story of a college student who used his credit card's cash advance to buy stocks, a strategy that is to personal finance what Dr. Jack Kevorkian is to personal fitness. Anita, another seminar leader, remarks wryly that over the past year the guy's credit card strategy might have worked, even at the ridiculous rates that card companies charge for cash advances. Maybe he was paying 20 percent for that money, but the market's been up around 22 percent.

"So maybe crazy he's not," Anita says.

"*If* he bought the right stuff," Avi warns.

Of course, once he paid the commission to his broker, he might have discovered that he made absolutely nothing, and a bland passbook savings account could start to look a lot sweeter than his credit card play.

Most of the evening's session is devoted to analyzing the performance of the pharmaceutical company Pfizer. We plot. We check graphs of profits. Price-to-earnings ratios. We analyze trends. The great quest is to find techniques to help figure out what a stock is worth, its valuation, and to consider buying it if its prospects seem better than the price the market has currently set for it.

The numbers are comforting. They provide a framework so that the decision whether to buy or sell is based on objective criteria and becomes defensible before the group. The technique brings a sense of control. But does the NAIC's precise approach really allow an investor to foretell the future? Probably not. But as long as one's real portfolio is well managed, this is a less expensive hobby than, say, boating. And the process can give the small investor the vocabulary and skills needed to ask tough questions of brokers or administrators of retirement plans back at the office. These analytical skills can help temper counterproductive emotions, the ones that can sneak up late on a Thursday night when the all-news cable channel is talking of trouble in Asia, you start to feel your entire investment strategy is unraveling, and thoughts become dominated by an ill-considered impulse to sell. There is some very useful personal finance education going on at an investment club like this.

And the investment clubs do tend to stay firmly within the universe of stocks. It is about shares, not about boring bonds or the tedious money market. The clubs do talk about "asset allocation," slicing the investment pie into different chunks to spread risk in case any one of the slices goes bad. In the club context, asset allocation often means putting a quarter of the money into small companies, a quarter into large ones, and the rest into medium-sized firms. What is not generally discussed is asset allocation in the larger sense, the mix of bonds, money market funds, stock mutual funds, or real estate that can be part of a club member's overall investment picture. Look wider still, and asset allocation can include categories for money invested in one's education, on consuming, on charity.

But I am left wondering about the opportunity cost of this investment hobby. As it was, we were missing the host's opening monologue at the Academy Awards. And what does this kind of hobby do to you? On the way over in the car I heard the Rolling Stones' classic "Shattered" on the car radio and could swear Mick was singing, "The prime rate is going up, up, up, up, UP!" It used to be "The CRIME rate is going up, up . . ." This quest is starting to get to me.

As the investment club folks head for the exits, I hear a voice in the crowd asking if there is a way to use any of the course materials to predict which film will win the award for best picture. Absurd? Hollywood execs will tell you an Oscar is all about boosting the price-to-earnings ratio.

The Beekeeper's Tale

It is Maundy Thursday and the first order of business is to rendezvous with my guide and chaperon for the day, economist Gary Shilling. Shilling is a former Merrill Lynch man and one of the most emphatic bears in the business. If you have a lot of money that needs professional management and you are of a mind that what goes up also goes down, Gary is your guy. The long bull market has given Shilling pause from time to time, but it is undeniable that he has made some remarkable predictions: during the 1970s, for instance, when people were walking around with Whip Inflation Now buttons and thirty-year mortgage rates were in the double digits, Shilling was the lone voice talking of a time of disinflation to come. He was right. He was so right in his overall strategy that in one recent year the money under his care brought in a triple-digit return. In that year *The Wall Street Journal* anointed Gary as the top forecaster in their annual survey. He is tall, very thin, bald of pate, and in some lights looks for all the world like an early Puritan, sans buckled shoes. Spot him in his late-twentieth-century business dress, and your first guess would be investment banker.

But Shilling's upright, severe bearing and nasal, country club voice do mask a rather dramatic iconoclasm. For starters, Shilling isn't much of a golfer. Instead, he keeps bees. He drives a nine-year-old Lincoln Town Car that his children call the Barge. And he is a fierce do-it-yourselfer, from plumbing to yard work. When he first moved to his affluent suburban neighborhood in New Jersey, a woman spotted him in his work clothes and asked how much he was paid for mowing the lawn. He is said to have replied, "Well, the pay isn't too good, but I get to sleep with the lady of the house."

Dr. Shilling has publicly articulated his worries about how sophisticated small investors will fare when they are faced with a sharp market downturn. He has continued to say this right into the teeth of a market that from 1991 throughout much of the following decade has never seemed to quit. He is also very quick to barbecue Wall Street's sacred cows.

There is a plaque at one of the Broad Street entrances to the New York Stock Exchange that begins: "This marketplace for the purchase and sale of securities was formed in 1792 by merchants who met daily beneath a buttonwood tree that grew nearby."

"Do you know what they were talking about under that buttonwood tree on that fateful day, my boy?" Shilling asks with a twinkle in his eye. "Setting fixed commissions." In *The Wealth of Nations*, Adam Smith discusses how lotteries are always games of negative expectations of the sort that Anthony Curtis, the gambler turned publisher, avoids. "The World neither ever saw, nor ever will see, a perfectly fair lottery; or one in which the whole gain compensated the whole loss; because the undertaker could make nothing of it." Smith thought lotteries unfair because of the commissions taken out by those who run them. I know of a poker game at which the person hosting the game each week would take 5 percent of every pot to cover beer, pretzels, and general wear-and-tear on the facilities. At the end of the night, the host's "commission" would always be bigger than the winnings of any of the players. There is a lesson here for investors. That is where some real money is being made—middlemen and middlewomen taking a piece of the action.

Passing through security at the World Trade Center with Shilling is an elaborate process. It is like trying to make sure that everyone who comes into work in a city the size of Harrisburg, Pennsylvania, has a valid ID badge. Gary and I are on our way to have sandwiches with a managed futures man at Dean Witter. Managed futures are derivatives, a word with all sorts of pejorative and mysterious associations. Orange County, California, got into derivatives and went from being one of the richest municipalities to bankrupt within weeks. The word "derivatives" isn't much use anyway. Its formal meaning is a tautology, "a financial instrument derived from another financial instrument." In practice, derivatives are what you use to get fancy with your investments, the kind of thing that if the strategy pays off, people think you are a financial genius, and when you crash and burn, your significant other will quote Jay Leno's famous line to actor Hugh Grant and say, "*What* were you thinking?"

Over here at Dean Witter, the idea is that there are some forms of intricate neurosurgery best left to the professionals. The thing about futures markets is that you can use a little cash to control a lot of money; for $2,000 you might have the option to control your own $35,000 platinum contract. But futures contracts can be gnarly things if you don't have deep pockets. With stocks, the worst that can happen is that you lose the entire value of your investment; with futures and other derivatives, you can lose a lot more than your investment.

"The good news if you trade futures on your own is that you've lost all your money," Mark Hawley says. "The bad news is that you owe more."

This is not the kind of place where I would want to wing it with a surplus. But if you are *sure* that gold is going down or that the U.S. dollar is destined to spike upward against the German mark, you should be allowed to set up a position so that you will profit if events go your way. That's where *managed* futures come in. Just don't say you are betting on gold or the dollar.

"I never use the betting scenario in any investments," Hawley says. "I hire disciplined money managers who use risk allocation units."

So it is not betting. Is it playing a hunch? Hawley winces.

"Yes, I know, the perception is 'Get a hunch, bet a bunch.' But I hire professionals."

The time comes to leave the corporate paradise far up one of the World Trade Center towers and hit the pits.

Gary and I push the down button on the elevator and descend into hell. In television news, reporters are always being admonished to write to the pictures. In the trading pits of the New York Mercantile Exchange, this passage from Dante would sync just about right with what I am watching in the heating oil futures pit:

There sighs, lamentations and loud wailings resounded through
the starless air, so that at first it made me weep; strange tongues,
horrible language, words of pain, tones of anger, voices loud and

hoarse, and with these the sound of hands, made a tumult which is whirling through that air forever dark, as sand eddies in a whirl-wind.

The Divine Comedy, Inferno, canto I, l.22

Some of the traders seem human, if tormented. Others have the loutish intensity of English soccer fans. It is the same look you see if you turn from the dog track and look back into the crowd: this moment means *everything,* and winning is *everything.*

Not all the trading pits are crowded and loud. As we walk past the tiny platinum session, a handful of traders are sitting around what looks like the craps tables I saw in Vegas. A handful of traders stand in a circle around a small enclosure with a net in the center to catch order tickets.

Computers today could do this trading, and many financial markets, including the London Stock Exchange, have gone totally electronic. Their floors are quiet and orderly. Some investors believe electronic trading is more efficient and less costly than open outcry systems. But what open outcry gives you is the momentum, the feel for what the market is doing. Many traders like reading the buzz of the trading floor.

The principle is this: You might pay less if you walk into a flea market and the place is empty. But if the place is crowded and everyone is snapping up deals, you figure the prices are good, the supply is short, and you might be more willing to pay a premium. This is why the New York Stock Exchange, the Chicago Board of Trade, and this commodity exchange insist that humans still produce the best deal. As we are walking through the cramped, frenetic pathways along the floor of the Merc, I look up and see a familiar indicator: the Dow Jones Industrial Average is again down 1 percent.

As the afternoon wears on, Gary Shilling and I have the conversation a father and son might have while off on a fishing trip. If only this talk had taken place years earlier, I might have been able to confront a surplus with much greater aplomb.

I try out the theory I learned from Ed Thorp, inventor of card counting in blackjack turned hedge fund manager. He said that unless I was rich enough to get into one of his fancy hedge funds, I should stick my money in an index and, essentially, forget about it for several decades. An index fund is a fund run by computer. It mimics an index such as the S&P 500. If that index goes up 12 percent in a year, the index, which owns the stocks in the S&P 500, also goes up. Fees should be lower because there is no expensive, highly trained, active portfolio manager in command. The approach is not sexy, but it seems to get the job done: index funds have beat a lot of the active managers at their own game. Shilling, however, is skeptical. He thinks the interest in index funds is a sign of the overconfidence that could mean the stock market has reached saturation.

"When people get the feeling that things are so good that the stock market is going up forever, on autopilot, so that they say, 'Let me just buy the whole market,' that tells me there's overconfidence. That is the death knell."

But long term the indices have a good track record, I argue.

Shilling is not persuaded there really are all that many long-term investors. He says many of us may be what the pros disparagingly call "odd-lotters." They are typically small investors who trade in less than one hundred shares, primarily because they don't have the capital to buy more. They tend to react emotionally and often sell their shares at the bottom of a stock market sell-off, at the very point when they should be getting back in.

During several big stock market drops in the late 1990s, however, it was many professionals who ran scared and the individual investors who saw the buying opportunities that lifted the market from the abyss. In other words, thank goodness for the odd-lotters.

Shilling remains worried about the day individual investors do lose nerve. He says there is an old saying on the street about how a long-term investor is really a short-term investor whose position went against him. The idea is that the fool is hoping time will put right his or her mistake. This is one key way daytraders often go wrong. Hoping that time will heal their mistake, they are tempted to violate the cardinal rule that implores them to sell as soon as a stock starts to lose money.

"Everyone says they are going to stick it out," Shilling observes. "You make assumptions about your own reactions that you have no basis for because you have never been in that situation before."

This is one of the reasons many folks pay the full freight, the higher commissions that come with having their very own stockbroker. David Johnson, the Texas broker who accompanied me to the track, says a big part of his job description is spending time calming people down, blunting knee-jerk reactions by clients to sell at what is often precisely the wrong time, during one of those market troughs when business television is full of tense faces. Johnson also spends a lot of time talking people out of acting on stock tips they may have thought they overheard on a crossed cellular phone line, including the guy whose dog signaled him to buy certain stocks by wagging its tail.

A very skilled broker like Johnson may also take a holistic approach, working with a client's entire financial picture and life goals. But the chance of tracking down one of these brokers-cum-financial-advisers is not good. It is probably about as likely as finding a doctor who will listen carefully to your whole life story and medical history. It can take a good-sized surplus to attract their attention.

Gary Shilling pauses to call the office to order some midcourse corrections in the portfolio he is running. He is taking a short position, one that will make money if the security in question falls in value. As I watch him take care of business, two contradictory thoughts begin playing out in my head. On the one hand, the stock market over the long haul grows about 10 percent a year, on average. If the time line is shorter and the porfolio consists of something less than all stocks, as all portfolios do, there are no guarantees. The advertisements mean it when they say past performance is no guarantee of future return.

Gary is on the phone asking his assistant to set up another position to profit if the thirty-year bond drops. It is minute-to-minute stuff, a delicate undertaking, a bit like flying an airplane by remote control. The fellow back at the office has to keep his eye glued to the news wires, ready to hit the eject button if anything shows up suggesting weakness in the economy. Weakness would mean less chance of inflation and the bonds could rise, wrecking the strategy. How are the Dow, S&P 500, and Nasdaq composite? I ask.

"Slipping, my boy, slipping." The Dow is down more than 1.5 percent now.

Shilling puts down the phone in a more philosophical mood.

He talks of the time when he made a living exclusively as a forecaster and the great economic calls he made. He says forecasting is a hard way to live. Either your peers forget about your successes or they put them down to luck. A stopped clock is always right twice a day is their logic. But managing money for clients and himself is a very different beast.

One's wealth, Shilling says, speaks for itself because money is the way society keeps score. You need recognition, and if you make money, no one can deny your effectiveness.

"You may have done some things that deserve recognition in other areas, but there is no guarantee the world is ever going to know it. But if you make money, no segment of society, except some fellow in a Vermont commune, is going to do anything but have a reverence, an appreciation, for that."

This is a tough game and not confined just to Wall Street. You see it in Hollywood and many other places. But I am not persuaded I have to buy into the logic. It's a funny thing, Dr. Shilling's and my disagreement on this point. We both want in our own ways to improve an imperfect world. And I know him to be a caring, generous man who puts his money where his mouth is, through a number of charitable foundations in which he is involved hands-on. Maybe it is just that in my business, all we have is talk. In the financial world, talk is cheap.

Shilling is also very involved in his church and has created a program to improve the quality of Sunday preaching. It is through this connection that Gary is able to introduce me to one of the most fascinating figures on Wall Street, Dan Matthews.

The Parson's Tale

The Reverend Dan Matthews runs the Episcopal church that presides over the high end of Wall Street. As rector of Trinity Church, Matthews does not just have to minister to the spiritual needs in a neighborhood more preoccupied than most with issues of Mammon. He also runs a big Manhattan real estate enterprise. Trinity Church is fabulously rich.

In 1697 King William III of England gave Trinity Church its charter and a parcel of land to build on. He set the church's rent at a peppercorn a year. Its great windfall came in 1705 when Queen Anne bestowed a chunk of Manhattan Island to the parish without raising the church's annual rent. It wasn't just the land. The parish also got rights in perpetuity to all beached whales and unclaimed shipwrecks at the water's edge of these property lines.

The blubber and salvage biz hasn't been too profitable for Trinity parish. But the real estate business has. The church owns about six million square feet of commercial real estate on the Lower West Side, making it one of the city's top landlords. What has been sold off has been turned into an endowment on a scale that would make many private colleges weep with envy. What property remains is managed by Rev. Matthews's staff as a market-driven business. How does "CEO" and "man of the cloth" fit under one roof?

The Reverend's office is behind the church, to the left of the American Stock Exchange on Trinity Place. The room is spacious and spare. But it's the reception area just before you enter the office that offers the View. We are up more than twenty stories in a hushed, carpeted room with a spiral of wrought-iron railing leading to a set of stairs that descends from the middle of the room. A pair of gothic windows dominates the room, windows with panes arranged to resemble a pair of crosses. A blast of spring sunlight is projecting the shadow of those crosses across a couch and a rug. Stand in the beam of light and you see it: Trinity's spire lining up perfectly, so that Wall Street projects outward to a vanishing point directly behind it. From this elevation something else becomes clear: the big Wall Street buildings are much taller and more massive than the church. If a medieval architect had proposed to dwarf a cathedral like this in a European city, he would have been burned at the stake.

In walks a gray-haired, square man with shining eyes.

"Ver-ry *good* to *meet* YOU!"

He's a preacher, all right. The extra effort to make every syllable count must have been born of years of trying to communicate in churches with lousy acoustics. Rev. Dan Matthews sends out a beam of passionate charm and wit that reminds me immediately of the larger-than-life chairman of the board of Southwest Airlines, Herb Kelleher, but without the smoking or the swearing. Matthews's first thought has both "Peter Drucker" and "mystery of life" in it. I've come to the right place.

Matthews is not a Marxist and quickly sets out his emphatic view that money is not at the root of it all, the goal, the guiding principle. Figuring I'm sitting there thinking, "Oh, that's just what a man of the cloth would say," his first example is not religious. He mentions World War II, when the idea of making a lot of money was suppressed in favor of patriotism or fighting the evil of Nazism. Money is an enabler, he says. It is a tool for a higher purpose, education, security, and the Reverend suggests, the chance to be on a spiritual journey. Discussions like these got Matthews into trouble forty years ago at the Amos Tuck School at Dartmouth, where he had received a generous scholarship. He found himself in the middle of a set of students who were among the brightest in the country, an extremely sharp bunch who would turn into high-powered business types, he just knew it.

"We would sit around talking just about money and the dreams they had for success and their specific job orientations. And I sat there missing my old undergraduate debates about is there life after death, is it valid to kill using the electric chair, is sex outside marriage ever permissible, the sort of things kids talk about late into the night."

So Matthews went to a dean he remembers very fondly and complained that the students ought to be thinking more about their responsibilities as whole human beings and to think bigger thoughts about what it is like to be a contributing person to a culture that is leading the world. And the dean looked at Matthews and shook his head with a mixture of pity and admiration and said, "Oh, this young man will never break $15,500 a year." Fifteen-five in the early 1950s was a fine annual salary, but not rich. Forty years later Matthews is now hoping fervently that the zeitgeist is changing and that people will increasingly understand that answering "To make money" to the question "Why are you here?" is no answer at all.

"When I have a vision for my life, money is then a tool to make the vision a reality. If I have no vision for my life, then money is in fact the only way I can gauge my worth."

This statement is rather like an analogy another clergyman once offered me when this subject was on the table: money is like sex. Sex has the seductive power to persuade that it's an end in itself. But if sex is a part of total surrender and love, the combination can give life meaning. If you can't figure out that sex is supposed to connect with love, then you end up like a wretch wasting money at a peep show.

"Sex, like money, captures you and makes you believe it is the purpose. Or it frees you to discover the purpose," the minister had said.

I weigh the possibility of feeding this analogy into our conversation and Matthews gives the impression of a man earthy enough to embrace it. He is a married Episcopal minister after all, not a celibate. But then I look over to my friend Gary, who happens to be holding his face at this moment like a man who is about to deny someone a mortgage, and I lose nerve.

"But isn't money just our way of keeping score?" Gary asks.

Shilling, who has done better than most according to this measure, says he is not defending this kind of score keeping but stating one of the realities of the world as he sees it. Matthews agrees that, yes, if one says the purpose of money is to evaluate the worth of a product or service, money is a good measure. A hotel that does well by its customers should be making more money than one that treats them shabbily.

"But is my real value as a human so intrinsically connected to money that I have no self-worth if I ain't got any?" Matthews asks. "I'm challenging that."

Shilling wonders if money can ever be an end itself. Money to make money seldom succeeds, he says, and what works is to make money by providing a product or service that someone needs. The Reverend isn't so sure.

"Look at the street we are on," he says. "This is greed alley."

We hear the story of the young man from a working-class background who sat next to Matthews at a dinner, an apparently bright guy who could have gone into medicine or law to help people. What Matthews heard was a kid who only wanted to go to the place where he could make the most money. Imagine what he would have said if he hadn't been sitting next to a guy with a priest's collar on, Matthews wonders.

We are having the debate Matthews was denied in business school, and I am certainly game. If money is so seductive, why not bow out? Why devote so much of our lives to careers, such as business reporting, asset management, or running a parish on Wall Street, that force us to confront money at every turn?

"I'm not in the camp that says money is dangerous," Matthews says. "Money's fine. Plenty of it is fine. Give it away, get it out there, circulate it, spend it, do *good* with it. And it doesn't hurt to pay somebody well."

The Reverend is forced constantly to reflect on this last one. His salary, he says, is an ongoing source of embarrassment, and not the kind of embarrassment most members of the clergy suffer. He's talking high, not low.

"Nobody comes near my salary in the whole diocese; there's no one near in the whole nation. It's something I have to carry with me. It's not a lot in comparison with these guys," Matthews points out the window straight down Wall Street, "but it's still an embarrassing situation. I have to think through all the time how I'm journeying with my own—I don't have wealth—*alleged* wealth in relation to a guy running a small church in rural Nevada."

And if accumulating this kind of surplus is not the goal, what is? It is using his professional skills to encourage a high rate of return for the parish so it can give amazing amounts away.

Last night Matthews, his vestry, or board, and his management team put the finishing touches on 425 homes the church has built in a part of the South Bronx where conventional real estate developers and bankers fear to tread. Four hundred twenty-five families will get low-cost housing, and the transactions have generated another $800,000 for the church, which has just decided to use that as seed money for the construction of 250 more houses.

"It's what we are here for, to do good. And where did that money come from? Well, across the street there. Do we analyze carefully where every single cent came from? No. We should, but no."

It turns out that while Trinity parish manages its own real estate portfolio, it does not manage the investment portfolio of its endowment. That duty is ceded to an investment house. The Reverend says he trusts the investment people will keep the church's money out of anything that will embarrass them, such as gaming stocks. But the church does not formally have a portfolio screened for so-called socially responsible factors.

Matthews explains that he has twenty-two people on his board who are all experts in the markets. Conservatives, liberals, women, people of color, white guys. He says opening up this kind of discussion would be painful and probably counterproductive.

"We would spend most of our time arguing about this and not how we are going to help the poor. As it is, we have already gotten into knock-down drag-outs about how much of our portfolio is going into Japan or what the right portion of small-capitalization companies is. So now we let the investment company decide."

In contrast, he says he finds it much easier for him and his wife to talk about allocating their family's investment toward women's causes or whatever their personal priority is.

Gary Shilling believes it is a fiduciary responsibility thing and suggests that socially responsible investments historically underperform the market. Dan Matthews doesn't want to challenge a man with a doctorate in these matters but recalls that at his old church in Atlanta, the manager of a socially responsible investment fund would appear every year and demonstrate how his screened fund consistently outperformed the church's actual fund. But he was never able to get his vestry to go along with it.

If the actual makeup of a church's investment portfolio is such a terribly thorny issue, the other side of Trinity Church's operation is embraced with much more singleness of purpose. The real estate company is a company, not a charity. It is very straight, Matthews says, market driven in every sense of those words. Its business and performance are based on the performance of the rest of the industry.

"They don't give away space. If Trinity allows a year rent-free to a customer, it is because the market demands it."

Eviction notices, the whole shebang?

"If the market demands eviction notices, then so be it."

Ironically, the church itself failed to pay its rent to the English crown for more than two centuries. When Queen Elizabeth visited the church in 1976, she was presented with 279 peppercorns, the outstanding rent. Matthews recently flew to London to pay her another two dozen peppercorns, packed in a red velvet box. He wanted to square things with the monarchy before the celebration of Trinity's three hundredth anniversary.

Matthews demands honesty from his company. He says it doesn't lie and it doesn't cheat. Square footage is square footage, and the dimensions of a masonry office building won't mysteriously change, as can happen in New York's cutthroat real estate environment.

"This is a funny, schizophrenic organization. On the one side, we are as hardnosed and as market driven as possible. On the other side, we are as generous as we can be and we give away every single penny."

These are the sorts of contradictions that arise from attempts at rational discussion about money. The Reverend's overall point is that there is a whole world of truth that is not understood rationally.

"Money is the rational world that can help us open our eyes," Matthews says. "It's like sex."

I freeze. Gary seems unfazed.

"Sex is rational. But not *love*. Would you die for a child? In a *second*. Would I die for my money? Never. Once you start questioning money, you start understanding that there's something beyond." I have returned to the point made to me by the avuncular and socially responsible Jack Brill in the Rockies. The smarter one gets about money, the more the ambiguities and inconsistencies do not go away. Nor do you learn to live with them. You learn to recognize them.

It is late afternoon back in a borrowed office at the World Trade Center. Gary is on the phone shorting another bunch of bonds. The Dow is down 1.7 percent. My fatalism, on this day at least, is proving correct. Perhaps I should take up short selling.

But there is one last question for Shilling before getting back to the New York Stock Exchange to see how it all ends. Where do I put a surplus today, right now? He looks at me and considers the question carefully. It is shaping up to be the longest peacetime expansion of the twentieth century, he observes. It must be the end of the business cycle, if not now, then soon, says the forecaster.

"If you have new money, this is probably not the right time to invest," he counsels. He is telling me to keep it in cash, that is to say, a money market fund earning hardly any interest but as safe and as liquid as can be. After all this, I'm being advised to keep it in something only a notch slicker than a passbook savings account, at least for now. I'll never be able to face the folks at *Money* magazine.

Shilling's bearishness is not enough to scare me out of the stock market. I put hundreds of dollars in this month, as I do each and every month. This would prove, during the course of my adventures, to be a smart habit. But Gary's reminders that trees don't grow to the sky, that there are upper limits, does serve as an antidote to the pervasive tenor of the times that begs me to put every penny I have in stocks and do my utmost to trade as early and as often as possible in an effort to outwit the market. It is becoming clearer that the only way to "outwit" the market is to ignore all the drama and stay cool amid the hullabaloo. In an interview I once conducted with Microsoft CEO Bill Gates, the richest man in the world mentioned that his friend Warren Buffett, the legendary investor, has no use for computers and the Internet, except to connect with his sister for games of bridge in cyberspace. Buffett has done very well ignoring the noise. I got this message in even more blunt form on this trip during a visit to one of New York's exalted investment houses.

The Chief's Tale

The chairman of Bear Stearns does not have a touchy-feely reputation, but he is known for his deep understanding of the ways of investing. When I mentioned Alan "Ace" Greenberg's name to an old Wall Street hand, he smiled and said that I was sure to enjoy my visit.

"Ace," he said, "is the sort of fellow who eats nuts and bolts for breakfast and heartier fare for lunch."

The man who welcomed me in his office that opened onto the Bear Stearns electronic trading room in midtown Manhattan was charming, and his advice to Mr. Small Investor here was breathtakingly succinct: stick the money in a stock mutual fund.

Which one?

"A good one, one with a good reputation."

Nothing fancy, such as one of those funds that invests in a specific country or a specific sector like metal or gold.

"It's crazy."

Not individual stocks?

"No, the commissions on the trades are too much. The small investor ends up losing big."

Index funds?

"If the market goes up you win; if it goes down you lose."

What about something besides stocks?

"Bonds are ridiculous. The best you can do is break even."

I was getting the answers I sought, but I tried to connect a little more with Mr. Greenberg. I told him the story of a visit to my office by another man who knows his way around Wall Street, Treasury Secretary Robert Rubin. I recounted Rubin's exhortation to stay away from short-term thinking. Does the Treasury Secretary pay attention to what the Dow Jones Industrial Average does every day, I had asked. No, Rubin replied, and I shouldn't either. Should I stop reporting the Dow's daily rises and falls and maybe catch up with it quarterly or even annually?

"Sure," Rubin replied, deadpan. "And you would be doing your listeners a favor."

What did Mr. Greenberg think? Do media guys like me contribute to short-term thinking? Should I shut up with the Dow, already, like the Treasury Secretary said?

"Silly statement."

Was it?

"Tell him I said so."

I was glad Mr. Greenberg wasn't my doctor. ("Bypass. Quadruple. Tomorrow.") But I greatly appreciated his directness.

Still, Treasury Secretary Rubin may have been on to something, and further research during the New York visit yielded some information about investing that was so explosive, it had the potential to bring down the entire system as we know it. The voice of my deep throat source on this at a big New York–based personal finance publication had gotten tense when the subject turned to this and was suddenly full of whispered "I thought we agreed we'd never discuss this on the phone/I'd tell you, but then I'd have to kill you" kind of stuff. I was persistent, but when I finally learned the truth, I wished I had not been. The source would only point me to a cryptic citation in a decade-old academic journal.

I managed to track down volume 53, number 3, of the *Journal of Personality and Social Psychology* in the fourth subbasement of a university library. With trembling hands I turned to page 490, fully expecting to find the article razored out. It was by a Harvard social psychologist, Paul B. Andreassen, and its title, "On the Social Psychology of the Stock Market: Aggregate Attributional Effects and the Regressiveness of Prediction," failed to fully capture the powder-keg nature of its findings. Professor Andreassen had tested human subjects on mock stock portfolios, giving some of the group bits of good or bad news about the companies in question. Another group of test subjects were given no news as they traded. My heart stopped. There was the abominable conclusion, in black and white: Investors who listen, watch, or read business news make less money than those who don't. The more you know, the worse you do. This would ruin it for everybody. This had to be suppressed. I resolved then and there to keep my mouth shut on this particular point.

Somebody says, "My boy."

It is Shilling, trying to tell me the Dow is falling further. Sitting with the venerable forecaster on a nervous market day, things seem more complicated. Resisting the temptation to "time" the markets, despite all I have learned, remains very hard work. How long term is my stomach, really? Against all advice I am starting to care about which way the market is going, the way a Superbowl match between two teams you normally could not care less about inevitably gets you rooting for one side or another.

My contact at the NYSE can get me back in, but not all the way. It is the last hour of trading, and to get a visitor onto the floor during the first and last hour of trading almost needs a special dispensation from the pope. Ever since Yippies in the sixties stopped trading by tossing dollars from the gallery onto the floor, the exchange has been a little testy about just who gets to visit and when. I am allowed to stand where I can see at least some of the action, and what I can see is not pretty. The Dow continues drifting down . . . minus 2.7 percent, 2.9 percent, 3 percent. In raw points this looks impressive, but in percentage terms it does not hold a candle to Black Monday in October 1987, when the Dow fell 23 percent. But for reasons of both conditioning and tradition, a fall of several hundred points still makes people nervous, both the professionals and the amateurs. Rational percentages aside, losing hundreds of points on the last trading day before a long Easter weekend is bound to unnerve investors.

I have the impulse to continue rubbernecking as the carnage goes on, but too much is at stake, and I leave the building just in case I am somehow responsible for any of this. I walk back onto Broad Street, hoping that a little distance between me and ground zero will break the jinx. I pace outside as the trading day approaches the final bell.

Four P.M. A great metal folding door clatters open, and a stream of brokers and runners tumbles directly from the floor onto the sidewalk. I call out to a woman wearing a broker's vest.

"What happened?"

"A little bounce at the end," she shouts back.

The Dow has closed down 2 percent. A clutch of the NYSE folk mill around the sidewalk, smoking, pacing, not talking, like a troupe of actors winding down backstage after a performance. One man is holding a half-eaten sandwich supported by a copy of Sun Tzu's *The Art of War.*

The parson said that money is a means, not an end. The same applies to the markets. There is a television ad for an on-line brokerage that has a charming woman clad in black lingerie lying in bed showing rather more enthusiasm for her laptop computer connected to the markets than for her bemused husband. The stock market is an effective way to grow a surplus, but I am not going to adopt it as a lifestyle, am I? Perhaps I already have and that needs to change. I cannot let the pilgrimage end here.

The Boatman's Tale

Silly me. Somehow I have completely forgotten this is Mayor Giuliani's New York, where—with apologies to Mr. Keillor—all the homeless are housed, all the sidewalks are clean, and all the criminals are above average. Even though night has fallen, it is not Gotham City anymore. So why am I walking toward the Port Authority Bus Terminal with such trepidation?

I have bad memories of that bus terminal. I once found myself stuck in a traffic circle in Ghana during a firefight between flatbed trucks full of soldiers on opposing sides of a coup d'etat and was still not as anxious as I get at the Port Authority Bus Terminal. The place is all about street smarts and survival, and the Fellini-esque characters there can detect the scent of hayseed on a passing traveler down to a few parts per billion. As a budding adolescent, I was accosted by a Hari Krishna at this bus terminal and pressured into buying, with my last twelve dollars, some wretched record album with "Avatar" in the title. I knew then that I had flunked my rite of passage, and I remain to this day, at some level, perturbed.

I am on my way to meet Delcy and Delcy's Uncle Mike, and the bus terminal is the meeting point. Delcy is a performance artist, a vegan, and an investment analyst in Woodstock, New York. She is a marauder for the use of capital to fix a very unjust world and finds no conflict between her fierce social activism and her ability to effortlessly catch the ENE (Enron) symbol flying by on a crawling stock ticker while engaged in a completely different conversation. I met Delcy at the socially responsible investment conference in Wyoming, and she said that whatever I do, I must meet her Uncle Mike, a man with some insight into the origins of how humans cope with a surplus.

Adjacent to the bus terminal is another world entirely. Inside a plate-glass storefront are wooden benches, woodworking tools, sawdust, and about a dozen handcrafted rowboats. Oddly, nothing is for sale. This is the temporary headquarters of Floating the Apple, an outfit that has very little to do with profit. The idea is to allow people to walk in off the street to lend a hand building the boats. The boats will later be used to turn the waterways surrounding Manhattan, primarily the Hudson River, into a public space. And the connection between Delcy's uncle, Dr. Michael Davis, a University of Chicago expert on the archaeology of ancient Turkey, and this free boats for New York outfit? Uncle Mike's rallying cry provides the answer:

"The Bosporus is alive with skiffs!"

What works in Istanbul could work around Manhattan.

After learning I'm good with wood, Uncle Mike gently asks if there is any way I can take a sabbatical for a summer to help kids build and float the boats. My instant reaction is to say how completely out of the question that is. My supervisors would never buy into the concept. And think of all that forfeited income across two-and-a-half months of summer. It could chew straight through a surplus.

As we sit on stools submerged in sawdust in the dimly lit space, surrounded by the looming skeletons of the partially completed boats, it occurs to me this place is a lot like one of Uncle Mike's archaeological digs. It is layered, like an ancient site. First it was a Chase Manhattan Bank branch, and an old vault is extant in the basement. Then it was a Jerry Brown presidential campaign headquarters, and some of that grooviness still hangs in the air. Later it became a trendy restaurant that failed, leaving remnants of a bar and a bright red tile floor punctuated with black. Each time the capital ran out.

But where did capital begin? That is the big question Uncle Mike is trying to answer in southeastern Turkey. He believes archaeologists have tracked down an early sign of capital from nine thousand years ago at the village of Çayönü. That's where and when humans moved from agriculture and hunting to herding cattle. Capital is not vegetarian.

Capital is wealth that builds more wealth. That's what herding goats, sheep, and cattle does. It is a way of storing up an extraordinary amount of labor. With livestock production, the more head you have, the less labor you have to put in per head. Herding encourages a future sense and opens the door to possibilities wider than just plant one seed, raise one plant. A fertile goat can produce many offspring, and growth can be, theoretically, exponential. You can, in modern-day, middle-class terms, finally get ahead.

Dr. Davis points out that in northeastern Africa, when herding people are forced from villages into cities, many show an entrepreneurial knack beyond that of their peers who are from a strictly agricultural background, where the experience of wealth-makes-wealth is not so well understood. The herders seem to have a better understanding about how to invest, how to do it to improve their political standing, and what kind of return they can expect when they spend to impress others.

Something else happens with this initial capital accumulation through herding. Uncle Mike argues that you get a much higher incentive toward rustling, thievery, raiding. Under an agricultural and hunting system, how much could you steal? Perhaps you and your nefarious pals could walk off with a week's worth of someone else's grain. But swipe a person's flock, and your loot can represent a lifetime of accumulated labor and other inputs. Uncle Mike points out the difference between the ways ranches are posted in Texas and apple orchards are posted in upstate New York. The Texas signs read, "Rustlers will be killed on sight." Stumble into an orchard in New York, and you are liable to be greeted with a wave and a smile. How much wealth in the form of apples can you really carry away?

Uncle Mike digs in his pocket and pulls out a chunk of something that represents a deep irony. It is a piece of terrazzo from an ancient public building in Çayönü. It's handcrafted, cement flooring with a white cement base welded to a layer of crushed red rock that was subsequently polished, very similar to the technique used in the modern foyers of big buildings. The point is, the public building with its fancy terrazzo comes from the Çayönü period *before* the advent of herding. Communal space and community institutions were needed when hunting was the norm so that the animals could be shared and regulated by the village. When herding began and sparked capital accumulation, the community-based civilization seems to have stopped dead. Individualism began to triumph, and wealth began to be pooled within the household, not the village. The public buildings disappeared. No more lovely terrazzo.

"Pecuniary" comes from the Latin word for cattle. "Fee" is the Old English word for cattle, property. "Cattle" and "chattel" are near synonyms, and both derive from the Latin *capitalis*, from *caput*, or "head," the origin of that fine English word "capital."

I pick up a big wooden clamp used to bind pieces of wood that are being glued together. It is a fine tool, as lovingly carved as many of the projects it is used to prepare. The sawdust from the room has left a pixie-dust coating on the hair on the back of my hands. It has an aromatic, woodsy tang, and it is seductive. I have just learned more in an hour in this room than I have in many months of shuffling to and from the office. Would it be possible to take up Uncle Mike on his offer? What would I discover if I spent a surplus some summer with Uncle Mike, his boats, and the young volunteers? That is the riskiest kind of investment, one for which the return, if any, cannot be described at all until after the fact. And it would be awfully tough to explain that, yes, I was adjourning from the rat race for the summer, and if you needed to get a message to me, you could find me next to the Port Authority Bus Terminal. It is a good thing Uncle Mike isn't pushing the hard-sell, time-sharing condo sales technique on me tonight, for I would rashly sign on the dotted line.

I would explore this theme of using a surplus to jump out of the rat race during a trip to Texas, later on my pilgrimage. But first, as a more immediate antidote to the sight of those defibrillator cabinets I witnessed at the stock exchange, I needed a dose of something more sedate, something with a much more long-term perspective. Putting a surplus into residential real estate could fit the bill.

Souvenirs

My first individual stock: a voided certificate for five shares of the Fruit of the Loom Corporation from May 1946, with the famous apple and grapes intricately engraved in blue by the Central Banknote Company.

A commitment to ignore the daily drama of the market when making my own investment decisions.

To do when I get home

Find out who owns the company that makes the portable defibrillator on the floor of the New York Stock Exchange and begin the research with a view toward an investment.

Doing the numbers

The average annual return of portfolios run by nationally affiliated local investment clubs: 13 percent. The average length of time members hold a stock: 7.2 years. (Source: The National Association of Investors Corporation)

8

Getting Real

Dying for a mortgage in
Levittown, Long Island

From the clipping file: A public works mechanic from Avondale, Louisiana, received $565,500 from the lottery, after taxes. The *Times-Picayune* quotes him saying, "We finished cooking dinner, we ate and then we left to go look for a brand new house." November 19, 1998

The progression to adulthood starts when you begin growing a beard or breasts and ends at the closing, the day the cash is released from escrow following a ritual exchange of signatures. The biggest single check many of us will ever write is the one for a down payment on a house. I own one and don't bitterly regret it. But I confess to taking delight in an expression from the Tuareg, a nomadic people from the Sahara, who like to say that "houses are the graves of the living." The question is, do you begin dying or living when you plow a nest egg into a mortgage? In the interests of fairness, I am not even going to mention the fact that "mortgage" is derived from the Latin word for death.

Still, some people have it made with real estate. I know an investigative re-

porter and screenwriter, an American, who owns a spectacular property in Tuscany. Bob's country house is wall-to-wall ancient beams and terra-cotta. Bob has a sweet barter deal going: he gives much of the Chianti grapes that grow on his land to local folks in exchange for a portion of the wine they produce with them. What a perfect place to invest a surplus. You could come visit; I would serve you some of my Chianti; and we could regale each other in person with stories of money found or fortunes lost as the fragrant Tuscan afternoon wafts by.

Tragically, my friend Bob's not selling. In lieu of this fantasy, I figure why not investigate the next best real estate alternative in—I am sure you are ahead of me on this—Levittown, New York. This Long Island community, the cradle of postwar suburbia, happens to be celebrating its fiftieth anniversary at the same time as my trip to Wall Street. I am looking for a sign about where next to consider applying a surplus, and the anniversary is it. If it makes sense to put the cash into buying a house, trading up, or paying down a mortgage in this former potato field, then it will make sense anywhere.

As I venture east along the Long Island Expressway, the radio comes to rest on a familiar frequency, 1130 AM, the old dial position of WNEW, a dapper station that for decades wrapped the eastern seaboard in a warm, velvety blanket of Sinatra and Mel Torme. Now, as the century draws to a close, things at 1130 are a lot more urgent, with radio business news pouring out the speaker with the metered precision of a ticker tape machine. Phillip Morris is up one and an eighth, the poor fellow on the radio is stuck saying. Doesn't he know there is more to life than business news? You can hear it in his voice, a man trapped in wingtips, dying for his Birkenstocks and the chance to talk about life, art, and politics. Why would anyone willfully limit himself to the business beat? I catch my eyes staring back at me in the rearview mirror and see them wince.

The businesscaster, undeterred, presses on. The yield on the benchmark thirty-year Treasury bond is up to 6.95 percent. Given the returns being advertised by the stock market this particular season, that bond yield is looking pretty sad. Flip that equation and start thinking like a borrower, not an investor, and that 6.95 percent looks like a much better deal. The money is cheap enough to draw a fellow toward a real estate loan. And what would that loan buy me? Contentment? Security? I can see the evolutionary parade, starting from the profile of an ape, ascending through Cro-Magnon, then *Homo suburbanus* depicted as the silhouette of a man and his propane-fired barbecue. I note the creeping shadow of a bad attitude casting over me as I turn off the highway onto Hempstead Turnpike, a wide boulevard interrupted by shopping strips and traffic lights. One of the bolts is missing from the official green, reflectorized Levittown sign, and it droops from its post like a withered arm. I had surmised that I would need to find a way to embrace this place, and some historical research helped. It turns out that a very wealthy man, indeed, blew his windfall here.

The problem with William K. Vanderbilt, Jr.'s windfall was that it killed people. Vanderbilt's great stroke of financial genius had occurred on his birthday, the day he was born into the right family. As the great-grandson of Cornelius, the legendary railroad tycoon, Willie K. inherited a lot of money, which he used in part to indulge his automotive proclivities. In 1904 he used a chunk of his money to pay for the creation of one of the first international car races, which wound through the existing byways of Long Island. But the Grand Prix was too successful. In the race's second year, a race car mowed through a crush of spectators, killing two. So Vanderbilt and some partners came up with $5 million—about $82 million in late-twentieth-century money—to build America's first limited-access concrete highway that could also double as a racecourse a few times a year. The Long Island Motor Parkway stretched forty-eight miles from Vanderbilt's mansion in Lake Ronkonkoma to Flushing, at the edge of New York City. The parkway used such innovations as single-radius curves so that drivers could keep their steering wheel in one position as they took a corner, innovations that would inspire the design of the great concrete limited-access interstate highways that were to come.

Tragically, Vanderbilt's motorway was not limited-access enough. In 1910 four spectators were killed, twenty-two others hurt, and racing ended here for good. But for several decades after, Vanderbilt's project remained in use as a $2 toll road and served as a model for what happens when you mix people, cars, highways, and real estate developers: suburbanization.

As it happened, Vanderbilt's road was eventually consumed by the force it helped create. Another legendary tycoon, developer William Levitt, would erect his most enduring monument, the great postwar business opportunity and social-engineering experiment called Levittown, in the very set of fields where Vanderbilt had placed his race's grandstand.

The ghostly trace of the old raceway is said to have shaped some of the contours of this town, if only I could find it. I stop to ask directions at Rock-n-Glow Bowling, but nobody seems to be home. The fellow across the way at the Jellybean convenience store never heard of no raceway. Maybe someone at the library knows, but the clerk is not clear on those coordinates. "As long as I've lived here, I don't know where nothing is," he says.

I have managed to wangle an invitation to a home in the neighboring Levitt development of Wantaugh. There will be people there who made their decision to get into real estate before I was born and whose commitment to that decision has outlived the thirty-year loan that made it possible. As I look for the address, I wonder about the range of outcomes I may have to confront. Perhaps these longtime home owners will project smugness, the kind that comes with being the one smart enough to have purchased an original David Hockney back when he was a nobody. Or perhaps their houses have turned out to be a bad idea, causing the kind of fossilized resentment you might find in someone who, for reasons long forgotten, has stuck out a bad marriage.

Clare Worthing invites me to take a seat at a board-room-size kitchen table and offers some fresh strawberries. I've materialized in the middle of what might have once been dismissively termed a coffee klatch. If that term conjures up an image of something that powerless housewives used to do to the background music of Doris Day, then the image would be only partly correct. This group did start out as an embroidery club, meeting regularly since 1964. But like a kind of bowling league, this gathering has generated a powerful output of social capital, and many of the women who have participated here ended up wielding a lot of power in what became the main forum for public life in Levittown, the school district.

Levittown isn't a distinct city—it is a subdivision—and property taxes go to the larger unit, the township of Hempstead. The one key institution controlled by the Levittowners themselves is the schools, and it is here where fault lines once erupted, between those who thought the schools were too expensive and those who wanted the best education available resources could buy. The women around Mrs. Worthing's table are all resolutely in the latter category, even though all are a generation or two past the age of having children at school. It becomes immediately clear that when you use money to buy a primary residence, it is not just the roof and the plumbing that become your responsibility. You get everything that comes with a stake in a community, and the schools are just for starters.

I grope for an icebreaker and clumsily pull out a query about the old location of Vanderbilt's raceway grandstand. The five women look as if I have asked to see Levittown's space needle or Levittown's fourteenth-century gothic cathedral. But unlike the guy over at the convenience store, these folks know exactly where the library is if I wish to pursue this further. Next to me is a lady who is such a believer in this kind of community resource that she has endowed, in her name, a Mildred Cantor room at the local library. She has worked as hard for the institution's betterment as she did for the schools. I punt on the raceway thing and plunge in with questions about what brought these folks to this area in the first place.

Mrs. Cantor moved to Levittown in February 1948, first as a renter at $60 a month, then as an owner, with no money down and a 4 percent mortgage. To qualify for special terms like these, all her husband had to do was to fight in and survive a world war.

For the Cantors there was no Hamlet-like period wandering and wondering, turning themselves inside out about whether to be or not to be home owners. Rent at their seaside place in Long Beach, New York, ran $50 a month in the winter but skyrocketed to $225 when the resort community switched to its summer pricing. Her housing costs blew up and down with the shifting winds of the seasons and temporary shifts in demand. If you qualify for a fixed mortgage, everything changes. You will pay the same each month for the next thirty years. No matter how much inflation savages prices around you over the years, that mortgage check will stay the same. The mortgage becomes a given in a world of change.

The cost of renting can change at short notice; so can the mood of your landlord. The desire to banish the power a property owner has over you must be a prime reason we buy. The landlord with his master key. The landlord who gets a divorce and gives you two weeks' notice that he's moving into your place with his new mistress. Among the most biting memories I have from childhood is the time there was a knock on the door one evening at our single-family middle-class home. It was the sheriff serving an eviction notice. My parents, as always, were paid up on the rent. But the out-of-state owner had decided she needed the house for something and didn't have the decency to call or write before sending in the storm troopers. We are willing to pay a lot to avoid that embarrassment and disruption. Ownership can take some of the risk out of one of the few givens in any household budget: shelter.

Mrs. Cantor adds that her mother-in-law was a little skeptical about Levittown when she first came to visit, with her faint praise coming out "It's nice for a summer place." What Mrs. Cantor didn't say was the bonus that one's mother-in-law, and all the demands she represented, might not follow you out to the 'burbs.

Across the table from Mrs. Cantor is another elderly woman who came armed with a life story weirdly customized to throw lighter fluid on my smoldering neuroses about using my cash to get into real estate. Ruby Richman's husband is a newsman who before the anchor of Levittown had never said no to a promotion or the suggestion of a transfer. When Ruby first visited the model homes rising up from the fields here, she saw ownership of a Levitt home as a way of taking a stand against the nomadic life, a message to her husband's employer, the Associated Press, that her family was not to be pushed around anymore. This is a key point about home ownership. It's a way to take a stand and attempt, at least, to put down roots. It's a great excuse to use when fighting a transfer or a spur to look for other work if your company tries to force your hand. The strategy doesn't always work in this increasingly mobile society, but a house can be a tangible sign that you should no longer be considered as if you were in the military. Someone needs to present very compelling reasons before you will pick up and move.

So far, so good.

There were, however, trade-offs for Ruby's family. Her husband spent many of the following years sleeping at the Levitt house by day and working a desk at the AP by night. It's hard to believe anyone would take a night shift by choice, and I cannot help but wonder if Ruby's husband's career trajectory suffered when he planted his flag on the Levittown property. Being a newsman means going where the news is, and if you won't, they find someone hungrier who will. Ruby's story has helped me to put my finger on the horror. It's that the decision to buy will flash-freeze your life right where it now stands, with all the frustrations and disappointments of one's current arrangement stuck in a hellish, perpetual loop and no ability to move on, and no ability to seek out the kinds of new disappointments and new frustrations that keep us alive. Peggy Lee's warped ballad "Is That All There Is?" starts to play in my head, and a wave of anxiety ascends from my gut to my chest.

I try to buck up my confidence by starting to recite a silent mantra: "Dan Rather is a home owner. Peter Jennings is a home owner. Tom Brokaw is a home owner." These are suppositions, but I take comfort in the idea that these guys, whose lives are presumably full of life-at-the-edge and under-fire experiences, have not been held back by their signature on a mortgage document. I also take some comfort in a profound change to the tax law that Washington has now provided. Since time immemorial, once you bought a house, you pretty much had to stay an owner. If you sold a house and failed to buy one of equal or greater value, the money you made on the sale would be hit by a red-hot poker of death known as the capital gains tax. But now Congress and the President say I can keep up to a half million dollars of the proceeds of the sale of my house without this penalty, and I can repeat the feat every few years if I so desire. Being a home owner is no longer a one-time transformation, like the one from virgin to not. The tax code is giving me wiggle room, the kind of wiggle I need in my life.

"You can always rent."

Clare, the hostess, must have been reading my thoughts as projected on my face. If the chance arose to take a fellowship in China for a year or if Jerry Springer ever went on maternity leave and they needed me as a temporary replacement host, I could rent my place out. It's possible that the rental market at a given time will be soft and might not cover the mortgage payments and upkeep on my home, but the odds are in my favor.

The only thing is, home owners can rent their property, but how come they so often don't? Clare and her husband, Jerry, checked into this motel but never checked out. They bought a Levitt house at what they thought would be a temporary step until they could afford a bigger place somewhere else on Long Island. Since 1951 they have been bolted to this spot. Six or seven times when space pressures built toward a breaking point, the family put off the move by renovating and expanding. The wood-paneled kitchen I have been looking at was fashioned out of what used to a carport. The parquet floor is brand new, the latest of hundreds of improvements that have been made to a house that is now three times its original size.

I am transfixed by the parquet floor, which Clare and Jerry lovingly laid with their own hands; the Scandinavian wood is as blonde as a freshman class at the University of Stockholm. Especially significant to me is that it replaces carpeting. The history of rental housing for me has been a long, sordid tale of bad carpeting that could not be altered because I didn't own the place. There was the lovely apartment on an island in the San Francisco Bay marred only by a woolly floor covering that produced a disorienting three-dimensional effect like the view from a helicopter over the Brazilian rain forest. There was also the long ride I took up the escalator from a deep subway station in London, lugging a carpet-cleaning rig the size of an Austin Mini Cooper so that the landlord of our rented London flat wouldn't find his gray low-pile carpet kneaded with gummy bear residue and Cheerios dust. Then there was that floor covering in our last rental the color of meat, a color that eats away at you until you crack and start seeing the term "carpet bombing" in a new light.

When we finally joined the home-owning class, that place, too, came equipped with an evil rug that mocked us by creating stains where no wine or blood was ever spilled. But now there was a difference. This was *my* house and I didn't have to put up with it. Once we saved enough for the replacement Italian tile, I was free to abuse the outgoing floor covering to my heart's content—to carve at it, deface it, even stand on the stairs and micturate on it from a great height. It was my house, and I was answerable to no one when it came to venting my rage against this accumulation of interior-decorating travesties. As it turned out, we got out the Stanley knife and cut the vile stuff into rectangles for recycling at a local crafts fair. The final insult to the carpet, I am delighted to say, is that the tattered beige doormats didn't sell.

Of course, it isn't just carpet. It is paint the color of Cheese Whiz. Toilets that bite back. Doorbells that transport you back to the 1970s, every time. If you own, you can have control over these things. It is control simply to rid yourself of someone else's bad taste or to put a nail of any size in any wall at your discretion, on impulse. If you want to erect a HAM radio antenna on the property that rivals the Eiffel Tower in its baroque majesty, you can because you own your own home. And if you already own, it is very clear what you do with a surplus. You spend it 40 percent at Home Depot, 40 percent at Home Base, and the remaining 20 percent at a variety of True Value and Ace outlets that you happen to stumble across.

The handiwork of the owners is visible throughout the Worthings' house, to the point that it's less a dwelling and more a sculpture. "Our kids know we are never leaving and the house is part of their inheritance," Clare says. "It's also part of their inheritance that they will have to dispose of all the stuff we've collected." The house is perfectly tidy, but every cranny and usable bit of wall space displays family photographs, awards, and a startlingly diverse array of framed prints, from Japanese artists to Maurice Utrillo.

"The time I realized we were never going to look anymore was when I found a gorgeous house on the water in Amityville," Clare says without any detectable wistfulness. "You could see Fire Island. It had a canal along the side, a four-car garage big enough for a boat. I loved it. Then I realized that we had just started making use of the fact that we were earning reasonable money and taking trips to Europe, things like that." Home ownership made sense to the Worthings, but the way Clare did the mental spreadsheet, using a nest egg to trade up to fancier digs would be a financial trap. I am in the presence of a veteran fellow traveler on this money trip, someone who also keeps a weather eye out for the unintended costs of spending.

"I realized that in that house, to have the freedom I have here, I would need a full-time maid," Clare explains. "Because the freedom I had here was a community that knew me, that had children of similar ages, and if something came up, they'd keep an eye on them for me." This provokes memories for all the women of the elaborate babysitting circles that kept the mothers sane in the early years of their suburban life. Some neighbors with adjacent houses even wired intercoms house to house to help mind each other's kids. Some men were part of the circle, including an FBI agent, whose occupation made him trustworthy enough to leave with little ones.

Did someone say "babysitting"?

If home ownership brings with it the possibility that I will integrate into a community to the point that babysitters are easier to come by, I am willing to pay any price. Yes, home ownership means working to keep up the mortgage. It means time getting competitive estimates for termite control and attending city council meetings now that you are a resident, not a passerby. There are PTA meetings and all the other obligations of community. But if the payoff is an earnest FBI agent next door who will watch the kids in a pinch, I am hooked. In my case, the theory worked. We bought a house, and two things happened after we got the stuff off the moving truck. Loads of unsolicited offers for home equity loans began pouring into our mailbox, and babysitters began lining up at the door, like the interview scene from Mary Poppins. As any parent will tell you, no expense is spared for a babysitter when you are in a bind. They are, in a sense, priceless. But you can use money to buy a house, connect with a community, and harvest the spinoff. The babysitters will come, trust me.

Clare's husband, Jerry, was less concerned about babysitters and more worried about the sometimes vanishing character of "real" estate when he considered using part of a nest egg to trade up. The Amityville house that got away was on a barrier beach, he says, and he worried that in another ten years the ocean might have been right under the foundation. I didn't have the heart to ask if he ever ventured back to the property to see if that actually happened.

Jerry has now retired for the second time, and his story is a little disturbing to someone like me who assumes that doing your personal finance homework is the key to a predictable future. He is an electronics engineer who groomed a successful business and retired the first time in the 1970s, when he was just forty-four, after he figured out he had earned all they would ever need. The legions of Microsoft millionaires who also aim to retire at forty-four, take note: Although he is a whiz at computers, one of the assumptions contained within his planning went awry. The way Clare tells it, he hadn't reckoned on runaway inflation in the late 1970s and early 1980s, rising prices that whipsawed the carefully crafted early retirement plan. Jerry had to return to the workforce, primarily writing energy laws for the New York legislature.

Hearing that story, my skin grows cold. I can strongly relate to Jerry. I don't know from energy law, but like the man of this house, I have the reputation of being able to fix things that break. His handiness is legendary in the Wantaugh-Levittown area. Like Jerry, I can just see myself sitting down and working out some nifty software-based system to prove that I could retire at forty-four. I don't want to hear how someone as clever as this can get blindsided by the insidious inflation variable.

Buying a house in this development, however, was a smart move financially. The original homes here were advertised in a green-and-white Levitt and Sons brochure topped by a line promising "every modern city convenience plus country comfort at down-to-earth cost—$8,490." Eighty-four hundred dollars is a steal even when you factor in inflation. It's about $62,100 in today's money. Now these houses start at in the two hundreds, which is a decent inflation-adjusted return even when you include the cost of all the improvements folks have made to their houses over the years. The government, through subsidized Veterans Administration and FHA mortgages, gave these folks in Levittown what turned out to be amazing investments. It's probably only fair: they had to fight the fascist Axis powers to reap this sweet deal.

A clock chimes from the living room. Did these people get an especially great deal, or is just that they used the passage of time to their advantage? I got out the laptop and ran a few numbers. What if that original $8,490 for a Levitt Cape Cod had been invested for fifty years at the paltry T-bond rate of today? Out of the spreadsheet came the answer: At 6.95 percent, $8,490 becomes $271,474 in fifty years, or about the current selling price of many of these Levittown houses. The government, through bonds, is offering me the same deal as the vets got in Levittown. How could this be? I thought the postwar real estate boom was an unbeatable investment. Remember, the folks who brag they bought a house for a song and sold it for a symphony never bother to tell you about the inflation rate during the period they owned the house.

It was a great deal for the Worthings, but would it be such a great deal for those of us who were not alive during the Second World War? The time of runaway property value inflation does seem to be over. Coots get to cackle, "See this castle here, with tennis courts, underground swimming pool, and circular driveway, sonny? Bought it in 1968 for $35,000." But late baby boomers and Gen X'ers are unlikely to say that. There remain some fine real estate hot spots and some icy cold spots, such as Palmdale, California, the northernmost suburb of Los Angeles that was eviscerated when the Cold War ended. Folks there tell of enormous commutes, rising crime, and mortgages much higher than houses were worth. Upside-down mortgages are an appalling trap. You can never leave because you'll never get enough money on the sale to pay back your loan. Some declared bankruptcy; others just mailed the house keys to their mortgage lenders and walked away. Even if the home owner can cut a deal with the bank to accept, say, $175,000 when he still owes $200,000, he gets hit with a horrible tax penalty. The amount of debt forgiven, in this case $25,000, is considered by the IRS to be taxable income, of all things.

My assumption in buying a house is that there has to be a compelling reason to do it other than the expectation of making a killing on rising property prices. A reason such as we really like the house because it comes with a Wolf commercial range already in place with enough BTUs to become an issue in the global warming debate. Or we like the public values of the community or the quality of the schools. The folks now sipping coffee on the pair of gray corduroy couches in the Levitt living room are aware that times have changed and, for their children, the real estate equation looks rather different from what they experienced.

One of the folks sitting with me has a son who moved with his family to a college town and was paying $2,000 a month for rent. The family knew they would stay for less than five years, but even in two years, two-grand-a-month rent works out to $48,000.

"They couldn't see throwing that amount of money away," explains the mother. The conventional wisdom is that rent is money down the drain, while a mortgage payment is an investment. Why enrich a landlord when you can build your family's equity? This is the central thesis of real estate: you have to pay to live *somewhere*.

Jerry, however, has done this calculation and says that financially, buying does not necessarily have a clearcut advantage over renting. The son who was paying about $2,000 a month in rent, if he were to pay a similar mortgage, he could buy a $300,000 house with a thirty-year loan costing 8 percent a year. His 10 percent down payment is not an expense; it goes into the equity of the house. If the house holds its value, at least that $30,000 will tread water in terms of inflation. But he won't be accumulating much equity. Only about $200 a month will go toward the cost of the house, which is $4,800 over the two years. All those interest payments are tax-deductible, the great government subsidy for either home owners or the real estate and mortgage-lending industry, depending on how you look at it. "But if you put some property taxes into the equation, some maintenance, some closing costs, you are pretty much in the same place as renting," Jerry concludes.

I have run my own numbers, and I find that even with the wee bit of equity a person builds in the early years of a mortgage, renting is initially cheaper than buying. But it's not that the decision to use some accumulated wealth to buy a house is all about nail holes and ugly rugs. The real personal finance issue is that the government believes that home owners are better citizens, and to encourage them to buy, it subsidizes loans. That is what the famed mortgage-interest tax deduction is, a subsidized loan. You cannot borrow money cheaper than a home loan, once you figure in the tax deduction on April 15. As a middle-class American, you don't get much from the federal government anymore. There are few communists to keep at bay or fallout shelters to maintain. One of the last perks for taxpayers, cheap admission to national parks, is disappearing. But the government is willing to help underwrite a house for you, and that means your savings or windfall, when used as a down payment, provides some very efficient leverage that is tough to ignore. And face it, there's nothing worse than feeling like the chump who was left out when the government handed out the last door prizes.

Stockbrokers have a metaphor they like to share with clients who are tempted to put money into paying down their mortgage instead of giving the money to them to manage in the markets. They like to say that putting money into a mortgage is like digging a hole twenty-five feet deep and stashing your money at the base of the hole in a locked chest and covering it up with dirt. You can still get your money if you are in dire need, but it is not going to be easy. You have to find a buyer and there are major transaction costs. But the difficulty of getting your hands on the wealth tied up in a house is one of its major attributes. It's there if you really need it, but it doesn't tempt the way piling bricks of gold bullion in your living room might. Bankers have found a way around this.

There is another personal finance reason to own a home. You become eligible for home equity loans, or second mortgages, as they are often labeled. I may be lucky enough to be debt averse, but lots of people rather enjoy the cheap money that a second mortgage brings. And the thing is, much of our consumer economy is based on the assumption that folks will own a home and lubricate their liquidity with a home equity loan. Money manager Gary Shilling spotted someone driving by in a Ford Steroid sport-ute with its $42,000 sticker still exposing itself from a side window. "They're buying those with home equity loans, my boy," Shilling observed, shaking his head with resignation. He calls them "fifteen-year car loans." Eight years from now, when that four-by-four is headed for the compactor, someone is still going to have seven years left on the loan to pay off. It's easy to criticize. But it is a different story altogether when a home purchase later permits a home equity loan that helps pay for something worthy and long-lasting, such as medical care or a kid's higher education.

I strike out along the Hempstead Turnpike looking for Hofstra University, on my way to see Barbara Kelly, a history professor who has written extensively about Levittown. When I get to her office, she is dying to tell me her horror story about real estate. A few decades ago Kelly bought her first house in East Babylon, New York, and she recognized that one of the first things you do as a new suburban home owner is to attend a

Tupperware party to get to know people. It was her first Tupperware party, and once she got through the door, she says she felt like she had earned her Red Badge of Courage. Kelly had read in the paper that morning that this community was going to vote on a new library.

"But did you read what the new taxes will be?" one of Kelly's new neighbors said.

An extra ten dollars a year.

"For ten dollars a year, you could *buy* a book," replied the neighbor.

"I almost died," Kelly says. The library was voted down.

Does buying a house do this to you, I wanted to know? Dr. Kelly says it depends in part on the community's design. In the case of Levittown, the design reinforced what were seen as traditional values.

"Levitt's houses supported a particular notion of a normal American family and is less comfortable with alternative lifestyles," Kelly says. "The Cape Cod has a master bedroom. What does that say? Obviously, the master sleeps in the bedroom. In a normal, nuclear family that's okay because the master and the mistress sleep together and the little bedroom is left for the children, who are clearly inferiors. But what happens if two equals move in? A gay couple, for instance?" And it only works when the traditional, nuclear family is young. When the family grows older, there is pressure from working-age children who might like to live near the parents or from grandparents who may need to be cared for in an apartment nearby, but the rules on subletting and the division of properties into lower-cost duplexes are strict. A decade earlier the bishop of the Roman Catholic Diocese of Long Island had written a pastoral letter urging officials to allow duplexes on the island and called the lack of affordable housing a "serious moral problem." Newspaper accounts of the time depict a Levittown Property Owners Association unhappy with this suggestion.

And to move into the original Levittown, it wasn't enough to be happily married heterosexuals with one or two little kids. You had to be white. Painful, angry stories have been recounted of black veterans driving out to Long Island in search of the opportunity to move into the middle class that the houses afforded. But the covenants were unambiguous on the subject of "Caucasians only."

Kelly doesn't blame Levitt for this. She reserves that for the federal government, specifically the FHA, which as a matter of official policy mandated that to be a successful subdivision, the developer's target market had to be homogeneous and harmonious, which is to say, a particular socioeconomic level and a specific racial group. And in 1947 there was little debate over just which racial group that would be. Kelly says even fifty years later, society has not worked nearly hard enough to extend the original promise of Levittown to other disenfranchised groups. It continues to show up during polling. Fannie Mae is the company that pools mortgages to spread risk in order to make home loans cheaper and more accessible. It routinely asks folks why they don't own a house, and people always cite the inability to cobble together a down payment or job insecurity. But another reason that comes up shockingly often is the conviction that they will not be treated fairly by mortgage lenders because of their race or national origin.

Still, working-class people of all races are increasingly buying homes, and new immigrants will be one of the main engines fueling the housing market well into the new century. There seems to be an ongoing hunger to display the official mark of success that home ownership represents. You actually view yourself differently. Barbara Kelly says this is the crux of the Levittown experience, folks no longer identifying themselves as factory workers when they are down at the factory. "They see themselves as home owners who happen to earn their living at the Grumman plant."

But the experience transforms all of us, regardless of our relationship to the means of production. Buying a house is an ordeal, with pressures comparable to those present at a wedding or childbirth. I've seen grown men cry under the weight of juggling the various strands of money that will be woven into a down payment. Then there is the truly rapturous process when they put the proctoscope of death up your credit report to look for any magazine subscriptions you were late paying for in 1978. All this concludes in a bizarre, highly ritualized ceremony, the closing. There is a big table with an imperious clerk who shifts the official documents back and forth with a mesmerizing rhythm between buyer and seller for a series of signatures so endless that the handwriting becomes automatic, like a chant. "Signature. Date. Signature. Date." If you emerge intact from this rite of passage, you are looked upon differently.

Your in-laws see you as a provider; the credit-rating agencies swap your report from the tawdry manila folder to the fancy leather binding.

My last question as I head out of Kelly's office is about Vanderbilt's motorway. The professor agrees that there are some Levittown streets that follow its groove, but she can't offhand suggest where I could find those.

The Levittown library is right where Mildred Cantor had said it would be, adjacent, as it turns out, to the spot where William Levitt set up the first model home. A very shy but well-informed librarian takes me into the basement to show me some of the ancient artifacts, including an instruction booklet for the original-equipment Bendix washing machines promising "Workless Washdays." One can only hope the promise was naive, not cynical. Postwar families soon found out that when washers and dryers were introduced, society's standards for cleanliness rose as well, so that clothes had to be washed much more often, adding to labor rather than saving it. There was also a pamphlet warning home owners that if they failed to cut their lawns, the boys from down at the Levitt landscaping department would come by, cut it for them, and slap them with the bill.

The library is the rendezvous point for me and John Pergola, Levittown's real estate agent extraordinaire.

Pergola, rhymes with "payola," is a genial fellow who puts little note pads emblazoned with his phone number at the real estate agency in most of the pay phones in Levittown. In 1948 he overheard some folks talking when he was signing the papers to buy his Levitt house. They needed some part-time men to help show the houses, no commission, a buck and a half an hour. He claims to have been involved in every one of the 5,400 Cape Cod rental properties when Levitt decided to sell them outright. But, he hastens to add, he was not the salesman. Why would you need a salesman?

"There was no magic," Pergola says. "There was no down payment. None. We took a $10 deposit, but we gave that back on closing. No negotiating, pick out the colors of your tile and your paint scheme and sign the contract. It was the no down payment that made all the difference for these guys." He's not kidding. By the early fifties there was the Korean War, and the government was no longer encouraging these housing ventures. You needed a deposit of about $1,000 to get into the Levitt houses built a little later than the original Capes, and because of that deposit, the entire character of those later subdivisions was different. Levittown itself was mainly working class; the $1,000 deposit people were much more middle class. Here was the making of the class division that would soon tear at the area's school system.

Pergola lives in that same Cape Cod, with no thoughts of moving.

"I met so many people here. I just love it. I love it here."

We stop by a couple of taverns looking for "the guys," Pergola's American Legion buddies. We are having trouble finding them.

"I mean, David, this was a great community."

I get stuck on the "was" in this sentence, the same past tense used by Jerry Worthing earlier in the day when he remarked that he didn't recall any great pressure to keep up with the Joneses in his town. "It was a low-key community," he had said. Now it is just a place to live. In the early years of Levittown, the crime rate was remarkably low. Of course it was. All the kids were about the same age, and none was old enough to cause any major damage. But then they became teenagers, and Levittown's crime rate rose.

And what about the stigma of Levittown? Everyone remembers the searing criticism of Levittown as a "future slum" and the aerial photos of houses being set down in a row in plots denuded of vegetation. Even today the same Levitt house in adjacent Wantaugh is worth more than one in Levittown itself.

Pergola dismisses that as snobbery.

"They fought hard to get that Wantaugh address. Here in Levittown, we attract *everybody*."

Pergola and I enjoy half a beer each and talk about about the secrets of getting a good deal on a house. He stays focused on those wild postwar days when the fields were being plowed under for this community. I bring to the conversation some ideas I got from a friend, Ellen James Martin, a personal-finance guru and one of the women I would least like to try to sell a house to in America. She advocates what I call the Woodward and Bernstein approach to getting a good deal on a house. You go house to house in your potential new block, knocking on doors without an appointment and asking nosy neighbors what they've heard about the property. She says tongues tend to wag, and she once used some water-in-the-basement intelligence to get $20,000 knocked off an asking price.

Martin also warns about mortgage insurance. Folks who don't have a full 20 percent to put down on a home are often socked with this substantial fee, which has a habit of not going away even at the point that a person has paid off enough of a house to own more than 20 percent of it. This is a lucrative area for companies that provide mortgage insurance and a cost that can be avoided in a number of ways, including disciplined saving before a home purchase so that 20 percent can be put down. Or with some fancy footwork, it is sometimes possible to get a second mortgage at the time of the first mortgage. The first bank lends you 80 percent of the cost of the house; a second bank lends you enough money to bring your down payment above the critical 20 percent mark.

Martin is also a big fan of exclusive buyer's agents, who work only on behalf of the person doing the buying. Regular realtors aren't wild about these junkyard dogs, and they can be hard to find, but the few who do this often come up with some pretty clever schemes to knock down the price of a house. She also warns against falling in love with a particular house and tumbling into the pit of needing to acquire at all costs. And don't make the classic mistake of scraping together every last penny for the down payment and hoping closing costs will somehow be forgotten during the confusion of the closing process. Officially, closing costs can run between 4 and 6 percent of the cost of a house, enough to eat up the lion's share of a nest egg.

Fortified by four ounces of beer, I screw up my courage to face the ignominy one last time. Has Mr. Pergola ever heard of Vanderbilt's grandstand?

Pergola looks at me for a long moment, then beckons me out to his car with a tip of his Bryl Creemed do. From his trunk he pulls out a memento for me, a 1948 poster-sized map printed on heavy card stock: "Levittown, A Garden Community." I scan the print and find what I am looking for toward the center of the map. Looping from Bloomingdale Lane over to Orchid Road is an eccentric, mug-handle-shaped right-of-way labeled Old Motor Parkway. It is the tracing of Vanderbilt's raceway. Pergola points to the spot where the starting line and grandstand are rumored to have stood.

I jump in the car and find the location. There, in the center of this carefully designed, developed, and groomed community, is nothing at all. It isn't a park; it isn't a field. It is just a long, barren strip half a block wide bordered by a pair of wooden fences. It looks remarkably like the no-man's land between East and West in Potzdammerplatz before the fall of the Berlin Wall, minus the guard shacks and anti-communist graffiti. There certainly is no obvious hint of a grandstand. I kick at a small jagged rock the size of a walnut. With my heel I dig it out. It appears to be a shard of concrete, and one of its sides is flat. It is just possible that I have found a remnant of the old pavement, but what little I remember about archaeology includes the admonition "Thou shalt not take souvenirs from digs."

It turns out I am too early, two months early, to be exact. When spring turns to summer, the property owners association and the Levittown Historical Society put up a commemorative plaque right at this very location. I reach Richard Marconi, whose house is so close to the spot that he is able to read me part of the plaque through his cordless phone: "Site of the official grandstand for the fourth and fifth Vanderbilt Cup Races." I ask if he's ever come across any of the ghosts of the parkway. He admits that he has often stood in his backyard in the evening, straining to hear the sounds of the races. There's a tire screech from time to time, probably modern-day idiots driving too fast, but he wonders and smiles.

To paraphrase Gertrude Stein on the subject of Oakland, California, there *is* a here, here, and I can live with that. Levittown has a special identity, either because of the social experiment the community represented, the individuality of its residents asserting themselves out of uniformity, even the town's racy past. If it exists here in what should have been soulless suburbia, it exists in lots of more-likely places where one might choose to burn off a windfall. It definitely exists in the multicultural inner city where I own now just as much as if I had bought into a place surrounded by overpriced designer coffee shops, independent film theaters, and neighbors with names that show up in the credits.

Levittown may not have a fancy Nordstrom or a symphony that records for Deutsche Grammophon. But it does have a large underground reservoir of irony, which makes it a pretty cool place. As it turns out, the whole place is a monument to how even wily, wealthy business folk can royally screw up a surplus with the best of them.

The tragic irony comes courtesy of William J. Levitt himself, who was able, for a good while, to live very well off developments like this one. But he really hit the jackpot in 1968 when he sold his company to the International Telephone and Telegraph Company for $92 million in stock. It was an enormous windfall, and in the hands of such a savvy business player, it should have gone even further. But that windfall came with a price: a contract preventing Levitt from working in the construction business in the United States for ten years. With all that money burning a hole in his pocket, Levitt went shopping for construction ventures overseas. He invested it in buildings in Iran, Nigeria, Venezuela, and Israel, ill-starred projects it would turn out. Also, in the years that followed Levitt's windfall, ITT was hitting the iceberg and its share prices plummeted, taking much of Levitt's wealth along with it. It was not a pretty sight, and later, at the age of seventy-three, Levitt was charged with improperly using money from the family's charitable foundation, money that was later repaid. I figure it was that insidious wealth effect at work. Levitt had this bundle, and when you carry a bundle around, you can get intoxicated, the feeling you get at a mall or a casino, but on a global scale. And without careful consideration and planning, it can all turn out badly.

Changes in the federal tax laws in the waning years of the millennium are making home ownership even more attractive. Gone is the tax penalty for failing to buy a new, bigger house after you sell yours first. This means many of us will be able to move in and out of real estate with comparative ease and be able to move where opportunities present themselves. Even opportunities to be a slacker, as I was to find in Texas.

Souvenirs

A poster-sized copy of an original Levittown map, suitable for framing in 1 inch = 800 feet scale.

The understanding that real estate and long-term Treasury bonds rise at about the same rate, but you can't live in a bond.

To do when I get home

Get out the calculator and confirm the awful truth: If we stay in our house only five years, renting will have been cheaper than buying, even with tax deductions and home equity figured in.

Doing the numbers

On the year of Levittown's fiftieth anniversary, home ownership in America reached 66 percent, at that time the highest rate in the country's history. The biggest rate of increase was among female-headed households and African American and Hispanic families. (Source: U.S. Department of Housing and Urban Development)

9

Quit Your Day Job

On sabbatical in
Levelland, Texas

From the clipping file: An insurance claim processor from Garden Grove, California, won $85,250 a year for twenty years from the lottery. According to the *Los Angeles Times,* the woman promptly quit her job and, since she had played guitar since the age of six, now intended to record blues music. August 19, 1994.

One of the wonders of a surplus is that it sweeps away an enormous excuse for not acting on long-held yearnings. That is also the horror of it. What if the reason we never went back to school to get that extra degree wasn't the money after all, but general inertia or insecurity about our abilities?

One can debate the merits of the stock market or real estate, but there is no debate about the merits of education. I started out looking for an evocative place that would help me understand the return on investment of going back to school. But I had not forgotten my experience in New York, when the anthropologist beckoned me to come back and build boats with other volunteers. What emerged during my research was a broader question, about what one gets for using a surplus to follow one's dreams, perhaps earning a new degree, perhaps learning to fiddle. I came across a reference to a small college in Texas that offers both. It was a place that inspires grown-ups with perfectly good careers in such things as the law and medicine to up and quit and go to the place to get a degree in commercial music: country, bluegrass, gospel. At first blush, such a course would seem irrational, bordering on irresponsible. But the folks in this school shone with a contentment that I have never seen around the intense corridors of a typical workplace.

It was a contentment I also saw elsewhere on the trip to Texas, when I spent some time with a tenured professor who had quit to use her surplus to become a full-time mystery writer and a media executive who had spent his fortune creating a folk music festival.

"Partly sunny today, with highs in the sixties and a chance of blowing dust."

Blowing *dust?*

The deejay reading the weather on KRFE out of Lubbock doesn't seem nearly as surprised as I am about the chance of dust. He has bigger things on his mind, like spinning some country music.

Just hours ago a cold front moved through this part of west Texas, leaving a knife-edged crispness in the air. I am driving through a landscape of little churches, nodding oil wells, and cotton fields. But this trip isn't about picking cotton. It is about picking banjo. About thirty miles west on Texas Route 114 from Lubbock is the Levelland campus of South Plains College, one of the very few places on earth where one can earn a degree in country music. Or bluegrass or gospel, for that matter. I want to know why anyone would give up a perfectly good job and spend their nest egg to earn an associate's degree in commercial music. If there is something you know you have to do before you die, the time to do it is when you can afford it. Graduate school. Dying with socialites on a Himalayan peak. Sailing from the Bahamas to the Cape Verde Islands. Teaching journalism in Malawi. When the man with the good ol' boy accent comes on from the cockpit to announce that the rudder of your 747 has cracked off and that sometime in the next few minutes you have a 500-mile-per-hour date with a mountainside, what is the one thing you wish you had done that you did not do? That is, besides going the whole hog with (his or her name here) on that sultry night in Barcelona?

I pull back from infinity and refocus on the surroundings. They are not kidding about this "level land" business: the campus and the terrain that stretches out to the horizon are as flat as a pool table. Coronado came here in the sixteenth century looking for gold. It was here, had he known precisely where to look. On the outside, South Plains looks like any tidy, manicured community college with a hodgepodge of low red-brick buildings. Inside the Creative Arts Department, however, there are immediate indications the rhythm is different here. A sign over the drinking fountain in the hall admonishes: "This is NOT a spittoon. Deposit your 'dip' elsewhere." The blackboards in the music classrooms are missing the usual music theory class scribblings about Palestrina motets and Debussy. Instead, they are filled with lyrics from bluegrass songs. A piano shares floor space with a pair of steel guitars that look like industrial jigs for turning out stainless steel guitar necks. A name on one door indicates it is the Waylon Jennings studio. Nearby is the Tom T. Hall studio, said to be the best TV-equipped recording studio between Dallas and Phoenix. A plaque on the wall is dedicated to Redd Stewart, who co-authored "A Soldier's Last Letter."

"That song could bring tears to a glass eye," says John Hartin.

Hartin is a troubadour, a veteran of stages and roadhouses as grand as the Grand Ole Opry and as modest as a grange hall in Nebraska. These days he spends his Saturday nights wearing overalls and adopting the posture of a geezer as he plays from his repertoire of maybe 10,000 songs with a group of country and bluegrass musicians called The Coots. Hartin chairs the Commercial Music Department. He is credited with having built up this program from its humble beginnings in a broom closet near the gym. The curriculum ranges from performance to songwriting to the technical skills needed to survive either as a traveling player or in the big time in Nashville.

"It's not fine arts—it's crude arts," he likes to joke.

Hartin has attracted some very serious musicians to his faculty, folks that make professional musicians snap to attention and salute when their names are mentioned. Try "Alan Munde" on a banjo player sometime and watch what happens.

Hartin worries that folks tend to throw their anchor in too early, making it tough to explore new territory. Every year at graduation he meets parents who rue the fact that they never had the guts to do what their children are doing.

"Life," Hartin observes, "is not a dress rehearsal."

His office looks like any professor's office: the books, a sign-up sheet for scheduling office hours, fluorescent lights. Somehow it is about to become a stage.

Hartin picks up a well-worn guitar and gives it a strum.

"Gee, it was tuned when I bought it . . . in 1956."

As he begins to noodle on the instrument, Rusty Hudelson, associate professor of music, sticks his head in and wordlessly, as he chews his gum, picks up a squeeze box and has at it. Renowned fiddler and South Plains College professor Joe Carr comes in, rosins up his bow, and gets in on the action. Soon two other faculty members join the fracas, playing another guitar and a kind of acoustic guitar equipped with a steel resonator known by its brand name, Dobro. They are making it up as they go along, with Hartin cuing the others for solos and then signaling the end with a big-finish verse. Four more songs then tumble out, and a cluster of amused students gather at the open doorway. Hartin comes out of the decaying last chord of the last song with a high-pitched yee-hah that has pigs pricking up their ears as far away as Garza County.

"Some professors come in in the morning and talk philosophy. We pick," Hartin says. "Then we go have a cup of coffee, pick a little bit, maybe teach a lesson, then we pick some more."

His rich, down-home voice lets him cultivate the image of a hayseed, but he is in fact a fine manager with a master's degree in management and a savvy marketer. The same fella who just likes to pick is the man who once chased a *Reader's Digest* rep around the Las Vegas Convention Center in a hat so big it looked, I was told, like an ant carrying a potato chip. Hartin used his silver tongue to persuade the rep's secretary of the merits of his plastic "E-Z Chord" device, which makes life easier for novice guitar players. It eventually sold 80,000 units. Hartin has taken some nest eggs in his time and run them through the entrepreneurial mill.

The commercial music program at South Plains takes kids right out of high school. But the reason I have made the journey here is that the program also attracts a large proportion of older students, many of whom have jettisoned some serious careers to be here. I once spent a decent pile of cash satisfying a full-bodied infatuation with the idea of trying my hand at being a foreign correspondent. I suspect that I will find fellow travelers on this campus. Direct costs aren't the big investment if you want an associate's degree from South Plains College. A complete semester at South Plains is about $2,000. That's $8,000 for the two-year degree. That also covers room and board, but what it does not include is the opportunity cost of quitting your day job to spend the time necessary for this full-time program. Can that be balanced with the opportunity cost of not doing something you are called to do? For me there is also the matter of giving the lifelong assumption that I am musically hopeless one final test.

I have arranged to hold what resembles office hours so that I can chat individually with commercial music majors. Jennifer Ames is the first through the door. She is from a little town near Abilene, and I soon get to hear what Latin sounds like with a few extra Texas diphthongs thrown into phrases like *"Rin stolonis de verbi Latinae"* (Fools laugh at Latin words). Seven years ago Ames completed a master's in Latin with the unfocused goal of teaching somewhere. She entered a Ph.D. program, but cutbacks forced her to find part-time jobs to raise enough money to stay in the program. Data entry, waitressing, that sort of thing. Then she saw an ad: "You can make $50,000 in the first year." Ames called.

"We sell manufactured housing," said the voice.

"You mean, like trailer houses?" Ames said, appalled at the prospect.

"Oh no, *manufactured* homes. Please come to our manufacturing facility, and we can give you a complete sales training course."

It turned out that Ames was very good at selling trailers. She's smart, she listens, and she's low pressure. Her customers kept telling her she was "right pr'ty." She began making real money. Hartin is right, life is not a dress rehearsal, but it isn't ordered à la carte either. You fall into stuff. Places, relationships, jobs. The money starts to get better; your lifestyle follows along with debt not far behind; and you wake up at age thirty-two or forty-seven singing the Talking Heads line "My god, how did I get here?"

Ames made more money in three months than in four years on the academic track, so she said to heck with "Ph.D. land." Seven years later she was still selling trailers, earning about $65,000, with prospects for earning more than double that as manager of a mobile home sales location. Ames says she had no time to spend her money, so it all went in the bank. She was working seventy-five hours a week. She had hoped marriage and kids would enter the picture, but the steady relationship she had broke down. Then Ames asked a question many folks forget to ask themselves: What is it I really want to do?

Around that same time, she got it into her head to call around to music stores asking to buy a banjo. She'd never even held a banjo before.

"I didn't know how to play the *radio*," Ames laughs. Radio, a bar so low on the musical ladder you need a sump pump to keep your hairpiece dry. Ames is deep in her story and misses my wounded look.

Banjo had always fascinated her, an interest spurred on by her ninety-year-old grandma's confession.

"If I'd 'a known I was going to live this long, I would have learned to play the fiddle," her grandmother had once said.

She found a shop with two banjos for sale and chose a $250 model. On her first try, she put the picks on backward. It was clear she would need some tutelage, but even in Dallas, good banjo instruction was hard to find. Her inquiries led her to Levelland. About the same time Ames's bosses were dangling a huge promotion in front of her.

"I told everybody I was quitting, and they said, 'Have you lost your mind?' I said, 'Yes, what of it?'"

I ask if she would play. The tempered, metallic sound of her banjo is joined by the woodsy notes of a mandolin brought in by her pal Shannon Gritton, a fellow student. The pair hold forth with a bluegrass tune, "Shuckin' Corn." Ames already has enough confidence in her skill to have a blast playing, even for a stranger.

"It was like somebody lit a fire under me the second I really started doing what I wanted to do," Ames says. "The folks here are great and they get my jokes."

Oh, for a place on the planet where folks would get my jokes. It's a basic human need, like warmth and food. Jennifer was looking for—and found—a sense of community.

It is clear that Jennifer enjoys the company of Mr. Gritton. His mandolin has been an avocation ever since his mother took him to see the mandolin virtuoso Sam Bush. He played in a band but kept this hobby separate from his day job at the Heaven Hill Distillery in Bartstown, Kentucky. He worked seven days a week and had no social life. All he really wanted to do was play.

"I would sneak off when the other guys were going for a smoke. I'd go out to the truck to play a song," Gritton says. "But it isn't living. I'm, like, I can't do this for thirty years. It's only money. The most money I made in one year was, like, $32,000 and you can live pretty well on it. But I thought, I don't want to trade my life for that."

Then one November about a year before our conversation, everything changed. To borrow Jennifer's phrase, someone lit a fire under Shannon, big time.

"It was one of those weird days," Gritton says, "with fifty-mile-per-hour winds."

He had been working the third shift and was home trying to get some sleep when a friend called to say the distillery was on fire. News accounts of the fire describe a "tidal wave" of flaming 120-proof liquor the consistency of lava flowing down from one warehouse and engulfing six others, destroying 2 percent of the world's bourbon production, 95,000 barrels of whiskey in all.

"Welcome to hell," a Bartstown firefighter told reporters. Mercifully, no one was hurt.

"I was displaced, although I still had a job," Gritton says. "But it was a sign."

Yeah, you might say so. The kind of sign that comes notarized, engraved in silver, strapped to an anvil that is thrown through your plateglass front window. Here I am, probing my psyche for subtle hints that my vague ennui is actually a suggestion that it is time to switch gears, and this guy figuratively gets struck by lightning.

Even when the sign is as unmistakable as that visited upon Shannon Gritton, you need to be prepared to act. Gritton was. His savings, a few thousand dollars, is paying for his first semester in the bluegrass program. As soon as the sale of his house goes through, he'll have the money he will need to finish. In the meantime, he moonlights at a liquor store in Levelland.

"Just can't get away from that whiskey," he laughs.

All of this, of course, is completely insane. Imagine the boss of General Motors poised at the cusp of a crucial decision about whether or not the company should make a major expansion into China's Guangdong province. On his way to work in his Lexus LS 400, a flat tire forces the GM chairman to the side of the road, where he comes upon a discarded fortune cookie containing a slip of paper that reads, "Prosperity Comes Your Way." It must be a sign to go forward with the overseas venture. What else could it be? If he admitted this to his board, shareholders, or Wall Street analysts, however, the chairman would be lucky if the company kept him on with a job spraying Scotch Guard at the local Buick dealership. We are rational. We try to apply the principles of science to big decisions. The problem is, there is no scientific discipline that gives us the tools to approach major life decisions with so many variables.

So call me superstitious. Stuck for a job out of college, I ended up doing radio traffic reports from a Cessna 1400 feet over the Washington, D.C., Beltway. When a pushrod in the plane's engine developed a kink one morning and burning oil began billowing from the cowling, my pilot began scouting for a clearing below.

"You want to die in that landfill to the left or that highly restricted, military-only airfield to the right?" Tom had asked.

He answered his own question by getting the plane down, with some fanfare, at the air strip at Fort Belvoir, Virginia. As one of the base's senior officers read Tom and me the riot act about national security and piercing the virgin sanctity of a classified U.S. Army facility, I just stood there making silent promises to myself, having been given this precious second chance. Yes, it's time to get married, I vowed, even though I was dating no one at the time. And, yes, I must apply to graduate school right away. It is tough to think very long term, about retirement, for instance, when you have just been presented with a neon sign warning of your mortality. A couple of years later, when a double-deck portion of a freeway collapsed just behind me during the 1989 San Francisco earthquake, I resolved to quit my job and find adventure as a foreign correspondent abroad. I can't help seeing these students in Levelland as kindred spirits.

Next into my adopted office at South Plains College is Clay McIntosh, a former Rapid Deployment Force paratrooper and advertising copywriter. Perhaps you remember Santa in the United Parcel Service ad, with the line "Only one organization delivers to more destinations overnight." The line was Clay's. He is a lean fellow with a goatee who has no interest in becoming Garth Brooks. His model is Harlan Howard, a great country songwriter who is not a household name.

"So what if I convince somebody to buy two bags of potato chips instead of one," McIntosh says. "When I'm at my deathbed, do I really want to think, yeah, I did some great ads? Songwriting was something I always wanted to do; it was something I always planned on getting around to doing. And suddenly ten years had gone by and I hadn't even taken one step in that direction."

So he gave a month's notice, packed up, and moved to Levelland.

"I did have some money saved, so it wasn't like I was moving down here and I didn't have a penny," McIntosh says. Modest debts. Savings. It is a theme beginning to rap its knuckles on my skull. According to Mosaic law, the seventh year is the sabbatical year, a time to allow fields to go fallow. During the sabbatical year, lenders are also supposed to let debtors off the hook. Now before you call Mastercard International with this bit of news, you should know that by the first century B.C., Hillel the Elder had introduced a legal maneuver that gave Judaism a way around this rule so that lenders would suffer from less heartburn and borrowers would find it easier to get money. But there is nothing in Judaism or any other religious tradition to prevent you from using your nest egg to discharge your *own* debts. Take the cash, use it to get out of hock, and use the resulting freedom to do something different in that seventh year. Sure, that fellowship you've been offered pays only a quarter of your normal salary, but if debts are low, you might be able to manage with the reduced income.

Goatees are happening here in Levelland, and the next one belongs to Declan McGowan, a red-haired fellow with an accent that says Ireland and London. He got word there would be downsizing at British Airways, where he trucked freight between the planes and warehouses.

"My life sort of flashed before me," McGowan says. "I was working with guys who had been there for twenty years. They were just, like, *desperate* people. They would fight for overtime to pay for the cable television, the updated cars, and whatever. That just doesn't interest me. So I thought, you know, I don't belong here, so I'm going to do what I want to do for a while."

McGowan had saved, and he also had some severance from his three years with the airline. His itinerary routed him through Las Vegas. On the way over, a flight attendant took dollar wagers off each of the passengers. That got him primed. He blew a chunk of his nest egg at the casinos. Fortunately, there was still enough left to polish his bluegrass chops in Levelland.

I also meet the nomads, who are not a band but a pair of wanderers named Bob Noblitt and Cynthia Rivera. Noblitt, tall, blue-eyed, and bearded, was a corporate lawyer in Houston for twelve years. At thirty-nine, he had had enough. It wasn't some cataclysm that provoked the change. He says he'd always had a desire to free himself from the career life and was tired of forcing himself to be something he was not. Once he indulged in taking a Porsche racing class, but that was a diversion. He wanted to change his life. His goal was to retire at age forty.

To this end, Noblitt had a big yard sale and quit. Then he and Rivera, who had a newly minted degree in journalism, set out in an RV for points unknown.

Bob says if you brush your teeth and don't drink, you can always find work, and they have, serving as campground hosts on National Park Service land and as caretakers on a sheep ranch in Oregon. He worries about telling me too much, for fear it will attract others to his lifestyle. I think most folks don't have the nerve. The couple lives simply, and the guitar is their cheap form of entertainment. South Plains will hone their skills. I'm curious what they do for health care. Bob turns the question in lawyerly fashion, answering that their lower-pitch life—keeping their own schedule, in the outdoors a lot—has tremendous health care benefits. Their savings keeps them and their twenty-five-foot recreational vehicle insured.

For those of us living jammed up solid eastbound on the southeast-southwest freeway—lunch from a vending machine—on deadline lives, it is easy to hate these people. Where is the productivity, the civic responsibility that made this country great? If we all sat around like a bunch of hillbillies in overalls picking banjo, we would never be able to compete in the global economy. This isn't wealth creation. It doesn't generate innovation, jobs, tax revenue. You know we will just end up carrying them via Social Security. Where do these slackers get off having a blast while responsible folks slog away to support families, to service loans, keeping the vital engine of American industry chugging along?

And if I said any of this to the next person to step in the office, I fear she'd snap me like a bundle of spaghettini headed for the pot.

While Kenyatta Barnes attained what she describes as "only an E-3" rank in the navy, her bearing suggests a rank closer to admiral. She wears a red and black cutaway jacket with large brass buttons and a bowler hat. An elaborate scarf draped over her left shoulder reminds me of Ghanaian kente cloth. After she found herself raising children alone, she became desperate for work. She enlisted in the navy and learned to do electronic calibration. Ten years passed.

"Navy," she says, "Never Again Volunteer Yourself."

When it was announced that Reese Air Force Base near Lubbock would close, some of her navy colleagues were terrified, angry.

"Everybody thought I was out of my mind because I started jumping around, singing and dancing, after they said they were going to lay us off," Barnes says. "I guess I'm different from other people because I believe things that happen in our lives happen to make us better and they'll either make us or break us, depending on how you look at it. I just felt like God has things that He wants us to do in our lives, and when we're ready for them, they happen."

She was ready, and armed with her severance pay.

Barnes came to South Plains to hone her skills as an audio technician. But soon folks suggested to her that she may have a place on the other side of the mixing console. Her instrument is her voice and her genre is gospel. Without hesitation, she launches into a rich a cappella rendering of "Amazing Grace."

The next morning I'm surprised to find a coating of ice on the windshield of the car. The winds driven by the cold front are gone. There is a smell so strong it's becoming a taste. It's the tang of petroleum from the all the wells around here.

The motel clerk points me toward Wal-Mart when I ask where

"downtown" is, but I manage to find Levelland's real main street: a very traditional town square with a city hall in the middle surrounded by a perimeter of shops. In the square the sheriff's office has an aging fresco above the door that warns there's a $10 fine for visiting prisoners. At this early hour I'm not interested in interviewing any varmints. I need the coffee at A. J.'s Cafe.

The man who I assume is A. J. is a mature fellow with a florid complexion who wears a madras shirt with the tails hanging out. He is sitting with another big Texan in overalls wearing a baseball cap embroidered "Max."

"How'r yew this mornin'?" A. J. begins.

"Fine. And you?" I manage.

"Jess tur'ble."

"Sorry to hear that."

"And the thang is, I'm doin' better than before."

"Glad I didn't ask earlier."

A. J.'s state of mind seems to mirror the economic fortunes of the region. Few seem to be getting rich around here, and the booming stock market is, and feels, very far away. I recall the sticker on the pickup that passed me on Route 114 the day before:

Please, God, give us another boom.
We promise not to screw this one up.

Isn't that the problem. When you get it, it's hard to know what to do with it.

I'm due at a harmonica lesson in less than fifteen minutes. I suck down the eggs and country gravy. But a framed piece of paper propped up by the cash register slows me down. It's that poem attributed to Jenny Joseph about enjoying life while you can. It shows up on T-shirts, in high school yearbooks. It concludes:

BUT MAYBE I OUGHT TO PRACTICE A LITTLE NOW?
SO PEOPLE WHO KNOW ME ARE NOT
TOO SHOCKED AND SURPRISED WHEN SUDDENLY
I AM OLD AND START TO WEAR PURPLE.

Here it was again, carefully retyped and put on display at A.J.'s. It's tempting to see this as an epicurean oath, an exhortation to burn up what you have as you have it, a version of the magnet that reads, "It's cheaper than psychotherapy: Mall of America." But the word "practice" in the paragraph strikes me as I think ahead to my appointment in a practice room over at the college. If this course is just another kind of consumption, wouldn't it make more sense to spend the money on Club Med, where the beaches are nicer and there is no homework? Perhaps this little gem isn't really about buying stuff but about learning to follow your true nature before it is too late. I substitute "play blues harp" for "wear purple" and decide there is a difference between spending on something like a car or a series of restaurant meals and investing in yourself the way students are doing at South Plains. I pay the bill and hurry to my lesson.

Rusty, whom I met at the improv session in the chairman's office the previous day, is pleased to show me which end to blow into on a harmonica, or for my purposes, a blues harp.

I learn that harmonicas are tuned to certain keys diatonically. The one at hand is in the key of D, but if I can just learn a little "cross harp," that is, the blues way, I can get the key of A out of it. Rusty gets the keyboard going on a preprogrammed blues riff and starts wailing on the harp. I can barely purse my lips tight enough to confine my blowing and sucking to a single note. The embarrassment is starting to flow back. As a kid, I learned to clumsily play flute by rote, could never read music, and could never sing, despite some nightmarish appearances in high school musicals. The professor is encouraging. He says that now that I know the basics, I can try a harmonica video and practice book, and if in a year I still can't play, he'd at least be able to get me going on a Jew's harp. With my Italian last name, little did he know.

On the bulletin board over his shoulder is a photocopied handbill for a country group called The Knights of the West. Hudelson points himself out in the group. I squint. It is hard to correlate his professorial visage, with his well-manicured, academic beard and wire-rimmed glasses, with the clean-shaven, longer-haired piano player wearing a hat and tux in the picture. His daughter, Tania, is in the picture, along with his wife, Schahara, and his son-in-law. The Knights of the West had been a family show band in search of a regular venue. That is, until Schahara took the entrepreneurial plunge by recently purchasing them their very own theater in the Old West town of Post.

After the music lesson I ride out to Post along with Schahara. Striking in her scarves and flowing clothes, Schahara blends a note of Gypsy with her country-music-star aura. It turns out she and Rusty know something of the Gypsy life.

They simplified their lives decades before it was the nineties thing to do. Tired of the big city grind, Schahara and Rusty moved with their little kids to a ranch house in Wyoming that cost $50 a month to rent. With some other couples they started the Close Encounters Coffee House in Sundance, Wyoming, near the place where Spielberg landed his alien spaceship as Richard Dreyfuss gaped. The Hudelsons' music really took off, although with three families in on the venture, no one got rich. Schahara still had to do extra jobs, including driving a school bus for a while. The goal was to play music, live simply, and not focus so much on *things*.

An impulse to go back to college in Lubbock was the only thing that dragged them from this lifestyle. Eventually their daughter, Tania, auditioned for a spot in the commercial music program at South Plains. Her father accompanied her during the audition, and Hartin and his colleagues were knocked out by Rusty's combination of erudition and breathtaking musical chops. He was asked to join the faculty.

Schahara, however, is the restless type. She has flung herself into the development of their venture, a recently renovated fifty-year-old theater. Post was founded by C. W. Post, the cereal magnate, as a social experiment in 1907. He wanted to create a small community of farmers who owned their own land. At that time title to most of the surrounding countryside was held by just a few large ranches. Post also experimented with rainmaking, although his attempts to create a lush landscape by seeding clouds failed. Decades later the city of Post is emerging as a bit of a west Texas hot spot. Every month the town hosts an impressive crafts and food market located in the warehouses of a disused cotton processing plant. Productions are regularly mounted at the

Garza playhouse on the main street. The Hudelsons are mounting their Knights of the West review, along with other traditional country acts, at the Tower Theater, their venture across the street. What the Tower has is charm, air conditioning, a dance floor, and a nifty western mural that serves as a backdrop to the stage. The idea is to make Post the Branson of the Southwest. Branson, Missouri, has turned a little town in the Ozarks into a kind of Disneyland for American music.

How did the Hudelsons pay for this dream? Savings. Where did they get the savings? Oh, here and there. The Tower Theater hardly cost them anything.

"I always invite people to come on down, if not for the music, then to see what a thousand dollars buys you these days," Shahara says. That's not a thousand down payment; it's a thousand outright. She was the only bidder at the auction. Call it a *grand* experiment.

Their $1,000 bought quite a bit. On the time-honored business principle that it's often better to be second into a market than first, so you can learn lessons from the pioneers, much of the renovation for the Tower had already been done by previous owners. She made the case to the former owners and the elected officials of Post that she was bringing promotions expertise, drive, and vision to the project, not just her thousand dollars.

I'm crossing my fingers that the Tower takes off. I'll keep practicing my harmonica, and although the Hudelsons allow only high-quality acts to perform, perhaps they'll let me get on the stage one day. Who am I kidding? At the very least they might be willing to open up the theater on a quiet weekday to let me blow my harmonica into the darkness so I can imagine what my life might have been like, had I been given even a dram of musical talent.

The front that passed through Levelland has not yet made it to the Texas Hill Country. Here, in the farmland north of San Antonio and west of Austin, two days of downpours have blended all the edges. Low clouds set the hue in that narrow range between purple and gray. A guy with a Celtic accent doing the folk show on public radio in Austin keeps using the word "dank." I wouldn't have reached for dank, which, for me, implies the cold, chilly wetness of a drafty Scottish castle. Here in Hill Country it is warm and humid as a womb.

The idea is to track down a couple of people who have a longitudinal perspective on spending money to feed an inner fire. Using cash to go back to school or to do development work with indigenous people in the Mexican state of Chiapas instead of turning the money over to a responsible mutual fund manager may seem a good idea at the time, but does it stand the test of time? For some, dropping out has been more than a sabbatical, a term that suggests something temporary.

Susan Wittig Albert's double-wide trailer is at the end of two miles of dirt road that curves along the shore of a small lake. Instead of returning to academe to follow a dream, Albert has left academe to do the same. She is a medievalist who was dean and vice president of Lyndon Baines Johnson's alma mater, Southwest Texas State. She held the only secure job left in America, academic tenure. In her forties Albert quit to return to writing fiction. The music students in Levelland are acting on faith that they can spend their money to willfully derail their careers and live to tell about it. Susan Wittig Albert and her husband Bill have been doing this long enough to have a track record.

"People always think we must be running dope or something," Susan says as we clomp through the muddy stand of pecan trees adjacent to the trailer. "We don't have any visible means of support."

"We match the profile of a methamphetamine lab so perfectly that for years we've had people flying over with helicopters," Bill adds with a twinkle. One day a pair of guys with heavy wing-tips, a new Ford Bronco, and no sense of humor pulled up at their gate, claiming to be lost. The Alberts assumed they were narcs, scoping the place. That is axiom number one for those who want to drop out of the career track: you *will* be suspect.

Rather than meth, my guess is that the narco boys were acting on a vague tip that went something like "the professor lady and her bearded husband are growing serious herb up there." In fact, Susan grows just about every kind of herb except for *Cannibas sativa:* comfry, rue, Texas mint marigold, lantana, love-lies-bleeding. These herbs are the basis for what is, literally, a cottage industry. Susan has a mail-order herb bookstore, a widely circulated herb newsletter, and a successful series of mystery novels. The main character in her books, China Bayles, is a lawyer who has dropped out of the rat race to grow herbs and run an herb shop in a small town in Texas Hill Country. Unlike the author, however, the heroine is reluctantly called upon to use her skills of deduction and detection to sort out all manner of murderous skulduggery. Narcs take note, that's heroine with a final "e."

Susan Wittig Albert's mysteries are as far as you can get from Chandler and Elroy and remain in the murder mystery genre. Reading her books, you learn a lot about Albert's fiercely independent heroine and much about herbs. Among the titles are *Love Lies Bleeding, Thyme of Death*—you get the idea. The one I brought with me on the plane, *A Rueful Death,* is set mainly in a rural Texas abbey where an order of nuns grows rocambole, a highly prized garlic. A merger of two disparate convents has created a poisonous atmosphere at the monastery. The story has suspicious deaths, threats, and arson. Poor China Bayles. All she wanted was a quiet retreat at the abbey to recuperate from a frantic holiday season.

There is a power in getting away from routine. When my father was diagnosed with tuberculosis as a teenager, he was forced to rest for a year—no radio, no books. Until then he was an okay student. After the year of forced isolation, with no study whatsoever, he emerged the kind of world-beating student who roared out of his working-class Italian American neighborhood and swooped into a very successful career as a professor of American literature. He admits that something magical happens when you get away, break the routine, and try something challenging in a new environment, which is probably why any extra cash my folks ever had while I was growing up was poured into travel and many years abroad. They didn't even buy their first house until I was in high school.

Susan points out two kinds of basil in one of her lovingly groomed herb gardens: the lemon- and cinnamon-scented. She says she'd like to have China get involved with this herb, but the story has yet to suggest itself. I mention that my Neapolitan forebears had an interesting word for basil, or *basilico* in Italian. Spoken quickly, the word in that dialect mutated into the more affectionate *vasenicola,* which is understood as slang for *vasa Nicola,* or "kiss Nicole."

Susan brightens. "We could call the book *The Kiss of Death!*"

It's too bad *Basil* Rathbone can't play China's husband in the movie version, I observe.

Susan gives me a look that suggests I refrain from using that line if I should ever be asked to address an herb convention. But then all is forgiven and I'm allowed in for some warm muffins around a farmhouse table. If this sort of place is what Jennifer Ames, the banjo player in Levelland, wryly referred to as "manufactured housing," I can't tell from the inside. The Alberts' double-wide has the feel of a summer cottage. The kitchen is decorated with handmade wooden and fabric crafts. The living room is lined with books. Susan's résumé notes her Ph.D. from the University of California, Berkeley. She was dean of Sophie Newcomb Memorial College, the women's college at Tulane. Later she became vice president for Academic Affairs at Southwest Texas State I ask if her trajectory might have naturally led to a position as university president.

"That was my career path, no doubt about it."

Now, the job of senior official at an academic institution has been likened to a person standing in a graveyard: there are lots of people under you, but no one is listening. Still, the job usually comes with an excellent, often furnished residence and an august title, such as chancellor or president. Why bail?

Susan spent a lot of time considering just this question as preparation for a book she wrote a few years back called *A Work of Her Own: A Woman's Guide to Success off the Career Track.*

"I heard women say they did not like playing competitive games in organizations to either salve someone's ego or preserve their budget," Susan says. "I didn't like those games. I just wanted to do the work, but it was always a power struggle and it became wearing, physically. I have a bad back. I had stress headaches." There was a divorce along the way as well.

"It got to be too much. I just wanted time for myself."

But quitting must have brought a whole new set of stresses.

"You know, I was never scared of the money part of it. I did have some concerns about the part of me that had identified myself with the job, who wore the label of college vice president," Susan says. "It was the loss of the professional identity that frightened me more than the loss of the money."

I pressed ahead with some rudely invasive questions about how Susan paid for the transition.

Did she have savings at the time she left the warm embrace of tenure?

Yes, but the $40,000 she had was used to close out some debt from an old entrepreneurial venture, a typing and copying service. She has a separate small retirement nest egg that she has never touched, which has grown eighteenfold over eighteen years: the pension plan to which she contributed while at Tulane.

She met Bill Albert, who ran the computerized death and birth records at the Texas Bureau of Vital Statistics. A cautious and bearded man with hands stained the color of iodine by the pecans he was harvesting this morning, Bill is a fierce saver. He thinks it has something to do with his heritage.

"My relatives were the tightest bunch."

When he was in the army, he often found himself with three uncashed paychecks in his locker, figuring he didn't need any spending money because the government was feeding and sheltering him. His one indulgence is the purchasing of used woodworking tools. ("The cost of a two-by-two and a two-by-four is roughly the same, so if you cut it down the middle you can double your money.")

Bill's savings, however, are considered his, and if the family, meaning Bill and Susan jointly, needs money, it's borrowed against the savings, as if Bill were the bank. They have no debts, and credit cards are used only for managing business-related expenses and are paid off each month. The first trailer home on their property, which they lived in before purchasing the double-wide, cost $4,800. The septic system cost $2,000, the well $4,000. Installation of electricity was just $200 because a neighbor had already strung the lines. The land, located in a part of the Hill Country remote enough from hip Austin or the quaint towns of Kerrville and Fredericksburg, was cheap. When they upgraded to the double-wide, which cost $36,000, they paid cash from the Bank of Bill (Bill's long-term savings) and paid it back out of their business profits in eighteen months. Figuring in inflation, the Alberts in the 1990s paid for their homestead about what a G.I. Bill veteran would have paid for a Levittown home in 1947.

Through trial and error, the Alberts have gotten the bill for food, clothing, and shelter down to $1,000 a month. They have a small-dish satellite for TV, but otherwise they have to entertain each other, living way out in the sticks. Susan says a genetic abnormality also helps the couple live simply: she abhors shopping and can't fathom why anyone would consider it recreation. That $1,000 a month, however, is just a third of their expenditures. The other two-thirds consists of health, life, and car insurance and taxes. Bill, an Ayn Rand reader, hates taxes. He complains bitterly about property taxes being the one reason one can't live wholly off the grid and be self-reliant. He uses the metaphor of the British hut tax in colonial South Africa.

"They needed a labor force, but people were more interested in subsistence living, so they introduced a hut tax so that people had to take formal jobs to raise the cash necessary to pay the tax," Bill says. Property tax was the first wedge; now there's the need for health insurance, Bill argues. "You've got to have a real-world job to survive."

The other thing that can stop an attempt to quit the rat race and downsize your life is children. Susan had three kids when she was eighteen, nineteen, and twenty-one years old. All had already hit their most expensive college age before their mother decided to pull the plug on most of her income. Susan is quite tough on this point, however.

"I educated myself, and I always assumed that my kids were going to do that. I never assumed that I was going to put my kids through school." Two have college degrees and one does not.

Still, the Alberts aren't just surviving off their herb garden. Susan's newsletter has 1,200 subscribers; the mail-order bookstore does well; and aside from the China Bayles series, there is also a Victorian mystery series she co-authors with Bill. Publishers have been doling out increasing amounts of advance money for each new China Bayles book. The lawyer-turned-herb-gardener-and-investigator is now providing most of the couple's income. Bill recognizes the one essential ingredient in any successful entrepreneurial venture: good fortune. It turns out herb folks had a hunger for their product.

"That was the one piece of luck that we had," Bill says. "We had no idea what the herbal market was once we started, and it turns out the contemporary herbal is outselling the historical five to one. We might have picked the wrong market."

Susan likes to say Bill has an "imagination of disaster." His planning is full of doomsday scenarios. This makes for robust forecasts. Many of the slings, arrows, and other surprises of life are already in the script, so that a forced march back to the workaday world of staff meetings, performance reviews, and commuter traffic seldom looms as a real threat. When this "bit of luck" comes the Alberts' way, it's gravy. So far, Bill's disaster scenarios remain untested, possibly because of their planning or possibly because they haven't been at their new life quite long enough. But what if the gentle mist of this morning ever turned into an extended deluge? That happened to Rod Kennedy in another Hill Country town an hour and a half away. A quarter of a century ago he quit his day job, and it has been a wild ride ever since.

It is pouring as Rod and I tear down Texas Highway 16 in his Ford Probe GT in search of a sandwich and a smoothie. Luckily, Rod has equipped this pocket rocket with seven-inch-wide sticky Goodyears, and so, Rod brags, he can take a right turn at 70 miles per hour. He's had the car for two years, and he's on his second set of these tires at $1,000 a set.

"I'm beginning to think I should slow down."

Sixty-six-year-old Rod Kennedy is a businessman who was instrumental in getting John Tower, the late conservative Republican senator from Texas, elected to national office. He is a combat veteran of Korea who believes the welfare system does more harm than good. He is a race car driver who won the Sebring Twelve Hour race for his class in 1970 in a Facetti-tuned Lancia that he got for cash plus one of his Ferraris.

Yet the Probe's license plates read "FOLK."

Rod Kennedy is also the founder and producer of what is arguably America's top folk music festival, held every year in Kerrville. The *Dallas Morning News* calls him a feminist. Kennedy's best friend is the Peter of Peter, Paul, and Mary.

How Kennedy got from A to B is a fascinating enough story. But the ups and downs of his long B period are a gut-wrenching example of just how hearty you have to be to take your money and punt in the direction of doing what you want to do.

"Peter Yarrow says I'm not a Republican. Tom Paxton says I'm a damn Republican. I'd say I'm a moderate Republican," says Kennedy.

Kennedy, a compact man with a gray beard who seems to have kept a lot of the upper-body strength that served him well as a marine, has a low-key way of talking about his own remarkable exploits. The marine supply clerk honed his skills as an impresario by bringing musical entertainment to his remote base in the Mojave Desert.

When he returned from Korea, he auditioned for LBJ's big 50,000-watt station in San Antonio and was told to get some experience and come back. What he did instead was turn to a classical music station because his musical parents had taken him to the symphony all his life. He became sales manager and then bought the station for $21,000. Some people are born businessmen. For all those thousands of hours I sat alone in radio studios as a young fellow, gazing into space waiting for what seemed like eternity to put in the local station identification for the Red Sox game or the Texaco Metropolitan Opera broadcasts, it had never once occurred to me to figure out a way to actually buy a radio station. Kennedy didn't think twice.

He also got into some serious event promotion, as Rod puts it, "from Roller Derby to the Lipizzaner stallions." Along the way he used his promotional skills to get public television started in Texas. Later he moved on to politics. He had Maseratis, Porsches, V-12 Jaguars. He owned a dealership for Formula One cars. In 1972 he was tapped to go to Kerrville to see if the private sector could come up with funding for a folk music festival to supplement the crafts fair the Texas Commission on the Arts and Humanities was funding in Kerrville.

"So I sold my home and bought the ranch, as they say." This is exactly what I was afraid of. It is this fear that stops most of us from demanding a sabbatical or going all the way and dropping out.

Here's what happened. In years one, two, and three of this venture, the crowds came. By year three the festival was moved outside to accommodate the folk pilgrims who came from across the country to see people like Carolyn Hester and Jerry Jeff Walker perform. Then in years four, five, and six, the rains came and the crowds did not. The weather wasn't all that cooperative in years seven through ten either.

"In sixteen years I lost a million dollars." Kennedy was forced to drive junk cars. The bankruptcy filing came in 1991.

Now the festival has turned around. Big stars like Nancy Griffith showed up for a twenty-fifth reunion concert. More than thirty thousand people have turned out for the festival in recent years, and the debt is down dramatically.

I look out at the drizzle from the protection of the Coca-Cola umbrella under which we are eating left-wing, sprout-laden sandwiches.

"What if it rains again?" I want to know.

"Well, that wouldn't be very good. We don't buy rain insurance because it's outrageous."

What Kennedy has done is to set up a foundation, in part to support the Kerrville festival. A substantial part of the financial backstop comes from the proceeds from successful New Folk concerts he puts on.

Kennedy's savings account at the moment has just $200 in it. But he is about to be paid $10,000 a year for nine years to give someone else the right to run the festival under its current name. His corporation will also be paid for some of the buildings on the ranch, and some of that will come to Kennedy because the corporation owes him money. And once the festival gets out of debt, he can raise his salary from its current $159 a week. For seventeen years he took no salary, but the bankruptcy court has mandated that little amount.

What's he going to do with the windfall, if you can call it that, after all he's invested?

Kennedy gets his personal finance advice from the Peter of Peter, Paul, and Mary. Peter Yarrow suggests Rod put it into thirty-year Treasury bonds. At least he didn't say war bonds. I figure with all that risk that Kennedy has lived with all his years, Yarrow thinks it's time for him to put what money he has into a sure thing.

Still, finding yourself in your late sixties expecting more but actually having just two hundred bucks in your savings account is not going to make you the centerfold in the April *Money* magazine. In fact, Kennedy could probably make extra cash selling This-Could-Happen-to-You posters of himself so that stockbrokers could finish off prospective clients by unfurling the image to the sound of an orchestra playing an ominous chord.

I consider myself warned. But I am left with a question raised by my conversation here in Kerrville. Who would I rather be, the former Rod Kennedy, rich business tycoon destined for a financially secure retirement? Or the Rod Kennedy that we have now, doing exactly what he wants to be doing, looking fifteen years younger than he is, living the kind of life that some of the students over in Levelland dream about? The choices for most of us probably don't have to be this polarized, but before I can begin to answer this key question, I have to take a crack at something I have never done before, even in passing: try to squint through the murk and discern the outlines of my own retirement, perhaps three decades hence.

Souvenirs

A red harmonica tuned to the key of C.

Professor Hartin's wisdom that life is not a dress rehearsal.

To do when I get home

Call Floating the Apple in New York to see if they still need volunteer carpenters.

Doing the numbers

A survey released the same month as my Texas trip found that 38 percent of Americans have seriously considered cutting back their working hours. (Source: *U.S. News & World Report*/Bozell Worldwide Survey)

10

Seek a Gray Area

Putting it toward retirement in
Tucson, Arizona

From the clipping file: A fifty-four-year-old former Nestle worker from Granite City, Illinois, won $3 million. The *St. Louis Post-Dispatch* quoted him saying, "Now I can retire early." February 27, 1997.

One of the reasons teenagers take foolish risks, too often with tragic conse-quences, is that the idea of death at their age is so abstract that immortality seems almost as plausible. For me the idea of retirement is almost as abstract.

My parents are not yet retired, so it seems a generation early to be worried about it. Still, I am the guy voicing all the headlines warning about the Social Security system unraveling right about the time I am old enough to need it.

Applying a surplus to retirement is a noble endeavor. Thinking ahead and deferring gratification are seen as the mark of a mature individual. It is also the public-spirited course, in the sense that the more I take responsibility for my own retirement, the less money high-net-worth individuals will have to pay in taxes to support me in my dotage. After all, I do want to go out of my way to make life as easy as possible for high-net-worth individuals.

But I will never take the idea seriously of using a surplus in this way if I cannot even visualize my retirement. What will a retirement community look like in the year 2040, when I am eighty? It occurs to me that if all the warnings about global warming are to be believed, my retirement will have to be in a kind of artificial world in a bubble, surrounded by a geodesic dome to keep the superheated toxic environment away from my elderly lungs. Such a place already exists, although it has yet to house old people. I arranged to visit Biosphere 2, in the desert outside Tucson. The place also happens to be a manageable drive from the site of an innovative experiment in retirement living that helped me make the idea of my own retirement more concrete. As luck would have it, the visit took place on the day the stock market nearly crashed.

The retirement explorations were later broadened when I met up with a traveler from Africa who would discuss a very different vision of life toward the end of life, one that requires a much more modest surplus.

Living in the moment is not the way to start thinking about my distant future. Well, tough luck, because at this moment I have achieved perfect harmony. It is a Sunday night; there is no traffic on the highway leading north from Tucson; the flavor and temperature of the double cappuccino is *precisely* where it should be; and the car radio has a nice lock on Vin Sculley calling the ninth inning of the seventh game of the World Series. The Marlins and the Indians are tied, and the tension stretches into extra innings. With nothing to do but drive into the blackness, I am visualizing the game in three dimensions from field level, way beyond what even high-definition television could ever provide. I must have been slipped caf instead of decaf. So much the better. With two out at the bottom of the eleventh, two things happen simultaneously. Edgar Rentaria hits a line drive behind first base and the Marlins win it, and a green highway sign announces my destination: "Biosphere, 2 miles."

I had figured why stay at a Ramada when it is possible to pay for a room at the Biosphere, the famous three-acre terrarium in the desert between Tucson and Phoenix? I'm not retiring for at least thirty more years, and by then the environment may be so degraded that I and all my contemporaries could be spending our last years cultivating oxygen in big sealed bubbles like this.

It is very late, but the security guard at the gate of the Biosphere campus is expecting me and directs me to my bungalow. The facility is now a tourist attraction, a conference center, a working environmental laboratory, and an earth science training program run by Columbia University. But the Biosphere reached its pinnacle of fame a few years ago when billionaire Ed Bass helped bankroll an ambitious experiment. Eight volunteer scientists were to be locked up for two years in a self-sustaining Earth-under-glass, an experiment that was beset by problems, including an atmosphere that became so degraded it had more carbon dioxide and less oxygen than the space capsule had during the *Apollo 13* disaster. Since 1996 Biosphere 2 has been run by Columbia, but its new managers still seem to be having trouble regulating enclosed environments: the temperature in my room is hovering near 55 degrees on this October night, and the little button marked "Heat" seems to be having no effect. Bundling up in my fleece jacket and two layers of blankets, I switch off the light and hunker down for some sleep, a process soon interrupted by a noise.

"Mmmmmuurrrrooooooooh."

Again, twelve seconds later, another long breath pitched between a moan and a growl. It is just five days to Halloween and feels like it.

"Mmmmmuurrrrooooooooh."

I switch on the light and grab a map of the facility. The sound seems to be coming from down and west of my room, and that, according to the map, is the direction of the Biosphere itself. The map position marked "e" provides an answer, the location of what are called the "lungs," a pair of big balloons that allow the atmosphere inside the biosphere to expand and contract. It is the sound of the Biosphere breathing. I sleep fitfully with my limbs tucked closely at my side.

The next morning I discover one other possible interpretation of the terrifying noises. They were perhaps the distant death rattle of investors in the Hong Kong stock market, which had been crashing overnight.

I am pleased to see that chill has not actually caused ice to form in the toilet and dress quickly to beat the dawn over to the main Biosphere building. As the second hand on my watch hits the mark at precisely 7:00:00 A.M., a spotlight of sun crests the ridge of the Catalina Mountains and paints left to right across the glass front of the main Biosphere.

The desert biome gets the light first, followed by the ocean biome and finally the rain forest biome. The "human habitat" gets the light last. I had expected something twenty-third century, but the Biosphere gives an almost retro impression, like a Victorian crystal palace crossed with a pair of Mayan temples. The modernist touches come from two geodesic domes flanking the structure, the lungs.

The Biosphere was built between 1984 and 1991 for about $200 million. Visionaries saw it as a prototype for a Mars colony; others wanted to see if, given the right ingredients, one could brew a self-sustaining little planet. But it was never really self-sustaining; there was always a need for light from the sun and a lot of power coming in from the western grid. And while the media made a big deal when it emerged that one of the Biospherans had slipped out to seek treatment for a cut finger, at a more profound level the whole thing just didn't work right. Most of the insect species bit the dust, leaving the place overrun with crazy ants and cockroaches. Among the insects that died were the pollinators, so agriculture was compromised. The ocean turned alkaline. And a combination of microbes in the soil and not-quite-cured concrete in the structure ate much of the oxygen out of the air, making it difficult for the Biospherans to breathe. But just because the premise of the Biosphere did not work does not mean it was a disaster. The world was left a vivid scientific reminder that technology may not offer much of an alternative if we screw up the planet.

As I stare into the misty humidity of the rain forest biome, huge tropical trees seem to menace the windows like caged, snarling carnivores. The impulse to try to manufacture a living, breathing community begins to seem arrogant. What would it have been like to be bottled up here with seven others for months on end? How would I know in advance if this is for me? Is there a way to choose your companions and choose the activities within the Biosphere to make a life by design work, the kind of life by design one would find in a retirement community?

Ever since Wall Street, I have been trying to train myself to avoid focusing on the moment-to-moment moves of the stock market, a tough discipline for someone in my trade.

On the day the U.S. Treasury visited and wryly suggested I not mention the Dow's daily movements in an effort to encourage longer-term thinking, I tried to uphold the principle. The Dow rose twelve points, which is, on the great time line of civilization, hardly another signing of the Magna Carta. So I didn't say anything about it for the first five minutes of our radio program, and I immediately began feeling out of sorts. Ten minutes went by and still no Dow had passed my lips. My gut started feeling as though it were being squeezed by fireplace tongs. After fifteen minutes I was shaking all over, and about seventeen minutes into the program, I caved and spilled the beans about the Dow's very modest gain. I had been conquered again by habit and convention. I am part of the problem, feel bad about it, and the guilt continues to manifest itself in annoying ways. Like the way I am now behaving in the desert southeast of Tucson.

A group of very nice people are taking a tour of a small part of what used to be called the Rocking K Ranch and is now the future site of the Academy Village, part of a nonprofit called the Senior Academy. It will be a retirement campus for the sort of folks who might have "emeritus" in their title or for artists, writers, and other interesting professional people. It will be assisted living for people with active minds who want to continue using their minds in retirement in a Medicare-approved setting that is affiliated with the nearby University of Arizona. The group is on a fact-finding mission to see just how all their retirement savings and investments can be specifically deployed here. I tag along, with one ear plugged into a little Sony, announcing aloud the Dow every fifteen minutes, like a persistent, overgrown gnat. The market appears to be crashing, and I am bent on getting a rise out of these genial people.

Harold Abel, in his early seventies, has been president of several colleges. He is wearing a fishing hat and a beige windbreaker and stands on a bluff by a saguaro cactus so regular in its symmetry that it suggests a menorah. Dr. Abel and his wife are gazing down the gravelly hill at a piece of white PVC pipe that marks the spot where their future Senior Academy retirement home will be built. They squint to help imagine the view from what will be their living room, and their heads are filled with the lively, smart community that could be.

"Hoo, baby. The Dow is now down 172 points." I have just saun-
tered into the Abel's dream wearing dusty boots.

The couple appears unimpressed by my statistic. Abel's latest project
is serving as chancellor of a distance-learning university via the Internet.
The couple has a condo in Naples, Florida, and they like their tennis and
enjoy their neighbors. But they miss the camaraderie of the campus environment and the intellectual stimulation that comes with it.

"How often can you discuss the weather?" Abel wonders when I ask
what is missing from his life in Florida.

"The Dow's off 233, captain. I canna holder her much longer," I report from engineering.

Elizabeth Zinser, chancellor of the University of Kentucky's Lexing-
ton campus, is the only plausible Trekkie in the group. She laughs and
says she would never put herself into a position in stocks that would either succeed or fail based on one day's market movements. Will she take
any action based on the market today? Maybe it's a buying opportunity,
but only that.

Zinser is here with her husband, Don, who lives in another state.
She is clearly much too young to be thinking about immediate retirement, but I can imagine that there must be a longer-term plan to end the
commuting that a long-distance marriage requires. She wants the Senior
Academy to share her general values about community while attracting
people from as diverse backgrounds as possible.

"That's what I love about the academic environment," Zinser says.
"That's what I want in a community in which I would live during what
I might not refer to as retirement because I don't plan to retire. I want to
write, I want to stay involved in teaching, I want to get involved in volunteer work, I want to learn Spanish and start studying some things
from that perspective, and so I've got a lot of ambitions, mostly intellectual and volunteer, and I'd like to live and work and study with other
people who have the same interests." The Senior Academy is working on
a formal structure that will allow residents to volunteer in leadership
roles in Tucson and at the University of Arizona.

I soon learn about one subject she would like to write about. I'm awful with names, but Dr. Zinser's seems eerily familiar. She notices my
gaze lingering on her name tag and reminds me of an incident that

gained headlines in 1988. She had been forced to resign after only five days as head of Gallaudet, a university for hearing-impaired students in Washington, D.C. Only one credential had been in question: Zinser is not deaf. There is no bitterness in the way she briefly recounts the story, and she says she remains close with Gallaudet officials and many of the students of the time. She makes it clear she expects the Academy Village to be a place full of people of diverse backgrounds, disciplines, and culture, or she won't sign on.

My radio tells me the Dow is now down 320. I make sure that Zinser and the rest of the group appreciate the fact that if the index drops to minus-350, the stock exchange's circuit breaker will pop for the first time in history.

"They have stopped trading for a half hour," I announce in a sepulchral tone.

Harold Abel looks at me, shakes his head, and announces he'll need to get to the airport.

"Yeah, if that's the case, we will have to go home now," he says somberly.

"Because of the market?" I ask, nervous now that I have actually frightened somebody, a senior citizen, at that.

"Well, sure, I can't afford the hotel now, let alone buy another retirement house." Abel eyes are twinkling. He is a long-term investor who has no plans to call his broker anytime soon.

"Look, if you can't brush off a day like today, you are in trouble," he says. "Unless I'm having what I like to call a 'senior moment' here, I'm still way ahead for the year. If you forget about the fact that 'If I would'a sold at the peak,' I think we are in relatively good shape. Second, from everything I read and understand, I think the economic fundamentals are sound and this may be a good opportunity for some people to buy."

Apparently the amateurs are calm; it's the pros who are having the bad day.

As we climb back in the cars to return to the hotel to learn more about the financing of the Senior Academy project, I snag the closing number. The Dow Jones Industrial Average has tumbled 554 points today, the worst point loss ever for that index. It is what will become known as Gray Monday. It's killing me that I'm not back in our newsroom at the helm. But it occurs to me that the real story is out here with real people, calmer than many of the expert traders and analysts I would normally be speaking with right about now.

Paul Lewis is driving. He is not much older than me and is the fellow who is turning the idea of the Senior Academy into cinder block and stucco. He is the project director for the Academy Village. He works for Pennsylvania-based US Retirement Communities, Inc.

"Well, David, you and me and our kids will now have to look forward to careers at McDonald's," Lewis says. Everyone's a comedian. I start to get defensive now that the tables are turned. It is only a drop of 7.2 percent, I insist. The crashes of '29 and '87 were three times the size of that.

At a hotel conference room, the ten couples are seated firing questions at Mr. Lewis.

- Will the library be a traditional one with lots of physical holdings or more geared to interlibrary loans and virtual information available via the Internet? (He's not sure.)
- Will there be a lot of nooks along the interior wall of the house plans? (Yes.)
- Linen service? (Yes.)
- Who will determine what the community's two vans will be used for? (The community itself.)
- And one show-stopping question that young families shopping for their first house rarely ask but perhaps should: How long is the ambulance trip to the university hospital? (Twenty minutes.)

Then it is the bottom-line stuff. One applies for membership to the Senior Academy. The founders seem to be looking for interesting life accomplishments coupled with a commitment to remain active and involved in the new community and the surrounding neighborhoods. You pay a $1,000 refundable fee when you apply for membership in the Academy. Then there's a $5,000 deposit on a spot in the Village itself. The next step is to really commit yourself and put up 25 percent of the cost of the house in preparation for the start of construction. The two-bedroom Mesquite will go for $195,000. The three-bedroom Saguaro goes for $310,000. There are models and another line of townhouses in between. Once you are in, there are monthly fees.

Some of the folks are a little queasy about tying up their money in the project before all the final financing is secured. That's the gamble: do it now, and you are committing to a project at a juncture when there are some loose ends, including an exact date for groundbreaking, which is set for five months hence. Wait too long and this place could become a hit and space could become rare. Lewis argues that those who put in their money the earliest are getting something else in return: the first pick of the properties. The assumption is that folks will sell a house they own already to buy one of these outright, often with no mortgage. And one other wrinkle in the financial arrangements here: Many retirement communities charge a sizable and nonrefundable entrance fee. The subtext is that it will be the last move that you will ever make. The Senior Academy does not charge this kind of fee because the project's organizers are well aware that their demographic is not shopping for a place to go to die.

The project's contractor then appears, waving a magic wand. It turns out to be a conduit, unraveled into a spray of individual cables to show in a literal way just how the houses of this community-to-be will be connected to the world. It is wide-band stuff, enough to Web- and channel-surf with abandon. In another era the contractor might have been tempted to demonstrate the newfangled icebox or later the hi-fi, but it's the end of the century and we are given a moment to worship the blue and yellow stands that will keep us wired. There is a murmur of admiration from the crowd when Paul mentions one Academy member who wants to fit one of the optional outbuildings, or *casitas,* with a dozen personal computers. The piano in the parlor tinkling away at ragtime in a traditional retirement community seems very remote indeed for a demographic that plans to be surfing electronically 'til the end.

It certainly seems to be the case for Neil in the denim shirt, blue jeans, and longish not-all-that-gray hair. Neil graduated from medical school in 1969. He paid money for Peter, Paul, and Mary concerts and James Taylor concerts. "Vietnam" is still a word with deep resonance for him. Why in tarnation is a youngster like this taking notes at a retirement project? Neil, it turns out, has been learning from his parents' experience with retirement and is now doing some very explicit early planning for himself and his wife, Edie.

For twenty years his parents have led a physically active retirement life full of travel. But now, twenty years into retirement, their age is beginning to curtail the travel and they have put down what are essentially permanent stakes.

Neil, a physician who teaches and is an administrator at a medical school, has properties in Montana and London and is ready to embrace the first phase of his retirement when it comes around in a dozen years or so. But it's the next phase that he's doing research for on this day in Tucson, the less active phase. His parents were forced to sit on a waiting list for more than a decade before they got a spot in their retirement community of their choice. Neil figures if he has the money, it doesn't hurt to at least consider putting in early dibs on a place like this that is supposed to encourage continued intellectual involvement and where there is no snow to shovel.

After dinner at the hotel, a music student from the university has been invited to perform some classical guitar pieces. The passionate music provides the right background to hear from the man spearheading the Senior Academy, Dr. Henry Koffler, a Viennese-born biochemist and seventy-four-year-old president (emeritus) of the University of Arizona. The idea ignited from the friction of two conflicting forces, the need not to lose the experience and institutional knowledge of older faculty members rubbing up against the legitimate need to make room for younger blood.

"When people retire, they are put out to pasture," Koffler says. "This creates disconnections between generations and leaves an enormous amount of talent unused." The idea of a retirement campus associated with a university arose from this. But bringing talented people together into a community with the hope that they will go on working and staying creative also requires that they stay healthy, which explains the second crucial element in the Academy, the continuing health care part.

But money alone won't get you into Koffler's community. It is open only to Academy Members, and to be a member one must apply. And people who have lived the kind of lives that were long on accumulating a surplus and short on community involvement may have trouble getting in.

"We are interested in past accomplishments, but more important, how people plan to remain engaged, and past experience indicates to us that individuals are likely to wish to remain engaged," Koffler says. "The assumption is that people who have led active lives and enjoyed their work are more likely to continue doing so [after retirement] than others who haven't enjoyed it."

The Biosphere scientists had trouble engineering a community. Will this visionary academic administrator and biochemist have better luck? We like to think of campuses as high-minded places to share knowledge, but anyone who knows anything about academia can tell you about departments mired in backbiting politics, plotting, and fierce competition. Koffler agrees that this is a concern but has two answers. First, he argues, in his Academy department barriers will not exist. Second, academic tenure and promotion also will not be a factor.

"Our people are already at the peak of their influence, and they need not strive. They are also in a position where they can return to society some of the benefits that they have received. And certainly, having now met literally thousands of individuals who might be interested in participating, they strike me as an exceptionally attractive and pleasant group of people."

But while the Academy will try to keep its population diverse, there is one implied bit of homogeneity that is striking. Everyone there will be older. Koffler recognizes this limitation. In a perfect world the Senior Academy would actually be located on the University of Arizona campus, in direct contact with students and current faculty. But there are practical problems with this. Costs would be high, and the Senior Academy would need to be placed in a high-rise apartment, and Koffler is pretty sure he could not attract folks to Tucson to retire in a high-rise block of apartments. Instead, the Academy will try to encourage the mixing of ages through its outreach projects. In theory this should mean all the mentoring a resident can handle without the noise of late-night frat parties. If they want to hear the sound of student music, they can always hire a music student for an hour.

The guitarist attacks his guitar with rising tension and drama. The little stock ticker I have implanted near my pineal gland sounds an alarm. Fifteen time zones away the Asian markets are getting savaged again. I beat a retreat to the television in my hotel room. CNBC has bumped the usual Geraldo-on-the-left and Chris-Mathews-on-the-right polemic and scooped gobs of heart-in-mouth reporters onto their prime-time schedule to talk about the renewed march of grim numbers now coming out of Hong Kong and Tokyo. The Hang Seng Index at the moment is down 16.7 percent.

"We'll be back with more of the market meltdown in just a moment," the anchorwoman says amiably into the camera. It is like the legendary TV news tease from the movie *The Groove Tube:* "Moscow in flames; missiles headed toward New York; film at eleven." I angle the laptop in view of the TV so that I can plan for my retirement and witness the apocalypse at the same time.

This trip to the desert is working. When I stand at the intersection of Bob Hope Drive and Dinah Shore Way in a place for older folks such as Palm Springs, California, retirement has nothing to do with me whatsoever. Now I have seen a concept that I might be able to live with, if they would have me. And it has a specific price. Let us say I am able to sell whatever home I own later in life to raise the capital to make a purchase in Koffler's village. It is an even swap, minus some real estate transaction costs. Now, the Senior Academy brochure here says I will be charged a fee of $2,455 a month to cover two people in the 2,157-square-foot Ironwood model for all the costs of the community, the library, the tennis courts, and most important, the assisted-living health facilities. I am ashamed to admit this is the first time in my life I have done even this rough kind of back-of-the-envelope retirement calculation.

- So $2,455, plus about $500 a month bare bones living expenses.
- That's $3,000 a month, or $36,000 a year.
- I won't want to move in for about another thirty years, minimum.
- If inflation rises at about 4 percent a year for the next thirty years and the Senior Academy's fees rise with inflation, then the fees will be about $120,000 a year.

- What kind of investment will be big enough to throw off $120,000 a year for my retirement expenses? At 6 percent interest (I can't have it in a very aggressive instrument at that age), I will need $2 million to generate more than $120,000 a year if I don't touch the principle.
- I forgot about paying tax on the capital gain. What is the right figure? Given the population bulge just ahead of me and if the government doesn't trim Social Security and Medicare benefits, I'll be paying about 70 percent taxes.
- But there is another problem: those retired boomers will have enormous political clout and they will ensure that the tax burden is shifted to the younger, working population. So I'll figure 30 percent, combined federal and state taxes.
- With all that figured in, I will need about $2.55 million.

How do I get two and a half million dollars in thirty years? Take the kind of surplus I once squandered away in London as a starting point, $17,000, and contribute $1,000 a month, without fail, for the next thirty years, and pray the stock market will generate its promised 10 percent appreciation, which is optimistic, given investment expenses, commissions, and my luck. If I can realize only a 6 percent return over the next thirty years, I'll need to contribute $2,400 a month. The huge difference between contributions necessary at the two rates of return is another example of the miraculous effects of compounding. The reality of the situation is that, with pain, there is the faintest chance I might be able to do the extra $1,000 a month, but there is no way I can do the $2,400. The point becomes clear: I am not taking irresponsible risks or being greedy or lazy by opting for the stock market over bonds. If I want to live in a Senior Academy someday, I do not have any choice. And this doesn't include other goodies that I might want in my life between now and then, including an education for my children. If I should get lucky with a surplus, there is now a fine argument to put it right here, retirement.

Over on the television, the market is not generating 10 percent a year. In parts of the world, it has fallen by that much in a matter of hours. The only thing to do is switch it off.

✳   ✳   ✳

Ambulances. Retirement community home owner association meetings.
A place to die. It remains a little macabre planning for the later retirement years, like writing out a will. It is, of course, the fear of death at
work. A few weeks after my trip to Tucson, I catch up with a man who is
less neurotic about death than anyone I have ever met. Dr. Kofi Asare
Opoku was my professor when I studied briefly at the University of
Ghana during college. He is a renowned authority on African religion,
folklore, proverbs, and indigenous knowledge who is able to mix good
humor with a gravitas that is anchored in bedrock. When Flight Lieu-
tenant Jerry Rawlings of Ghana rang in the New Year of 1982 by seizing
power in his second coup d'état, the university near the capital closed
down and I was forced to return abruptly to the United States. Professor
Opoku was at a conference in Bali and I never had a chance to say good-
bye.

One day meandering in cyberspace, I typed in Opoku's name and
out popped his present location, as visiting professor in the religion department at a college in Pennsylvania. Lucky for me, his next academic
conference would not be in Bali but only a short flight away in San Francisco. At our meeting spot in Union Square, Opoku appears with his International Academy of Religion name tag still pinned to his
blue-and-white batik *dashiki*. He likes to play a joke on his students by
getting them to guess his age. He looks forty-one and turns out to be
sixty-four. "I have eaten more salt in my life than you can carry in a ten-
ton truck!" he teases his classes.

Opoku and I wander around San Francisco's tony shopping district
talking about materialism and his feeling that many Americans seem to
have lost the sense of purpose he saw during his visits to this country in
the 1960s. We pop into what is probably the city's fanciest store, Gumps,
where we have a chuckle at some $1,350 Pratezi bedsheets for sale on the
second floor. We linger the longest at a mixed hardwood and softwood
Polynesian sculpture located by the store's ground-floor elevators. The
work is the one thing that is not for sale. He worries about the influence
of consumerism and television on his teenage son, who is staying with
him in Pennsylvania, a son who gets to hear a lot of proverbs from his

father about responsibility, community, and money. There is the one about savings, for instance. "The animal who does not trim his claw will be able to scratch his itch."

Did I know that among his people, the Akan, debt is considered a very bad thing? Opoku asks. In America, if you go in to buy something and have no credit, the impression given is that you have done something very bad. Opoku finds too many people in North America lacking in passion, be it for politics, issues, or even values.

We are pretty interested in money, I suggest.

Opoku wryly agrees.

"But you've got to leave something behind when you go, David," Opoku says. "And I don't mean just things. I mean a legacy of what you have done, how you have contributed to your community."

Opoku is officially retired from the University of Ghana, from which he receives a pension of some 171,000 Ghanaian cedies a month. All those zeros are misleading: that's about $100 a month. So he accepts visiting professorships with a view to eventually retiring to his farm, fifteen acres of tropical forest in Ghana.

"I am going to disturb only three acres. The rest will never be touched," he says. "When I die, I will be buried in the forest so it becomes a *sacred* forest that cannot ever be developed."

There are many of these sacred forests in his country, areas for burial where trees and other plants have been discovered that botanists once thought extinct. Opoku's plan is to make sure his patch will stay, even if all the rest of Africa's tropical forest goes. In recent years he has planted eighty-nine seedlings he picked up from the Ghanaian forest service that may not reach maturity for hundreds of years, his gift to the world.

"You asked about money. I want to make a little money so I can fence the property. You are not supposed to venture into the sacred forest because the ancestors are buried there, but at the moment I'm not buried there and people now go in to take firewood, and I want the property to be for everybody in perpetuity."

"How are you going to eat when you retire there?" I inquire, not able to resist at least one bottom-line question.

Dr. Opoku has a plan. The lower part of his farm's valley is very

damp, perfect for raising a simpler kind of livestock that can both provide sustenance and be sold for cash.

"All I will do is raise snails," he says. "They are not like chickens. You
don't need to give them medicines and what-not. No, the snails can take
care of themselves. Snails are big business. And then I will write."

Opoku is intent on continuing to learn from people with the kind
of indigenous knowledge that Western scholarship has usually scorned.
And he is writing much of it in his first language, Twi. In his lectures
around the world, he likes to emphasize the point that traditional
African people do not live by superstition or guesswork; they lived on
the basis of knowledge, knowledge with ongoing moral and in many
cases environmental utility.

"When I appear before my ancestors, I want to be able to tell them,
'I did something with the language you left us; I put it into writing,
which was a form of communication in my day.' I want to be able to say
to my ancestors that I have chronicled as much of our people's wisdom
as I could. This is what I have to do in my 'retirement.' "

The professor has a future sense that puts mine completely to
shame. I can barely discern middle age, let alone retirement. The professor is thinking beyond retirement, about ways to use his skills to generate enough income to position himself to fulfill his *post*-retirement
goals. The word "retirement" has little meaning for him. His plan is to
build a legacy in the way he lives his life—a plan that for most of us
would not await age 59 1/2, when the government officially allows us to
start drawing on retirement money without penalty. The tragedy of considering a surplus is that it gets you off this track. It has come time to
pursue some simpler ambitions.

Souvenirs

A small flat stone I found at the desert site of the Academy Village
that will make a nifty pendant. Some see in it the neat flame of a
candle; others see praying hands. The concentric series of ocher and
beige ovoids imbedded in the little stone suggest to me something
from Georgia O'Keeffe. I take it as a sign the land is anything but
barren.

The understanding that even if you are too cool for shuffleboard, you are not immune from the cost of long-term care.

To do right away when I get home

Take some money and put it into a supplemental retirement account. Why fool with other investments that require after-tax money if I still have room left to contribute to this sweet tax-deferred deal the government permits? I'm not even close to the $10,000-a-year limit.

Doing the numbers

The average fifty-year-old has saved $2,300 for retirement. (Source: President's Council on Sustainable Development)

- -

11

Go Conservative

Saving in Seattle

From the clipping file: A thirty-five-year-old electronics industry technician from Cherry Valley, Massachusetts, won $8.5 million in the lottery. The *Boston Globe* reports he planned to put his check in the bank and "think about it for a while." June 27, 1995.

*J*ust weeks before the 1987 stock market crash, the state where I reside was so flush with cash that the governor persuaded the legislature to return to taxpayers a billion-dollar budget surplus. A rebate check for $232 eventually arrived in our mailbox. I remember the windfall, but I have no memory of how I disposed of it. Certainly it purchased nothing of permanence or significance. Four years later the same state was paralyzed by a bitter political fight over how to cope with a gaping budget deficit. If only the state had saved its surplus for the rainy day to come.

As that governor learned, one of the hazards of a surplus is that it demands some employment. My adventures are based on this very assumption, that you cannot just leave a surplus alone. Or can you?

When I began to consider saving it for the unexpected tragedies and opportunities that come our way, I got stuck on the "rainy day" part and imme-

diately thought of Seattle. The place is also the hub of a modern-day thrift movement, now dubbed "voluntary simplicity" and promoted by folks who argue that living with less is good for you. The movement decries consumption, exalts savings, and actually cherishes such colorless places to store money as passbook savings accounts and government bonds.

In keeping with this theme of thrift, I wanted to spend as little money as possible on this trip. To feel the effect of every cent I would have to spend, I resolved to use only cash except for the airline tickets. Seattle would prove to be full of more humble (rather than humbling) lessons about money. It was also a trip to retire this quest to understand the utility of a surplus and to let go of the obsession.

This was a bad idea.

It's wet, it's cold, and I've had to abandon my family after wolfing down a Thanksgiving meal so I could catch a plane to Seattle. I am now just through the front door of a rooming house on a residential street north of the Space Needle, and it seems I've stumbled into Mad Max's lair. A hairless young man with Doc Martins and many metal accessories welcomes me by feigning a punch to my teeth. Something between a laugh and a screech comes from a woman wearing sleeves so long her sweater would make a handy straitjacket if that should become necessary. Two guys, one in leather, one in a lumberjack, are using oversized cans of Foster's lager to block my path to the stairs. I timidly say I have reservations.

They think this is very funny. If I have reservations, then I will have to talk to Greg. The lumberjack beckons me toward the closed door of one of the hostel's bedrooms.

"Greg doesn't like to get woken up," the lumberjack warns, and before I can stop him, he takes his boot and delivers to the bedroom door three heavy kicks that freeze all activity in the hallway. The door opens and out steps a big, bleary-eyed fellow with eyebrows bigger than Neil Young's. Greg doesn't like to get woken up.

Now, it wasn't the concept that was wrong. I had figured a trip to Seattle to consider frugality, voluntary simplicity, and savings should not include a room at the Four Seasons. I had heard about the Green Tortoise backpackers hostel from a British friend, and at $16 a night it would be cheaper than camping. Still, even my groovy Seattle contacts thought this was not a good idea. What about a phone? What about your stuff? They didn't know to add, "What about Greg?"

Greg stares at me for a moment and shakes his head.

"Man, I hate to tell you this, but you've got the wrong Green Tortoise." The one I wanted is on this same street but about three miles south of here, downtown. The Internet and the guidebook addresses had disagreed, and for once the Internet was right. Greg turns out to be polite and helpful. He finds a map, gives me the directions, and wishes me well.

At the other Green Tortoise it also postapocalyptic, but in a more optimistic, *Star Trek* sort of way. As part of a convivial Thanksgiving night film festival in the hostel's common room, they are showing the very rare first *Star Trek* pilot episode, "The Cage," a film that was too cerebral for NBC in 1966 and never broadcast. I would have paid money to see this. This place is going to work out, after all. It is dormitory style, with four men to a room. They keep coffee and tea going for free in the kitchen at all hours. Who knows, maybe I'll meet some folks.

I pay in cash for two nights in advance plus an extra dollar for a two-day rental of a top sheet and blanket. Had that amount gone onto a credit card, I would have passed the next two days deluding myself that I still had this $33 left to spend. There was also a $20 room-key deposit, plus a $9 deposit for the bedding. True, I am tying up $29 in a no-interest situation, but it is just for two days, and this way there will be twenty-nine fewer dollars in my wallet crying out to be spent. I cannot remember the last time I paid cash for a room. I resolve to see if I can completely avoid using credit cards for the rest of the trip.

The irony is that the Puget Sound area, awash with the vast billions of both Boeing and Microsoft, can also arguably call itself the capital of savings. Grunge may be out, but voluntary simplicity and its corollary, savings, remain a growth industry. The *Simple Living* journal is headquartered here. There are study circles galore for those who want reinforcement from peers as they seek their cures for consumption. It is the home of the Learning for Life project and the New Roadmap Foundation, helpful resources if you want to associate with folks who won't look askance at you for preserving your 1977 living room sofa and 1986 Honda Civic wagon even though you can afford new ones.

So it is with great annoyance that I notice in the early light a distinct rainbow arcing over Lake Union and coming to an end at the University Village Shopping Center. A pot of gold will be found at a *shopping center*? It is said that this Main Street–themed mall has more than three times the patrons in a year than an entire season of Seattle Mariners' baseball games. I have arranged to start my day over coffee at the Starbucks, which in Seattle is like saying that we'll meet at the bus stop without specifying which one. Eventually I find the Starbucks that contains Sherry Avena, who runs Save for America, an organization that encourages kids to set up bank accounts and put money away. Avena is on her way to Grandma's house on an island in the Puget Sound on this day after Thanksgiving, and the only spending we will be doing at this mall is the $2.25 for the latté.

Avena doesn't have much faith that most of us will ever learn to save. Little kids you can teach, she says. From her hard experience, by the time children get to junior high and high school, it's all over. The consumption messages are just too strong. Once she ran a savings promotion at some high schools. The students were offered their chance at a grand prize if they put some modest savings into an account on a Tuesday. By Friday many had withdrawn the money to pay for weekend dates. And we grown-ups? Avena just shakes her head.

Kindergarten through third grade, however, is a different story. These kids can be taught the savings habit. They just need a regular, easy system for doing so. It's like brushing and flossing, Avena says.

Flossing suggests another approach to the problem entirely: arrange for dental hygienists to threaten folks with sharp stainless-steel implements every six months if they fail to save.

There is a theory that most people will not start saving until they turn forty-six. David Anderson, a down-to-earth economist in Missouri, once showed me a graph that tried to prove this phenomenon. It showed the postwar birth rate moved forward in time forty-six years to approximate the number of people turning forty-six on a given year. It follows the contours very nicely of the inflation-adjusted S&P 500. Anderson's analysis goes this way: on your forty-sixth birthday you wake up, slap your forehead, and yell, "Holy, moley, I'd better start socking away money for retirement." It was poignant for me to note that, once again, demographics are against me. The number of people turning forty-six, and perhaps then the stock market, reaches a nadir right around my retirement year.

Avena hears this tale of woe and regards it as even more reason to encourage my children to start saving now. But could she really mean we should tell our youngsters to make the great personal finance mistake of the late twentieth century, that is, put money into a passbook savings account earning an interest rate that just might equal inflation if we are lucky? Avena says big rates of return aren't really the issue; it is getting the children to put the money away for the future. The little interest payments are just a nifty bonus. Furthermore, passbook savings are not necessarily the final resting place of the kids' saved money. When the account gets high enough, the children and their parents are encouraged to consider buying thirty-year U.S. Treasury bonds on-line. More mature savers might even want to experiment with a stock mutual fund. A special fund for young investors is mentioned. Personal finance starts with savings, Avena says, but does not have to end there.

One of the problems with this system is that banks are famous for turning up their noses at piddling kiddie savings accounts. Save for America has done its research and can pull out charts that show that banks that are nice to children get business from their parents. In other words, participating banks get free advertising and get an inside shot at selling loans to the parents. One might argue that this means that even as the children are being encouraged to be frugal, the parents are being drawn toward debt. Still, if a family is going to take out a home equity loan to renovate the attic anyway, why shouldn't the child-friendly bank get the business?

Save for America helps schools coordinate all this through its Crayola-colored Web site. I ask Avena if she's encouraging saving as a habit by making it fun. She pauses, then shakes her head.

Saving, ultimately, isn't fun, she says. "It is like training for a sport. It is something that requires some discipline. It is about deferring gratification and teaching people that there are other reasons to take actions in life beyond fun." That is not what I wanted to hear. I half-hoped she would say saving is exhilarating, like a ride in a hot-air balloon, only with interest. Instead, it is rather like a DPT shot, a little painful but good for you.

In the car I foolishly hit the radio's first preset and find myself tuned to the station at AM 880, my personal idea of hell. It is Seattle's official source for Christmas tunes from the forties and fifties interspersed with what seems like the full 18 1/2 minutes per hour load of commercial spots, most with tags that follow the "No payments whatsoever until June of next year!" theme. My discomfort stems mostly from guilt, for I, too, have perpetrated this kind of programming. During several Christmases during my precollege years, I was the very fiend broadcasting a solid wall of holiday music and commercials to indoctrinate you with the spirit to spend. My punishment for this was more than swift; it was concurrent. For six hours a day I was chained to the studio, forced to listen to everything I put into the transmitter. As a result, "White Christmas" has a worse physiological effect on me than sucking down a doggy bag's worth of MSG.

As I wait for Vicky Robin to answer her front door, I manage to quash the rising urge to hum the chorus of "Little Drummer Boy" to myself. What a shocking faux pas that would be. This is the nerve center for Robin's New Roadmap Foundation, an outfit dedicated to help people break the cycle of consumption that can make even wealthy people feel they are falling behind.

The house in a neighborhood north of the University of Washington is pleasantly spartan. A Japanese rice-paper room divider. A serviceable couch. Robin invites me to sit for some tea at a dining room table covered with a brown plastic tablecloth. I search in vain for signs the fancy Waterford crystal has just been stashed out of sight or the Range Rover hidden under a camouflaged tarp. She walks the talk. Her black dress has an Amish note to it. She has chosen granny glasses that draw attention to the gray that is creeping into her hair. Vicky Robin says she lives on $625 a month; she takes in $1,000 a month. The rest goes into thirty-year Treasury bonds. The money from a book she co-authored with the late Joe Dominguez, *Your Money or Your Life,* has gone into the foundation that now preaches the gospel of simplicity and ratcheting back consumption. She believes that most of us are living on a diet of sugar alone, or spending and debt, and that a financial diet could leave us a lot healthier. She wants people to see their money as an expression of their core values. There is also a green subtext here.

"Environmental sustainability and frugality are very linked words," Robin says, "because sustainability is about spending today as if there is going to be a tomorrow. Frugality is the same thing. It's the understanding that if I spend all my money and I max out my credit cards, there is no more. Sustainability is about living within the limits of what the planet can provide."

Record amounts of money are pouring into the stock market via 401K plans and the like. Surely Americans are finally saving. What more does she want from us? Vicky is not wild about the stock market. She worries that it encourages folks to believe they can get something for nothing or to take bigger risks than they should, based on the feeling that stocks always go up. What she has a soft spot for is bonds.

"They are for people who really do not want to obsess about money," Robin says. "They want their investments straight up, meat and potatoes, earn some money, save, free up their time."

There can be a big opportunity cost for the stock market if it turns you into one of those folks who spends every waking hour checking the Internet or cable TV ticker, and *Barron's* and Rukeyser start to supplant real relationships. I think about our bedroom with my pillow, my wife's pillow, and our third partner, a computer connected to the markets. It can get perverse rather quickly.

But what about inflation? Stocks are supposed to be the great conqueror of inflation, while bonds, by design, often merely compensate for rising prices and not more. Robin points out that the end of the millennium has been marked by very low inflation, and what inflation there is is probably overstated. Even the powerful chairman of the Federal Reserve has wondered aloud if the government's main index of inflation, the Consumer Price Index, is exaggerating price rises. The CPI measures a predetermined basket of goods. Vicky Robin argues, simply, "Don't buy that particular basket of goods; buy a different, cheaper assortment of necessities." Car prices are rising? Don't buy a new car. Apparel prices going up? Get your stuff at a thrift store. Oil it or fix it yourself.

Also, Robin says, government bonds are safe. "Unless the whole world financial system collapses, the government is not going to reneg on its debt obligations." This principle should work unless you live in Russia, which did—effectively—default on its debt obligations, to the shock of Wall Street, as the century drew to a close.

Of course, there is an ideological issue at stake with bonds. Does not buying the government's debt encourage public profligacy in the name of our personal frugality? Vicky's not buying that. She responds that people who buy government bonds are helping to keep government expenses down by creating demand for the debt that lowers the interest rates the Treasury has to pay.

But if we do not consume much, we will put good people out of work and the economy could fall into recession. Isn't saving un-American? I ask.

Saving, Robin says, is inordinately American. Until the last forty years, the highest compliment was to be called frugal, one who makes good use of resources. Anyway, Robin says we don't actually spend money in a patriotic effort to help the economy.

"I do not know anyone who eats a high-fat diet to keep heart surgeons employed. We do things because we've become convinced it is good for us or that we will enjoy it or it passes the time. And targeting these myths can help us get our finances in order."

Still, $650 dollars a month. Let's not be unreasonable here. That must mean housing is taken care of. What about insurance, property taxes? Clearly, children cannot be part of that calculation. Just as the dean-turned-mystery-writer Susan Wittig Albert has taken a hard line about giving offspring a blank check for the cost of their higher education, Vicky Robin is pretty tough on this subject too, suggesting that offspring who contribute more to the cost of their education value it more. She talks about a doctor who decided to give his children money that would pay the cost of either one year's tuition at an Ivy League school or four years at a state school, their choice. The point, Robin says, is that if I want to make education my family's priority, that can be worked into our financial plan. It is only important that the money for education be an expression of our values, not based on myths or social pressure. The New Roadmap Foundation's big catch phrase is attaining FI, which can mean financial independence, financial intelligence, or even financial integrity. It is not, Robin says, a pot of money at the end of the rainbow.

Since it is the day after Thanksgiving, I have to ask if she is going shopping. Will she be tempted, even a little?

"No, first of all, I am quite aware that everything I buy and bring into the house I am going to have to deal with. It's like I don't own things; things own me. It is just more stuff to take care of. Also, my time is so valuable to me, and I don't want to put myself back in a job in order to support a Nordstrom habit. I know people who can go out and spend two thousand dollars on clothing in an afternoon and some of those clothes end up in the thrift store with their tags still on them, and I get a beautiful silk blouse for four dollars. So let them pay," she says.

I told her about the rainbow leading to the mall just down the street at daybreak. "Well, you know how hard it is to pinpoint the end of those rainbows," she laughs. Maybe there was a parallax error and it had actually ended over here.

This time of year is a seasonal version of the conundrum I faced at the casino in Las Vegas. If you are stuck in a place devoted to gambling and don't choose to gamble, what do you do with your time? This time I have come prepared. I consult the guidebook for something that is free. There is Suquamish village, burial site of Chief Sealth, the Native American leader from whose name Seattle is derived. Nearby is the site of what was once a vast longhouse, burned down by officials in 1870 in a strike against communal living and for private property. I could make the trip for the cost of the gas and the ferry passage to Bainbridge Island, but the radio is saying the ferries are backed up for two hours because of all the mall traffic. I will have to make do with a trip to Gas Works Park instead.

On the northern edge of Lake Union, the park is a vivid way to see how the tension can resolve between industrial angst and a playground. The place is the site of an old gas plant that helped keep Seattle illuminated and warm until 1957. Some of it is protected by a gaily painted barn. The old machinery has been rendered harmless to little fingers by some thick coats of enamel. More stark and more intriguing is a huge rusting fenced-off section that looks like an after-the-fall oil refinery covered in graffiti. I'm not sure I would be tempted to sink a well for drinking water on a site like this, but for a weird, absolutely free place to stroll and shoot some frames through the camera, this will do fine. There is no concession stand, no Gas Works T-shirts to buy, but what do you know, the rain has stopped, the sun has come out, and it's a memorable place to spend an hour and a half goofing off, watching a few ferries plowing the whitecaps. It is hard to believe that those boats are filled to the gunwales with shoppers. It is my cue to venture back to see how Buy Nothing Day is going. That requires a trip downtown to—but not into—the Westlake Mall.

A stretch of sidewalk across from the mall is a designated "Shop Free Zone." A fellow on guitar is singing about keeping the sacred fire burning and rhyming, "No one must be allowed to put it out" with "for money's not what life is all about." Monica Woods is in a booth that reads, "The Dr. Is In." She is trying to cure "affluenza." There's a handy wicker basket within which to dispose cut-up credit cards. Alan Seid has abandoned the business suit he wears when he serves as a Spanish-English interpreter over at the courthouse for a blue watch cap and a heavy purple cotton peasant shirt with a white turtleneck underneath. Seid helped persuade the Canadian organizers of Buy Nothing Day, the Ad Busters Media Foundation, to move what is billed as a "celebration" from a day in September to the day after the American Thanksgiving. As a media strategy, it worked. Here I am, salivating on cue. A wire service man, some newspaper reporters, and a Japanese TV news crew are here checking out this odd band of people trying to swim upstream. Seid is sure there is only about a third as many folks milling around the shopping district compared to the same day last year, even though the weather, which has been challenging at times, is apparently not as bad as last year's. Seid doesn't know how much credit to take for tempering the usual orgy of spending. It could be in part the effects of mounting credit card debt.

Shoppers pause to find out what the event is all about. The participants repeat the carefully crafted message: Buy Nothing Day is an attempt to extend Thanksgiving, to be thankful for what we already have for one more day. It is a chance to reflect on whether loved ones want more stuff from us as an expression of our affection or would rather have our time. The group wants folks to make the connection between consumption and the environment.

I scan the urban landscape for signs of local merchants roaring after these protestors with hatchets, but there is no counterdemonstration. I poke my head into a few shops to inquire, and the reactions range from "I wish they hadn't picked today" to "They've got a point about all the credit card debt." Outrage is absent.

I locate Seid again to ask about how he copes with surplus.

His personal conversion into a saver occurred when he was getting out of college. Money's only value, he says, was what he could buy with it at the moment. But five years of living more simply has piled up a big enough stash in government bonds that he says he is now on track to quit his day job by the time he is thirty.

"I was not trying to save, exactly. The savings came effortlessly when I turned the focus away from accumulating money to making sure that my expenditures are in alignment with my values."

Do the people on his holiday gift list hate him for being a cheapskate? Seid looks at me blankly for a moment, finally replying that this has not been an issue for years. His whole family is supportive of what he is trying to do. At the holidays he makes gift certificates redeemable for him to come by and do the laundry for a week or a pledge from him to pay for a certain number of long-distance phone calls between them.

It is 3:30 in the afternoon, and a very black cloud has parked over the city. The breeze has turned chilly. The Sharper Image gadget store across the street could provide shelter, but I am not making that mistake. My Christmas and Chanukah lists are not going to get filled by random hours of impulse buying. The guidebook suggests another free place to go.

Snoqualmie Falls is about forty-five minutes from Seattle toward the Cascades. There's a fancy hotel there, the Salish Lodge, but it is the falls themselves I want to see. I make it there as dusk is falling, and there they are: the mesmerizing tumble of water from David Lynch's *Twin Peaks*. At the head of the falls is what was billed in the television series as the Great Northern Lodge, but to my profound regret there is no Sherilyn Fenn in this version. The actress was once quoted in a British newspaper admitting that her worst vice was shopping. She said she once spent the equivalent of $15,000 on clothes in a Los Angeles store. A friend, according to the account, told Fenn it was like she was on drugs, with her eyes glazed over as she kept repeating "Yes, I'll take that" over and over. The bass notes from the falls are luxurious. This pagoda built over the canyon wall would be the perfect spot to discuss with Ms. Fenn the importance of savings.

About a mile down the road, the neon says, "Big Edd's Diner," not to be in any way confused with "Big Ed's Gas Farm" in the TV show, and this place is serving marionberry pie, not cherry.

As I wait for the check, I tear off a scrap of paper and start doing a little figuring. One way or another, we get the kids educated and out of the house and living independently. The earliest that will happen is eighteen years from now. What did the mystery writer Susan Albert tell me in Texas? They bought their double-wide for about $36,000 in cash plus another $4,000 to get it plumbed and wired. So I need $40,000 for shelter, and if I get our expenses honed down as low as Susan's, what did she say, $1,000 a month? Vicky Robin here in Seattle says I should not worry about inflation, but remember what happened to poor Jerry Worthing, the longtime home owner in Levittown? He once did this very same calculation but got the inflation wrong and was forced back into a nine-to-five job. OK, let us inflate Susan's $1,000 a month by a modest 3 percent inflation a year. That means to live like Susan and Bill live in Texas, I will need $1,720 dollars a month. That is $20,640 a year in interest that I will need to be earning. How much of a surplus produces a return like that? A principal of $337,000 at a plausible thirty-year bond interest rate of 6.125 percent would do it. I shouldn't forget that trailer I will buy. At 3 percent inflation in 18 years, the same trailer will cost $69,000. Throw in $25,000 more for some outrageously cheap land some place. That is $94,000 plus the $337,000 for a total of $431,000 I need for "financial independence" eighteen years from now. If I took that $17,000 I once squandered on my family's lark in London and put $1,000 of after-tax money a month into something that earned that T-bond rate, I would have just a tad more than my goal in eighteen years. All I have to do is figure out how to live in the meantime, allow the family to thrive, and pay for the kids' education while saving $1,000 a month.

If only I could really trust the stock market to return 10 percent on average over the next eighteen years. Then all I would have to put away for my goal is about $550 a month. The waitress at Big Edd's would like me to settle up for the coffee and pie. That bill is easier, $3.95 plus gratuity, in cash.

It is now early evening back at Green Tortoise backpacker's hostel, room 106. A couple of young northern European guys have moved in, and one has taken my lower bunk. "I am afraid of the heights," Jorgan says sheepishly. I move to the top. I inadvertently exact retribution, however, when I misread his accent.

"What part of Germany are you from?" I inquire.

"The *Danish* part of Germany" comes the reply.

In the common room a radio plays all Rolling Stones all the time, in harmony with the big event in Seattle that night: The Stones are playing the Kingdome. In a chair in the center of the room, a woman with a long skirt and a suede vest has her face attached at the lips to a young bleached Rod Stewart. Two fellows speaking French stir hot water into their ramen soup at a table under a blue crayon rubbing of the Hendrix grave: "Forever in our hearts. 1942–1970." In the corner sits a time machine, a green computer monitor and keyboard that is about to pull me back out of the sixties into the late nineties. I tumble into the World Wide Web.

Http://www.publicdebt.treas.gov

It is everything I ever wanted to know about buying government debt with a surplus. Want one of those thirty-year Treasury bonds of which the New Roadmap people are so fond? You can snag them right here, commission free, through a government service called Treasury Direct. Auction schedules, terms, fairly up-to-date prices. One button is marked "Take Me to Your Leader," and the link leads to a smiling Dick Gregg, Commissioner, Bureau of the Public Debt. It turns out he is not my leader; he is my servant:

"We are a small agency within the Department of the Treasury. Our customers are your neighbors, co-workers, and most likely you, too. You are our customer if you have ever bought any type of Treasury security for yourself or, as millions have done in the case of savings bonds, as a gift for someone else."

Well, lessee, a bond that matures thirty years this month is paying 6.125 percent a year, according to one of the Web pages here. If I bought seventeen of these thousand-dollar bonds, it would generate $1,070 a year with virtually no risk, and this does not even count what I could get if I reinvested the proceeds. Treasury Direct caters to folks who want to hold the bonds to maturity. You could sell in advance, but you would have to find a broker.

It occurs to me that the Treasury is talking about both the maturity of the bond and of you. If for a moment you forget that thirty years is a long time, there are questions to answer when you sign up that include "Will this bond be passed on to your surviving spouse?" "How about other beneficiaries?" In other words, what will happen to this bond when you are dead? You had better dig the interest rate payments, sucker, because you ain't ever gonna see the principle. The green time machine is spinning again. Suddenly I am transported ahead thirty years to November 2029, the date that bond matures. I am sixty-nine years old. I have hair in my ears, my pants are too long, and the kids here in the hostel's common room are staring in horror.

It turns out their horror is not directed at me. Someone has slipped another sci-fi tape into the VCR in the hostel's common room, and it is the film that is causing the reaction in the room.

So what if I am old. They say saving is supposed to be a way of shifting income from fecund to fertile periods, shifting the surplus from the peak earning period of one's life to the time when you can or have to ratchet back. Will I have to? A steelworker's back or a letter carrier's knees might give out, but a knowledge-based worker like me should be able to keep going, barring some medical lightning strike. A few weeks ago I passed through Missouri on business and had the opportunity to meet the great radio voice of Kansas City, Walt Bodine, who in his mid-eighties and nearly blind is still asking probing on-air questions and making connections. Walt's tip about a surplus for me is a warning about what he calls "automotive indigence." That is a phenomenon in which your car runs fine until an unexpected windfall comes your way. As soon as the extra money is available, a specially designed sensor somewhere under the hood notices the bulge in your bank account and immediately triggers the need for an expensive repair approximately equal to the amount of the extra cash available. This is the basic principle: Don't spend it if you are not forced to, because one day soon you may have to.

Like car repair and financial markets, life is unpredictable, and it is that understanding that makes saving seem like a rational course. Outrageous opportunities and awful challenges occur, and there are only two ways to field them, by taking on debt or by paying from savings, that is to say, the expensive way or the cheaper way. I could say the irresponsible way and the responsible way, but doing the right thing for country and family tends to lose when it goes bare knuckles with the more seductive opportunities for immediate gratification. One of the things I do know about myself is that I truly, madly, and deeply love a bargain. Saving saves.

Before logging off the net, I fill out the form on the Web directing the Treasury Department to send me a packet of registration material. I can get OK interest rates elsewhere, but a system that strongly encourages you to keep your mitts off the money for three decades is a powerful tool to foil consumption.

Noel, an artist from Texas, flits into the hostel's common room like a moth. He will lead an official Green Tortoise pub crawl through the adjacent neighborhood of Belltown. I am too exhausted for a beer, but somebody grabs the sleeve of my sweater and I find myself in the middle of a pack of good-natured free spirits roaming north along Second Avenue. At the first place even I get carded, but I think they are just being polite. The band Big Pink has actually released a CD, and the American lead singer is trying hard to simulate working-class British punk vowels. It's too loud to talk.

Next door at the fifties-diner-style bar, I spring for the three dollars cash for an order of nachos deluxe, which I share around as a woman in a black hat demonstrates her skill at folding newspaper into hats. Her name is Mary Wages, really, and she prefers to be called by both her names. Soon the Green Tortoise group can be easily identified by their

Mary Wages hats. They range from the traditional sailboat triangular peak hat to a fancier pillbox variety. Bradley, a waiter at a four-star restaurant at a Canadian ski resort, is very pleased with his hat.

"Perfect! Super! Amazing in an origami sort of way."

I get bestowed with a paper bishop's miter. I search the *Seattle Times* sheet from which it was rendered for some sort of significance, but it is only the sports page.

The rest of the bar is now grooving on Mary Wages hats, and strangers are leaning over the backs of our booth clamoring for hats of their own.

"I need one, I need one," a woman cries.

Unprompted, Bradley's buddy Jonathan, another Canadian, leans over his beer and says with hushed solemnity, "What we are learning from the hats here is the need to distinguish between 'need' and 'want,' ay?" David from Idaho really likes this observation.

David is a quiet fellow with a graying mustache and a blue hat with a kayak logo. I am pleased to learn he's forty-two, so I am not the old man of the bunch. Jonathan reveals he is from a town called Moose Jaw. The word "moose" has a lot of resonance for David. It prompts him to recount a shocking story from just over a year ago. He had been watching the downright depressing *Leaving Las Vegas* at his weekend cabin and set off to return home to Coeur d'Alene. Some forest rangers were just ahead of him on the highway when they noticed David's car take a sudden turn. The rangers were unaware of any side road at that location, but they drove five more miles. Finally their sense of foreboding got the best of them, and they returned to find the roof of David's car and the top of David's head torn off. A 1,280-pound moose had walked into his path. The moose was dead and David was nearly so. His brain was exposed and his left eye lay by his ear. His skull is now patched by an invisible layer of titanium. David offers to let Janet from Connecticut feel the rivets under his eyebrow. She shrieks but then gamely gives it a try.

After a respectful pause, someone speaks up. "I'd just like to be the one here to say on behalf of the group that we're all very pleased that you've come through as well as you have." It is Jonathan the Canadian, and he is ready with the most pressing question for the man from Idaho. "I hope, Dave, you won't feel I am being in any way disrespectful by asking, but I was just wondering, does your head now set off the metal detector at the airport?" The small bit of titanium, for the record, does not.

There is a commotion at the front of the bar, some guy getting kicked out for spitting on the pinball machine. David from Idaho and I take that as our cue to leave. Why is he here in Seattle? Because he checks Southwest Airlines' home page every day and they had a super-cheap deal if he flew on Thanksgiving. Why is he really here? Because he is trying to spend a surplus. I get the story on the walk back to the hostel at 1:15 in the morning.

By day David Hunt counsels teenagers and teaches music in the Coeur d'Alene public school system. By night he is a broker, but not of stocks. His card says "Idaho Marine Brokerage." He sells boats, kayaks in particular. He has no debt other than his mortgage. What money he has accumulated has gone into a number of modest real estate ventures, including a cabin built by hand on a lake just south of the Canadian border. He buys his cars very used, part of his generally spartan approach to life. But after his accident and the long recovery, he took some further time to reevaluate his life and plan for the rest of it. He now wants out of his kayak business. He is here in Seattle to spend that money. With his surplus Hunt is buying a boat, and it is no kayak.

He pulls out a dog-eared photo from his wallet as if to show off a loved one. The object of his desire is a thirty-three-foot blue Nauticat. I ask the boat's name and instantly wish I hadn't. It's *The Nutcracker*. He's going to live with that appellation, despite its jib-right-where-it-hurts image. Changing a boat's name, Hunt says, is bad karma. How is it that a mild-mannered counselor and cello player from Idaho who now drives an '81 Saab is in a position to buy a boat? He answers with one of the few bits of advice he remembers his father passing down: "Don't concentrate on how much your earn," his dad said. "Concentrate on how much you spend."

Here is Hunt, capping a long day on which I have managed to keep at least one foot on the ascetic path I mapped, spending a huge chunk of money on a *thing*. And not just anything but in fact the classic thing that guys blow money on. Should I give him the sermon that I have been practicing all day about affluenza and the hollowness of consumption? I don't think so.

It occurs to me that if a guy has been through a near-death experience and wants to buy a boat, let him buy a boat. Second, Hunt has saved, and for all his adult life he has, by his account, acted in a financially prudent sort of way. He has been doing what the frugal gurus have been telling him to, living beneath his means. But this exalted state of frugality is not, for Hunt, an end in itself.

What do I want from the poor fellow, to have him save so long that only his beneficiaries—and through estate tax, Uncle Sam—get to use the money? It is clear Hunt wants to use his assets to align his life to his priorities, and it is less about having a boat and more about the adventures it will bring. A sailing trip along the faraway coast of Maine is mentioned. David's boat passes what I am finally realizing is the important test for a surplus: he can answer "yes" if asked if he expects his use of his money to have a lasting, positive impact on the rest of his life. He is not buying a boat that he cannot afford, cannot keep up, and will seldom use. *The Nutcracker* is something he has wanted for a very long time and is an expression of who David Hunt is. Like the money I once spent on turning myself into a foreign correspondent in London. My pilgrimage has completed the circle.

Still, I want a tangible representation of the value of savings. A certain photograph I have in mind will do.

About a mile from my office in Los Angeles, I once spotted a rooftop neon sign that read, "Jesus Saves." In the foreground was a billboard for American Savings Bank. If He saves, then perhaps I will finally have the answer to the savings versus consumption question. The thing is, I want to see if Seattle has the same sign. A buddy at the public radio station here sends me north of the city, where I find a close, but not quite, "Jesus is Light." Downtown, the historic Pioneer Square District is the kind of place that would support the sort of missions that would sport such a sign. I walk for an hour in the chilly drizzle, surveying the rooftops in the neighborhood, and find nothing.

In the middle of Seattle's Pioneer Place, while contemplating a three-story totem pole, I decide to give up on the picture. You find what you find on these adventures. The guidebook tells the story that the first totem here was stolen from the Tlingits more than a hundred years ago, but it burned. When Seattle officials gave the craftsmen money to fashion a new pole, apparently the Tlingits took the cash and said thanks for finally paying for the old pole, now let's negotiate payment for the new one you want.

Next to me and the pole is an immense man sitting like Buddha in a lawn chair protected only slightly from the wind and rain by an umbrella. He is soliciting spare change and I toss a few coins into the cup. His name is Pedro.

"Would you mind, brother, going across to the coffee place over there to pick me up a large English Breakfast tea with three fake sugars?" The request is too specific to refuse. The coffee hop behind the counter identifies the genesis of this order immediately and shouts to his colleague, "One Pedro, large." Others have been down this road before. Back under the umbrella, my man takes the tea and returns the favor by handing me one of his leaflets. It is filled to the edges with compact writing set off by two words rendered boldly in outline in the sea of script. The two words, of course, are "Jesus *Saves*."

Some folks on their pilgrimages have to keep clear of the dragons. I had to keep dodging the troll.

I could feel his breath the strongest at the Mall of America, but he was never far, no matter where I went on my money trip. The troll cleverly conspired to mail me a catalog of jaunty clothes from Wyoming that arrived the day I returned home from Jackson Hole full of wistful thoughts of the Grand Tetons. On my way to Las Vegas, he made me stop on the pretext of dinner at southern California's newest and biggest complex of outlet stores. He lured me away from Wall Street to buy a Modigliani print from the Metropolitan Museum of Art that was too big for any wall in my house. On my way back to the Lubbock, Texas, airport I was encouraged to search for a guitar store, even though I had been a musician for only about an hour and a quarter and my only instrument was a harmonica. In Tucson the troll clipped a local magazine ad for a mission-style wood and leather armchair and slipped it subversively into my folder full of worthy notes about setting money aside for the long term.

So I feel a certain grim fascination as I am finally able to meet my nemesis. I have found him lurking beneath the Aurora Bridge in Seattle's wacky Fremont neighborhood. He is in the form of a huge concrete sculpture of a scowling ogre snatching the husk of a real VW beetle with its grasping claw as its metallic left eye gives off an unblinking, acquisitive glint. A sign warns that in the dark of night the ogre has been known to consume car parts that do not belong to him. I am sure he consumes a lot more than that. I have gotten much smarter about money during the money trip. Charity has become a much bigger part of the portfolio; I no longer feel the need to take an antacid when I sign the papers to lock spare cash for the next three eons in a retirement annuity; I do not expect the stock market to make up for my own shortcomings. But while I am much more deliberate about spending, conscious of a budget, and less compulsive with the credit card, the consumption thing is something that is managed, not cured.

Confronting the troll with me is a familiar figure, Eric Smith, the socially responsible certified investment planner from my first breakfast in Wyoming. He still has a face like the figure on the Shroud of Turin, but this time he is not wearing the bar code for a name tag. Smith lives in Seattle, and we arranged this meeting.

Smith and I seem to share a common burden, which is that the people we meet tend to want us not for our bodies but for our investment advice. He has the formal credentials to better answer those questions than me, a bachelor's degree in business administration, a general securities license, an insurance license, and a registered investment advisory representative license. But as we sit together on the troll's great knuckles telling jokes and talking portfolio management, I cannot help but notice the difference in my appreciation of these matters now as my adventure draws to an end, compared to what it was when I first met with Eric.

Now I realize that the call to a professional like Eric may not necessarily be the *first* move for someone juggling a surplus. People need to spend an evening, a weekend, or in my case a year and a half reflecting on the wide choices they have with a surplus, taking a hard look at their own financial situation, and begin the process of identifying some goals. Among the services many folks like Eric stand ready to provide is financial counseling by the hour, but he doesn't get much call for that sort of thing. "Most people who need this kind of basic sorting out of their personal finances are lacking in discipline, and since they are lacking in discipline they don't pick up the phone and call," Eric says.

I have come to believe that a money trip, even if is just over a couple evenings with some sharp pencils and a fresh pad of legal paper, is an important precursor to any formal financial planning. A case in point is an assumption I made prior my decision to take our savings to London all those years ago. I had imagined a financial adviser's eyes lighting up at the sight of my money. My surplus at the time had "home mortgage down payment" written all over it, I had figured. I try this on Eric: Young family living in a rental apartment with new baby, not much debt, finds they have squirreled away seventeen grand in a passbook savings account. Next step, house, right?

"Not necessarily," Eric counsels. "The money you put in your mortgage is locked in a steel box with a chain around it and buried twenty feet below your house, and in order to get it out, you have talk to the bank, which has a special shovel. And you have to pay for the use of that shovel in refinancing fees to get that money back out again." It depends on whether you want a house and how long you are thinking you might stay in it.

So is the socially responsible financial adviser now donning his stockbroker's vest? Surely if the money doesn't go into a house, he would say put it into the stock market.

"If you are deploying your money into the stock market and you think there's a possibility that you might be using it for a house down payment within the next year or two, that's gambling, not investing," Eric says.

A professional cannot define goals for you or synthesize the contradictions that are always a part of any big decision about money. That is what the detective work involved in a money trip does for you. When a financial adviser starts talking about the asset allocations in my portfolio as percentages of stocks, bonds, and money market funds, I am now in a position to understand that the slice dedicated to charity has a place in the conversation. Money for the offspring's college will obviously come up. But what about a reserve in case another chance to work with city kids building wooden boats comes along? You can't save for retirement unless you visualize retirement first. A key point about financial education, be it through travel or investment clubs or Friday evenings with Rukeyser, is that it gives you the tools to make the visits with your broker or adviser interactive and helps ensure that the portfolio reflects you and your family's agenda and not the adviser's.

Eric and I move our conversation out of earshot of the troll and end up sitting with big bowls of oatmeal down the street at the Still Life Cafe. Each of the tables sports snippy little placards warning patrons not to conduct business in the cafe if there are others waiting. Business, as opposed to what, pleasure? I know now there is no such clear distinction. There are folks waiting for tables, so we obey the letter of the law by keeping our conversation away from the nuts and bolts of portfolio management.

Instead we share stories. Eric tells of the young man who earned so much so quickly in high tech that he was able to quit at age thirty and take an around-the-world trip. A few months after he returned, he found himself bored out of his skull, desperately missing the pace and the pressure of the software industry. So he went back to work.

I told of seeing the apparition in the midst of the chaos on the floor of the New York Stock Exchange, the cabinet marked "Defibrillator." I had identified one of the companies that makes the portable packs to restart people's hearts in restaurants, casinos, and long international flights, did the homework, tracked the stock carefully.

"How'd it do?" Eric asks.

It was up 13 percent in the first year of tracking it, but it was volatile and would lose that much in a day. Had I put a whole surplus into a fund tied to the S&P 500 index right after the market fell the day I was there, just before Easter, it would have been up 23 percent eight months later, the time of this conversation.

"Why didn't you?"

I figure I am a dollar-cost-averaging kind of guy. I put the same dollars into the market month after month, so when stocks prices are low I automatically buy more of them, and when they're expensive I automatically buy fewer. I have learned that I have little insight into market timing whatsoever, and I am skeptical of most people who say they do.

Eric tells one about a woman who comes in to his office looking to invest in a socially responsible tobacco company. This sounds to me a bit like looking for low-salt pork rind or cruelty-free plutonium.

Dutifully, Eric did track down a brand of cigarettes called American Spirit, which ties its business to the Native American ritual use of tobacco, as in a peace pipe in sweat lodges. Eric said the cigarettes have no preservatives, flavorings, or other additives, but alas, the company that makes them is not publicly traded, so his client could not invest.

I talk about the two Waynes, the janitor-cum-shoe-shine Wayne on Wall Street, who was barely making it despite the market boom going on around him, and the Wayne drifting through the charitable Nevada town that was trying to win the All-America City contest by building sweat equity through volunteerism.

"Did the town win?" Eric wonders.

If the question is, did the folks win their All-America City designation, the answer is no. Hawthorne did not even make the first cut. I took this as a sign that social capital cannot do it alone, but volunteerism in partnership with real capital from public, private, and charitable sources is a better bet. Still, one of the bowling teams from Hawthorne did win at the Nevada state tournament this year. And the town is moving on a plan to bring an arts center to their community.

Eric picks up on that word, community, and he speaks of an initiative in this very Seattle neighborhood to grow a bartered economy, a project known as Fremont Time.

It is funny. My adventures started from a premise of individualism, what *I* should do with *my* money. But for me the most compelling moments were in people's relationships with each other, enabled by money, usually in the form of savings. Banking based on human interaction, not strictly spreadsheets, as I learned in Wyoming. The professional gambler's desire to use his nest egg to go into publishing because of his relationship with his parents. The way community evolved among the new home owners of Levittown. The nurturing feel of the music department at the Texas college.

And how is the harmonica coming?

A tape from Texas Music and Video of Levelland had arrived with a nonthreatening fellow on it who is patiently tutoring me through the basics of the blues harp. I can now stumble through a baby version of "Kansas City Blues."

What is left for me, besides keeping at the practice so I can someday stand up and play a triumphant harmonica solo on a Saturday night at Schahara and Rusty's Tower Theater, is figuring out a business proposition for myself. The four Senior Corps of Retired Executives guys who put me on the grill for lunch never did get a viable business opportunity idea from me. Now I finally think I have it. The Green Tortoise folks who run the Seattle hostel where I stayed are mainly in the business of operating what began as hippie bus tours. Perhaps I could partner with them to run a series of bus trips for folks who need some time to figure out their own answers to the big question of wealth. I have got to believe there is a surplus in it for the person who serves as guide.

Souvenirs

A paper hat in the shape of a bishop's miter appropriate for a fellow on a pilgrimage.

The understanding that if debt is a trap, it is savings that is liberating.

To do when I get home

Comb through all the credit card statements from the past year and add up all the charges that do not stand up to the tests of time. Divide by twelve. Resolve to take this amount each month and bury it deep enough in my portfolio that I am not tempted to play with it.

Doing the numbers

Personal savings in America during the last months of the millennium dropped below income for the first time since the Great Depression year of 1933. (Source: U.S. Department of Commerce)

Epilogue

- -

What do you do with a surplus?

Our record in coping with a surplus is not a good one. When one of the two longest American economic expansions in history looked as if it could linger into the next century, a great debate erupted in Washington. The enduring boom had resulted in a budget surplus generated by all the extra taxes the federal government raked in. No matter that the national debt was still measured in the trillions of dollars. Politicians scrambled to build consensus about what to do with the money. There was a President who wanted to save the surplus until reforms were made to the troubled Medicare and Social Security system. There was a Congress that wanted to be sure folks got some of that money back in the form of lower taxes. Then a military campaign in the Balkans came along and decided for the politicians what a chunk of that surplus would be used for. It was a profoundly tragic version of Kansas City's octogenarian radio host Walt Bodine's concept of "automotive indigence," when your car senses that you have come into extra cash and, accordingly, breaks down. The world too often conspires to decide for us how a surplus will be used.

Before these adventures, I would politely avoid answering when folks asked for advice about what to do with the proceeds from some stock options they had just exercised, the capital gain they had made by selling a bigger house and moving into a cheaper one, the bequest they had been sitting on. There was even a single time I met someone who had actually won a medium-sized pot in the lottery, as statistically unlikely as that

might be. My dodge in these situations went thus: "Before asking someone where to put money, find out how fancy a car he drives." Then the
punch line:

"I bicycle to work."

This is a variation of the "If I were so smart, I wouldn't have to do
this for a living" confession.

Now, following my pilgrimage, I still avoid answering the question
directly, for what someone should do with money is all about who the
bearer of the money is, not who I am. But I do answer indirectly with the
following short story.

I was sorting through my in tray, a two-foot-high pile of mostly junk
and out-of-date news releases, saving anything that looked like fresh
news, listener letters, or memos from the boss and slam-dunking the rest.
After one particular fistful, I stopped for a moment, realizing that I had
failed to give that bunch even a cursory glance. Digging back through the
recycling bin, I managed to locate the unreviewed clump. It was a good
thing, too. Lodged therein was an innocuous-looking envelope addressed
to me. Oddly, my last name was spelled correctly. Intrigued, I opened the
envelope to find a check inside with me listed as the payee. The check
that I had nearly thrown out was written for the amount of $42,500.

Let me say that again, but this time with feeling: *forty-two thousand
five hundred dollars.*

Before my trips around the country to consider options for a surplus,
a check like this would have sent me into a disoriented, spiraling funk.
Could buy Mercedes, I doubtless would have drooled, dropping all personal pronouns and definite articles in my daze. Or must give whole
thing to broker before it is too late. Prior to my adventures, the sense
that I was missing the great secrets about what to do next with it would
have put me off my food, given me insomnia for several fiscal quarters,
and generally provoked a personal and family crisis.

As it was, I was able to confidently grasp that $42,500 check and
knew exactly what to do next.

I would have to donate to public radio.

The beauty of that strategy was that I could pledge to public radio at
a level I was comfortable with and still have $42,465 of it left over to
build the portfolio of my dreams. . . .

Modest dreams, actually. Perhaps the down payment on a dream. I could now look at a check like this and quickly realize that a spreadsheet would make short work of such a paltry sum. Paltry, you say? The proof was in the spreadsheet.

The Windfall		$42,465
	EXPENSE	**BALANCE**
Early Retirement Savings Shelter in tax-free retirement account topped up to the government's limit	$3,500	$38,965
Federal and State Taxes	$16,132	$22,833
Charity Give away 10 percent of after-tax amount	$2,283	$20,550
Credit Card Debt Pay down high-interest debt	$300	$20,250
Frivolous Money—His	$500	$19,750
Frivolous Money—Hers Take just over 1 percent for each spouse and consider it fun money	$500	$19,250
Education Fund Use half of remainder to start a children's education fund with money put into bonds to mature before each child goes to college	$9,625	$9,625
New House Fund Use remainder to cover the transaction fees on a slightly bigger house with an extra bedroom, a study and a garage.	$9,625	$0

The spreadsheet lacks the emotional power of a lottery commercial, but it is defensible, mature, reasonably sober, incremental, and decidedly not revolutionary. For something more life altering, less Ward Cleaver, I saw two choices. One was to use the entire after-tax amount on something more dramatic. I could learn from the folks I met in Texas and jump off this train. A sabbatical somewhere provocative.

The other way was an attempt to reconcile two visions of what to do with this surplus. As I know from all the folks I met on the road, using money always involves trade-offs. It is not un-American to recognize that we cannot have everything. The trade-off involved the new house. If I replaced the last item in the spreadsheet, New House Fund, with Around-the-World Airline Tickets, something interesting happened.

An Around-the-World Airline Ticket	$2,399
Four Tickets	$9,596
New House Fund	$9,625

I would need five, not four, tickets to take the whole family. But the point was, there would be many other expenses for a venture of this sort, not the least of which would be room and board for six months to a year. The $9,625 would not cover it, but it would begin to cover it. It was seed money for a dream that could possibly be accomplished without completely abandoning my responsibilities. The other freelance gigs, moonlighting, and the discipline of supplementing this fund with savings each month out of the main paycheck might just leverage this venture into reality. But it would take work, not just good fortune.

I would stand a better chance making this more radical case for the money if I could prove that the big check was really a windfall in its truest sense, unexpected, perhaps unearned, and therefore less encumbered. For that, I needed to do one extra bit of research. I telephoned my agent to check the provenance of the sudden surplus. The call did not go well.

The check was a mistake, a pitiful, painful, shocking mistake. The $42,500 did not belong to me. I had in my hands someone else's surplus.

When asked what I did when confronted with the biggest surplus I had ever seen in one place, given what I learned on these adventures, I answer truthfully. I got out a black medium-point indelible marker and wrote "VOID" several times across its face.

About the Author

David Brancaccio is host and senior editor of *Marketplace,* public radio's popular and award-winning business program "for the rest of us," produced at the University of Southern California and distributed nationwide by Public Radio International. A broadcaster since puberty, Brancaccio has worked in San Francisco, Washington, D.C., and his home state of Maine. He has also served as London correspondent for *Marketplace* and the radio service of the *Christian Science Monitor.* He has a B.A. from Wesleyan University, an M.A. in journalism from Stanford University, and no M.B.A. whatsoever. He is a frequent lecturer and moderator and lives in Los Angeles. Links to more information about this book can be found at: www.squandering.com